Understanding Intercultural Communication

C000107912

UNIVERSITY

In this book, Adrian Holliday provides a practical framework to help students analyse inter-cultural communication. Underpinned by a new grammar of culture developed by Holliday, this book incorporates examples and activities to enable students and professionals to investigate culture on very new, entirely non-essentialist lines. This book addresses key issues in intercultural communication, including:

- the positive contribution of people from diverse cultural backgrounds;
- the politics of Self and Other which promote negative stereotyping;
- the basis for a bottom-up approach to globalisation in which periphery cultural realities can gain voice and ownership.

The book is accompanied by eResources, which are designed to support the reader's own understanding and can be found online at www.routledge.com/9780415691307. Written by a key researcher in the field, this book presents cutting-edge research and a framework for analysis which make it essential reading for upper undergraduate and post-graduate students studying intercultural communication, and professionals in the field.

Adrian Holliday is Professor of Applied Linguistics at Canterbury Christ Church University, UK.

OXFORD
BROOKES
UNIVERSITY

Understanding Intercultural Communication

Negotiating a grammar of culture

Adrian Holliday

Routledge
Taylor & Francis Group

LONDON AND NEW YORK

First published 2013
by Routledge
2 Park Square, Milton Park, Abingdon, Oxon OX14 4RN

Simultaneously published in the USA and Canada
by Routledge
711 Third Avenue, New York, NY 10017

Routledge is an imprint of the Taylor & Francis Group, an informa business

© 2013 Adrian Holliday

The right of Adrian Holliday to be identified as author of this work has been asserted by him in accordance with sections 77 and 78 of the Copyright, Designs and Patents Act 1988.

All rights reserved. No part of this book may be reprinted or reproduced or utilised in any form or by any electronic, mechanical, or other means, now known or hereafter invented, including photocopying and recording, or in any information storage or retrieval system, without permission in writing from the publishers.

Trademark notice: Product or corporate names may be trademarks or registered trademarks, and are used only for identification and explanation without intent to infringe.

British Library Cataloguing in Publication Data
A catalogue record for this book is available from the British Library

Library of Congress Cataloging-in-Publication Data
Holliday, Adrian.
Understanding intercultural communication : negotiating a grammar of culture /
Adrian Holliday.
pages cm
Includes bibliographical references and index.
1. Intercultural communication. I. Title.
P94.6.H648 2013
303.482--dc23
2012048807

ISBN: 978-0-415-69131-4 (hbk)
ISBN: 978-0-415-69130-7 (pbk)
ISBN: 978-0-203-49263-5 (ebk)

Typeset in Galliard
by Saxon Graphics Ltd, Derby.

MIX
Paper from
responsible sources
FSC
www.fsc.org   FSC® C013056

Printed and bound in Great Britain by
TJ International Ltd, Padstow, Cornwall

Contents

Contents by concept

Concept	Chapter and section	Summary
Cultural belief	3, Opening up to complexity	Thick description as a means for getting into the complexity of things
	8, Francisca, Hande and Gita: missing home, belief and disbelief, and following sections	Main treatment
	9, Cultural belief and disbelief	Disbelief and the fear of culture loss
Cultural prejudice	4, What we imagine	Fuelling historical narratives in **small culture formation**
	8, Prejudice	Main treatment
	9, Cultural belief and disbelief	At home, against cultural innovation
Cultural travel	4, Cultural travel and building	Abi and Tomos building culture in a new location
	4, Cultural travel	Examples of cultural learning through experiences across home culture boundaries
	5, Creative cultural behaviour	In dialogue with national structures
	9, Cultural travel and innovation	Main treatment
Duality	4, Dualities	Between acceptance and rejection of a new management practice – as a discourse which can be brought in in differing degrees
	5, Duality	People being more creative about cultural behaviour than they admit to. **Statements about culture** giving the impression that culture is more fixed.
	7, Managing and undoing discourses	Degrees of buying into discourses.
Historical narratives	4, What we imagine	Influencing imaginations about others in **small culture formation**, e.g. what is cosmopolitan?, who should know what?
	2, Anna visiting Beatrice's family	Beatrice's father imagining that 'American' is cosmopolitan
	5, Jenna and Malee: critical thinking	Jenna's friend referring to their history of revolution
	6, Historical Narratives	Main treatment
	7, Discourses as social constructions	Compared with discourses
Idealisation and demonisation	4, Idealisation and demonisation	As part of the Self and Other politics, demonising as exoticism
	5, How this works with Protestantism	Idealisation of Protestantism and demonisation of non-Protestantism
	6, Ivonne, Chung and Ning: simple things about food	Ivonne realising that the emphasis on individualism in Protestantism has led her to be suspicious of Exian culture

Concept	Chapter and section	Summary
Professionalism	4, Self and Other	Idealising the professional Self
	6, Kay and Pushpa: sociological blindness	Idealising the professional Self in opposition to a culturally deficient collectivist Other
	7, The objectivist myth	And professional discourses
Reification	2, Global trajectory	Beatrice's father takes foreign eating habits and establishes them as a normal part of family behaviour
	4, Reification	The new concept of Smart Project Management is reified within institutional practice
Resistance against expected cultural norms	2, Global trajectory	Beatrice's father adopting American eating habits
	2, Examples and factors	Influencing the formation of cultural practices
	5, Dialogue with structure	Main treatment
	7, Ramla, Ed and Jonathan: sticking to principles	Resisting the dominant voices in her company by pushing an essentialist picture of her own culture
	7, Cultural resistance	General analysis of cultural resistance throughout the book
	9, Safa: 'when are you going back?'	Against cultural innovation and against cultural conservatism
Self-Othering, self-marginalisation	3, The problem with stereotypes and a top-down approach	Francisca believes that cultural profiles help people define themselves in opposition to foreign influence. This can be interpreted as adhering to negative stereotypes about oneself
	5, Duality	Accepting the label of Westernisation because of its Centre status
	7, Nada, Jahan and Osama: getting it wrong?	Osama accuses Jahan of self-Othering by clinging to a stereotype
Small culture formation on the run	2, Being successful	Anna constructing a means of dealing with new cultural practices in Beatrice's family
	2, Dima and Christoff: future in-laws	Dima and Ehsan's families deciding to break with tradition and share wedding costs
	4, Abi and Tomos making a cultural event	All parties co-constructing the culture of the naming day
	4, Small culture formation on the run	Detailed discussion of the concept
Third space	7, Discourses of Culture	Main treatment, as a dominant discourse of culture
	8, Innocent beginnings	As an innocent discourse
	9, John abroad: politeness and space	Interrogated in John's experience of crossing boundaries

Figures and tables

Figures

Tables

Preface

The purpose of this book is to understand the nature of culture so that we can deal with unfamiliar cultural practices when we encounter people from different cultural backgrounds. The way in which we present ourselves culturally and deal with unfamiliar cultural realities is complex. It is partly to do with a describable difference between nations, but it also has a lot to do with how all of us negotiate the cultural realities of everyday life in very similar ways. This book concentrates on these shared cultural skills. The knowledge of how they operate helps us understand and engage with cultural behaviour wherever we find it.

The content is a basic sociology about how culture operates everywhere. It capitalises on the universal knowledge of social life possessed by people from all cultural backgrounds. Addressing this content requires a laying bare of everyday processes, many of which pass by without notice, and some of which occupy our minds as niggling problems, but which are rarely thought of as the building blocks of cultural engagement.

Another, more human and educational purpose which this understanding meets is:

- to bring together people from different backgrounds to collaborate in understanding and pooling their diverse experience and contribution;
- to promote a universal core in cultural competence through which people from diverse backgrounds can find common cultural ground while at the same time preserving the most positive aspects of cultural diversity;
- to see all of this within the context of the global politics and ideology which underpin cultural misunderstanding.

This is by no means the first book to have this purpose; but its approach is different to those that tend to compare national cultures so that we can predict and explain how 'our' behaviour will be different to that of foreigners. While the focus is on how to behave in foreign circumstances, this will not be informed by characterisations of particular foreign cultures, which I believe would result in over-simplistic and perhaps damaging stereotypes. Instead, the tone of this book is to encourage engagement across cultural boundaries, finding common ground and sharing experience.

Grammar of culture

The book is driven by a grammar of culture, which is a loose device for explaining how different elements of culture relate to each other within an open dialogue between the individual and social structures. This is looked at in some detail in Chapter 1 and becomes a model through which the rest of the book is conceived.

Narratives and categories of cultural action

Each chapter is built around ethnographic narratives. To avoid national stereotypes, and to emphasise what people share, the nationalities of the characters are only revealed on a need-to-know basis. The emphasis is more on processes than the particularities of location. However, as an author who is rooted in Britain, I have located some of the narratives there; and I have myself to avoid falling into the trap of familiar stereotypes.

The narratives are each analysed through categories of cultural action that are based on the grammar. Through this analysis, the grammar is explained and explored, and its complexities revealed.

Reflective activities

Throughout there are reflective activities which invite readers to interrogate the ideas and cases presented. A major function of these activities is to invite discussion about the many loose ends in the text and to prevent the authorial voice from getting above itself. In this respect the activities take the form of an *independent critical voice*. They are therefore staged at critical places in the text.

Some of the activities are expanded to encourage readers to carry out a piece of informal research to practice and sharpen the disciplines for looking at culture.

The activities and informal research projects are introduced discreetly so that they can be avoided by those who wish to be left alone with the text and to make sense of it in their own way. They can be carried out individually, or, far better, collaboratively by peers, and preferably from different backgrounds.

Chapter 3 focuses particularly on the research disciplines necessary to carry out the activities and generally to understand intercultural communication. Readers are encouraged to use these disciplines to write their own *ethnographic narratives*. A model activity is provided which can be used to do this based on the content of each of the other chapters.

Uses

The text of each chapter can be divided into

- explanatory and discursive prose;
- the narratives, the analysis using the categories of cultural action, and the reflective activities.

The narratives, analyses and activities can form the basis of materials that can be used in classrooms, seminars and workshops for a range of audiences. They have been trialled with second- and third-year undergraduate and masters students, curriculum developers and trainers. The prose sections are more suitable for private reading and further guidance and discussion.

Further reference, epilogue, glossary and cross-referencing

At the end of each chapter there is a further reference section which directs readers to further reading or material on the internet. The further reading is for those who wish to connect with a more academic discussion and indicates some of the theoretical research underpinning the chapter. Chapter 10 takes the form of an epilogue which presents a detailed account of the theoretical underpinning of the book.

To save too much cross-referencing within the body of the book, there are two locations which will provide readers with extra help to find their way around. At the beginning of the book there is a *thematic list of contents* which picks up concepts which are referred to explicitly in a number of places. At the back of the book there is a glossary of key terms which can also be found in the index.

Structure

The book is divided into nine chapters plus the Epilogue. Chapter 1 presents the grammar, which indicates the main concepts to be used throughout. Chapter 2, 'Cultural practices', sets the scene for the whole book by getting down to the complex details that we can all find both foreign and familiar, and helps us to find the everyday links between what we know and what we do not.

Chapter 3, 'Investigating culture', builds on the work on cultural practices in Chapter 2 to develop strategies and disciplines for approaching and making sense of the culturally strange. In so doing, it capitalises on the everyday complexity of cultural practices as something we all have an understanding of, and through which we might find a route to the unfamiliar. Chapter 4, 'Constructing culture', demonstrates that much of what we do when approaching the culturally unfamiliar begins with the everyday task of constructing culture. It looks at this process within **small culture formation** within the broader domain of **underlying universal cultural processes**.

Chapter 5, 'Dialogue with structure', builds on the notion of creativity in cultural construction within the context of the individual's potential dialogue with the structures often associated with 'national cultures'. These potentials will be looked at realistically, given that they may often be inhibited by circumstances and feed dominant rumours of 'national culture' dominance. Chapter 6, 'Historical narratives', looks at the way in which constructing culture in the present can be influenced very much by the historical narratives which we bring to the situation.

Chapter 7, 'Discourses of culture', explores discourses of culture as things that we construct in order to make sense of culture, but which then take on a life of their own and can easily begin to dominate what we think is real about culture. Chapter 8, 'Prejudice', will look at how we can so easily fall into the trap of prejudice when encountering people from other cultural backgrounds. Chapter 9 deals with the way in which cultural experience and competence can be carried from one location to another. It counters the common expectation that newcomers have an inherent disadvantage because cultural lines can never fully be crossed. Chapter 10 presents the theoretical underpinning of the book.

Acknowledgements

I would like to thank Asya Draganova, Ritu Mahendru, Sadia Ali and Yeonsuk Bae for being informants and for making particular contribution to aspects of the ethnographic narratives. Ardeshir Yousefpour, Duan Yuping, Fereshteh Honarbin, Gong Yafu, Haesoon Park, Sanam Rostami, and Shabnam Holliday and Brieg Powel and their family and friends, also contributed observed material. Ireri Armenta, Nadia Seemungal, Richard Fay and Yasemin Oral provided invaluable and insightful ideas regarding the structuring and content of the text. My grandchild Aara, the same age as the inception of the book, provided endless example of rich cultural learning in three languages. Staying with Safa Kassab-Hassan, Osama Jradeh and their family and colleagues in now war-torn Damascus also provided rich data for cultural travel and creativity. Bojana Petric, Jo Angouri, Chris Anderson and John Kullman allowed me access to their students to try out ideas. Teaching the students of the BA English Language & Communication at Canterbury Christ Church University, and the three-day seminar with Leticia Yulita, Zebo Niyazova, Saida Irgasheva, Kamola Alimova and Olga Kim, provided insight into the practicality and authenticity of the material. Anne Swan, Ayesha Kamal, Bill Sughrua, Haynes Collins, Irasema Mora, Lesley Wheway, Nasima Yamchi, Paul Hudson, and especially Stephanie Vandrick provided ideas and moral support through discussion and blog. Sage Publications kindly allowed me to use the grammar of culture diagram, first published in my 2011 book. I am forever indebted to my wife and friend for life, Mehri Honarbin-Holliday, for giving me purpose and inspiration.

Chapter 1

The grammar of culture

The book will be driven by the grammar of culture, which is represented in Figure 1.1. As linguistic grammar provides a structure which enables us to read sentences, the grammar of culture provides a structure which enables us to read cultural events. However, it is also an invention – a map which can guide us. This map must never be mistaken for the real terrain, which is too complex and deep to be mapped too accurately. Throughout this book, whenever mentioned, the items of the grammar are in bold.

With this unfathomable complexity in mind, the grammar is characterised by loose relationships which represent a conversation between the different domains. This conversation is sometimes harmonious and sometimes ridden with conflict, which is sometimes irreconcilable. Of particular interest to this book is the element of this conversation in which individuals interact with national structures. The grammar is spread across three broad domains, **particular social and political structures**, **underlying universal cultural processes** and **particular cultural products**. It is the interaction between the particular and the universal which will be the basis for much of the discussion throughout the book. There is both understanding and a dark side in the universal domain:

- It is what we all share in the universal which enables us all to make sense of, read and interact with the particular wherever we encounter it.
- However, the universal also underpins the architecture of cultural prejudice, which is a common mechanism for making limited sense through easy answers.

Below I will say something about each part of the grammar and the main places where they will be dealt with as the book proceeds.

Particular social and political structures

On the left of Figure 1.1 are structures which in many ways form us and make us different from each other. They include nation, religion, language and the economic system. These structures may in some circumstances map precisely onto each other – for example where a nation state corresponds largely with one religious group, one language and one economic system. Examples of these might be isolated communities which have been relatively untouched by global affairs. It may well be, however, that they are more imagined than actual, residing in our exotic idealisation of the 'tribe', or the lost civilisations of travellers' tales, or, as more scientific constructs, the ancient discoveries of archaeology. In these cases it is easy to think of a single 'culture' in which all the members really do share things that no one else does.

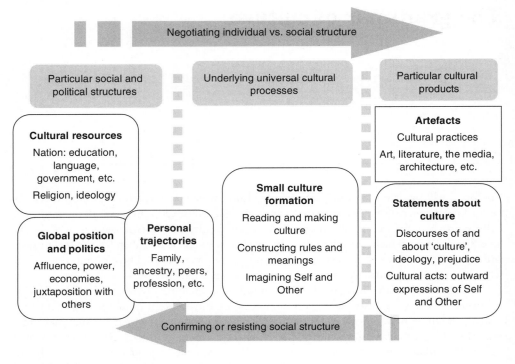

Figure 1.1 The grammar (source: Holliday 2011a: 131)

In most cases, however, the relationships will be more complex than this; and religions and languages will transcend nations or be minorities within them and within economic systems, even though nationalist statements may say otherwise. Degrees of the economic system may well be controlled by the nation state, but the variations of the other domains may well mediate the extent to which these can be culturally defining.

The first of the domains in this part of the figure, **cultural resources**, is the influence on our daily lives of the **particular social and political structures** of the society in which we were born and brought up. It relates to what many of us refer to as 'our culture', or national culture. The way we were educated, our national institutions, the manner of our government, our media, our economy and so on are different from nation to nation and will undoubtedly impact on the way we are as people. These are resources in the sense that we draw on them, but they do not necessarily confine everything we do and think.

Next, **global position and politics** concern how we are also influenced by the way we position ourselves and our society with regard to the rest of the world. The structure of this positioning may well come from the **cultural resources**. Examples of this are how people in the West view non-Western countries and how people outside the West view the West; at a more local level, how Britain and continental Europe view each other, how Middle Eastern nations view each other and the concept of the Arab World, and so on. This is a key area which is often ignored in intercultural studies texts. It is a major tenet of this book that almost everything intercultural is underpinned by this positioning and politics, which is very hard to see around because of the degree to which we are all inscribed by long-standing constructions of who we are in relationship to others – Self and Other – in our histories, education, institutions, upbringing and media representations, and that these are rooted profoundly in a world which is not politically or economically equal.

Moving into the centre of Figure 1.1, **personal trajectories** comprise the individual's personal travel through society, bringing histories from their ancestors and origins. Through these trajectories they are able to step out from and dialogue with the **particular social and political structures** that surround them and even cross into new and foreign domains. This domain thus crosses the subtle boundary with **underlying universal cultural processes**.

'Culture' and reality

Consider under what circumstances you talk about 'a culture', and what you mean when you do this. Then consider how far this notion matches reality.

Consider two countries with which you are familiar and compare how their social and political structures interact and overlap. How might the concept of 'culture' be therefore used in each case?

What factors would act against an easy use of the concept of 'culture'?

Underlying universal cultural processes

These processes in the centre of Figure 1.1 are shared by all of us. They are common across national boundaries. They involve skills and strategies through which everyone, regardless of background, participates in and negotiates their position within the cultural landscapes to which they belong. This is the basis upon which we are able to read culture.

Small culture formation is the major area where the **underlying universal cultural processes** come into operation. Small cultures are cultural environments which are located in proximity to the people concerned. There are thus small social groupings or activities wherever there is cohesive behaviour, such as families, leisure and work groups, where people form rules for how to behave which will bind them together. Small cultures are the basic cultural entities from which all other cultural realities grow. Wherever we go we automatically either take part in or begin to build small cultures. In this sense, **small culture formation** happens all the time and is a basic essence of being human. We might even think of **small culture formation** on the run – every day, everywhere, whoever we meet or even think about, we are always in the process of constructing and dealing with cultural realities.

Particular cultural products

Back to particularities, on the right of Figure 1.1, these are the outcome of cultural activity. The first domain, **artefacts**, includes the 'big-C' cultural artefacts such as literature and the arts. They also include cultural practices, which are the day-to-day things we do which can seem strange for people coming from foreign cultural backgrounds – how we eat, wash, greet, show respect, organise our environment and so on. These are the things which are most commonly associated with 'our culture' or national culture; but they also differ between small groups within a particular society.

The second domain, **statements about culture**, is perhaps the hardest of all the domains in the grammar to make sense of. It is to do with how we present ourselves and what we choose to call 'our cultures'. However, there is a deep and tacit politics here which means that what we choose to say and project may not actually represent how things are, but rather our dreams and aspirations about how we would like them to be, or the spin we place upon them to create the impact we wish to have on others. This is not to do with lying or deceiving, but with a genuine presentation of Self which involves a sophisticated manipulation of reality.

Cultural negotiation

The arrows across the top and bottom of Figure 1.1 indicate that throughout the grammar is a dialogue between the power of underlying universal cultural processes possessed by the individual and the influences of the particular cultural realities which derive from national structures. Moving from left to right, at the top of the figure, personal trajectories and underlying universal cultural processes enable individuals or groups of individuals to introduce their personal cultural realities into existing structures. Moving from right to left, at the bottom of the figure, the degree to which this can be successful will depend on how far existing structures are confirmed or resisted. Here I am particularly interested in the potential for newcomers to be cultural innovators.

How the grammar is used throughout the book

The ensuing chapters do not deal with each part of the grammar one by one. Instead the interconnection and conversation between the parts are demonstrated within the theme of each chapter.

Categories of cultural action

This interconnection is demonstrated through the application of categories of cultural action to each of the ethnographic narratives. Although they can be taken from all parts of the grammar, these categories always include **statements about culture, global position and politics, cultural resources** and **underlying universal processes**. The reason for focusing on these particular domains rather than others is that they best represent the personal, political, particular, universal aspects of culture, as I hope will become clear throughout the book. They serve to help break open what is going on in the narratives to expose the key forces which are at play. It is hoped that these forces will be recognisable to outsiders and help them to read culture wherever it is by referring them back to forces they can find within their own society. Other categories from the grammar will also be added depending on the circumstances.

Summary

- The grammar of culture represents a loose conversation between the cultural realities which are particular to national structures and the **underlying universal cultural processes** which are shared by everyone and enable us all to read and engage with culture wherever we find it.

- This conversation can take the form of **personal trajectories** in which culture is re-negotiated as individuals travel through life and collect their own cultural realities around them.
- Underlying all of these processes are **global position and politics**.
- A major focus which develops throughout the book is **small culture formation**.

Further reference

Holliday, A.R. (2011). *Intercultural communication & ideology*. London: Sage.
  — Chapter 6 describes the grammar of culture with examples. Also, throughout, there are ethnographic narratives which are analysed using the categories of cultural action in a similar fashion to this book.

Holliday, A.R. (1999). Small cultures. *Applied Linguistics* 20/2: 237–64.
  — The original paper in which I introduce the notion of small cultures upon which the grammar of culture is largely based.
  — Readers might be interested to compare the small culture diagram in the paper with the grammar diagram in this chapter and to try to trace the development.

Hall, S. (1991). The local and the global: globalisation and ethnicity. In King, A.D. (ed.), *Culture, globalisation and the world-system*. New York: Palgrave: 19–39.

Hall, S. (1991). Old and new identities, old and new ethnicities. In King, A.D. (ed.), *Culture, globalisation and the world-system*. New York: Palgrave: 40–68.
  — Both of Hall's works describe the global politics surrounding cultural issues, and the impossibility of defining culture as a neutral, objective, measurable entity.

Nathan, G. (2010). *Social freedom in a multicultural state: towards a theory of intercultural justice*. Basingstoke: Palgrave Macmillan.
  — Pages 44 onwards present another new picture of culture which might be compared to the grammar, especially with relation to complexity.

Chapter 2

Cultural practices

For many of us our first encounter with the strangeness of culture is with the different practices that can be found in different cultural environments. Cultural practices can be defined as ways of doing something which relate to particular cultural environments and may therefore be unfamiliar to newcomers. They concern everyday activities where there are choices about eating, washing, clothing, communicating, timing, surroundings, being together and so on. A cultural environment can be defined as a geographical or psychological entity from which an individual derives a sense of cultural identity at a particular point in time. This could be anything from a community, friendship group or occupation, to a notion of nation or civilisation.

This chapter therefore, by looking at cultural practices, sets the scene for the whole book by getting down to the complex details which we can all find both foreign and familiar, and helps us to find the everyday links between what we know and what we do not.

Cultural practices are located within the **artefacts** domain of the grammar, along with art and literature, under the general heading of **particular cultural products**. They are thus tangible items which are the produced outcome of the complex forces of culture which are indicated in the rest of the grammar. As such, part of their function is to be an outward show of how people wish to project themselves to others. They represent the special features of a particular cultural group, and can thus be flagships of cultural identity. In this sense people will present them as being very particular to who they are – their nation, their family, their company, their team and so on.

However, unlike the big-C items of art and literature, which are often very consciously created, displayed and even sold and bought, cultural practices can be quite tacitly created. We may hardly notice the practices which are close to us until we compare them with practices with which we are unfamiliar. They are often the things we think of when describing 'a culture' as being different from another. In this sense cultural practices may indeed be the most noticeable signs of difference to newcomers.

Foreigners and newcomers

These two words can be used to refer to people who come from somewhere else, with the implication that they will find the cultural practices they encounter in the places where they arrive as unfamiliar and strange. They do not, however, necessarily come from different countries. They may come from the house next door, the next street, community, village, city or province, from another sports or social group, or from another company or department. One of the strangest practices I have witnessed was carried out by employees from another department in my university:

> Three women came into the cafeteria each with their own mug,[1] which they gave to the person serving to fill with the coffee or tea which they were buying. One of the women was carrying two mugs, one of which belonged to her co-worker back in the office. The body language of the women and the people serving indicated a long-standing yet tacit protectiveness around the mugs and their ownership.

My own office was only a few buildings away from theirs; yet I was clearly the foreigner with respect to their cultural practice, which I felt I would have to be initiated into if ever I moved to their department.

Examples and factors

Examples of cultural practices are presented in Table 2.1. The first column shows domains of everyday living. The instances of each domain are randomly chosen from my own experience. The list of both the domains and instances could literally go on forever. Indeed, wherever one looks one will see examples of quite definable and different cultural practices. There are a number of things to note about these examples. Some of them are associated with particular societies or groups of societies. However, others are associated with a wide variety of other factors, such as:

- a decision not to be so formal on particular occasions, e.g. resistance against tradition, rules, parents, employers;
- a traditional view about cleanliness, upbringing or avoiding waste, which may or may not be associated with religion;
- attitudes to power, territory and space which may or may not be associated with religion or ideology;
- availability of resources, e.g. furniture, rooms, appliances;
- climate, e.g. ways of dealing with cold or heat;
- the tradition or ethos of a particular family, institution, business or activity;
- modernisation, social change, resistance against tradition, etc.;
- pressures of work or the demands of everyday life;
- tacit traditions with which people are brought up, e.g. showing respect to elders;
- the policy of particular institutions, e.g. how to treat customers;
- variation between families or generations within families.

Table 2.1 Examples of cultural practices

Domain	Instance 1	Instance 2	Instance 3
Eating	People take plates and cutlery from a central place and negotiate space at the table during the event.	Each person has a personal space marked prior to the event by a table mat and cutlery arranged in prescribed positions.	Each person goes to a table to get plates, cutlery and food, and then sits elsewhere to eat from their lap.
Dish washing	Dishes are immersed in soapy water and not rinsed.	Dishes are soaped individually and rinsed under running water.	Dishes are immersed in soapy water and then rinsed in a separate body of non-soapy water.
Furnishing	Chairs and coffee tables are arranged around the edge of the sitting room.	Chairs are arranged around coffee tables away from the edge of the room.	The floor is the major place for sitting, with low tables as a central focal point.
Offices	Doors are kept open and visitors are invited to wait inside the room.	Doors are kept closed and visitors are asked to wait outside and then called in.	One must always knock before entering, even when doors are left open.
Children	Children have different eating and sleeping times to parents.	Children take part in adult activities.	Children are allowed to roam freely.
Getting served	Customers crowd at the counter and try hard to get the attention of several employees so they can get served.	Customers wait in line and get served one-by-one by the next free employee.	Customers crowd the counter and several can be served at the same time.
Meetings	Members of the meetings address each other by family name and title.	Members of the meeting address each other by given name and rarely use titles, except for the Chair, when she or he is being referred to formally.	Members of the meeting address each other by given name and title and display affectionate deference to seniority.
Time keeping	Colleagues arrive at the meeting gradually up to ten minutes late, make excuses, and may not leave their previous location until the designated time of the meeting they are going to.	Colleagues arrive on time and look disparagingly at latecomers.	Colleagues come and go throughout the meeting and do not make excuses. Arriving and leaving is acknowledged by a friendly look from the Chair.

Linking factors and examples

Try and link the above factors governing cultural practices with each of the instances in Table 2.1.

While doing this, describe your own experience of similar cultural practices which help you to make sense of possible links.

Devise other factors which better explain particular cultural practices and add them to the list.

Looking around

Go to a public place where there are people, such as a café, a shopping centre or a sports event. Look around and see how many different cultural practices you can spot.

Label them and see if you can attach them to a factor listed above, or name new factors if required.

See if you can work out if any of the practices are foreign or just eccentric. Justify your decision.

Finding universals

Assess the claim made in the text that the factors listed above could apply across cultural environments.

See how many of them can be found in the cultural environments of you and your colleagues from different backgrounds.

Terminology

Why is the term 'cultural environment' used in the text instead of 'culture'?

Table 2.1 is by no means an exhaustive list and could be added to indefinitely. Indeed, it would be wrong to try and pin this down too much. However, what can be noted here is that all of these factors are common across cultural environments. They therefore also connect with the domain of **underlying universal cultural processes** in the grammar. All of them are the sorts of issues which *all* cultural groups need to deal with. They are at the centre of what we all do every day in forming and working with the **small cultures** that surround us and provide the fabric of our everyday social lives, such as families, work groups, leisure groups and so on. As **particular cultural products**, cultural practices are indeed the outcome of the needs of small cultural groups to have routine ways of doing things, and, as shall be demonstrated below, thinking about Self and Other. The rest of the chapter will explore how this universality is the key for newcomers to make sense of and read unfamiliar practices.

How to behave

There are two good reasons for thinking carefully about how to approach unfamiliar cultural practices. One is more instrumental – if you need to live and perhaps work with the people involved in the practice, or to join their group. Another is the more human need simply to understand people from different backgrounds to your own.

When faced with unfamiliar cultural practices when travelling to other societies, we can be overcome by a sense of unfamiliarity which is compounded by feelings of isolation due to being far from home.

However, what is often forgotten is that in the more familiar surroundings of 'home' we do in fact deal with unfamiliar cultural practices as a normal part of getting on with life. Perhaps the earliest conscious time we do this is when going to school for the first time and having to deal with the classroom and playground, where there are new rules for how to behave. We also encounter culturally strange behaviour when we visit our neighbours' or friends' houses and find that they have different arrangements for eating or rules about when things happen, or perhaps how to be polite to each other. They may seem more or less formal, more or less friendly. We might find that the linguistic expressions that we have grown used to at home do not quite work in someone else's home. Encountering new cultural practices continues when we learn to operate in more new social settings, in education, when we form relationships and perhaps marry and become parents, or when we take new jobs and move from one work setting to another.

Anna visiting Beatrice's family

The following narrative[2] explores such a familiar domestic situation which, though located within Britain, contains issues which will be familiar to all readers regardless of their cultural background, and demonstrates the universal nature of many of the factors determining cultural practices as listed on page 7.

Anna was 18; she had been friends with Beatrice for several months when she was invited by her parents for dinner at their home. Anna's first impression of strangeness was their use of rooms. Whereas she felt that her parents' home had the traditional arrangement of sitting room and kitchen downstairs and bedrooms and bathroom upstairs, their house was very different. Beatrice had her bedroom in the basement, the ground floor was a very large kitchen, the sitting room was upstairs, and the parents had their bedroom and a study on the top floor – altogether a basement and three further floors in a tall, narrow terrace (or row) house.

At dinner there were more differences. Whereas Anna's parents had fine china plates, theirs were heavy earthenware; and after she had already taken salad and put it on her main plate with everything else in the main course, she discovered that they all put their salad on a smaller plate at the side, which she had presumed was a larger than usual one than she was used to for putting bread and butter on. They had roast beef, but rather than slicing it very finely as she was used to, they cut it in what she thought were rather rough, thicker slices.

Anna sensed there was a distinct disapproval of her behaviour. While eating with a knife and fork was to her a very normal thing to do, fork in left hand to take pieces of food and put them into her mouth, with the knife in the right to cut and then guide the food onto the fork, she felt Beatrice's father watching her as though she was some sort of unworldly being who had never travelled anywhere. He was holding his fork in his right hand to take up his food and even to cut it with the side of the fork on occasion. His knife remained on the side of the plate until needed for more demanding cutting activity.

Afterwards, in her room in the basement, Beatrice explained that her father had this thing about breaking away from what he considered to be parochial British eating habits and that he had been influenced by his trips to America where, he said, people were more articulately informal about eating. Anna was reminded of the classic scene in the Second World War movie in which two escaping Americans were spotted by German soldiers because they were not eating with a knife and fork in the European fashion. Beatrice said that she felt her father was a bit extreme on this matter, but when Anna complained about the salad plate Beatrice said that she should know by now that a lot of people considered it more sophisticated to keep the salad separate.

Anna's eating habits were the least of the problem. Beatrice then told her that her parents thought that she lacked personality because she said please and thank you far too often. Anna was devastated. She had been on her best behaviour in the best way she knew. She also began to wonder how it was that everything she had believed about good manners were so easily in question.

Table 2.2 presents an analysis of the narrative using the categories of cultural action which derive from the grammar. The categories of cultural action reveal that although this visit to a friend's family might be considered to be a domestic event, there is evidence that many of the features of intercultural communication are in fact taking place. They indicate that this is indeed an intercultural event. They also immediately indicate the depth of complexity of everyday encounters – which is a major focus throughout this book – and that the reading and learning of culture, no matter how haphazard, is going on all the time and is part of its nature.

There are important personal identity issues. It is crucial to note how central to Anna's identity this encounter with a foreign cultural practice is. The 'good manners' she has learnt from her parents and upbringing are her major **cultural resources**; but they do not serve her well. The *Collins Dictionary* definition of manners is 'social conduct' or 'a socially acceptable way of behaving'. This tells us that she is being momentarily robbed of confidence that she is behaving-as-normal, which is central to **small culture formation**.

At the same time, it may well be that in any other situation Anna might not need to draw on the particular **cultural resources** of good manners. She is perhaps unusually in a family setting which on this occasion is marked by relations with parents, which mirrors her own, and within which the issue of manners is particularly important. In other settings she might even be rebellious against these manners. Nevertheless, whether we carry the manners of our parental family with us or not, it is the security of knowing what manners are and how they work that we can carry to other settings.

The last row of Table 2.2 shows all parties being engaged in the same **underlying universal cultural processes** – working out the rules for behaviour associated with identity. Anna does not belong to the small culture of Beatrice's family; she is only there on a flying visit and may well never go there again. It would be a very different matter if it was the family of a future spouse, or even of neighbours with whom there will be ongoing business. This is not, however, the whole point. The small culture may well not be a fixed place at all. It may be 'a kind of place', which is whatever cultural reality a particular person is involved with at a particular time. Each cultural practice, and the rules which it embodies, will be at the centre of the **small culture formation** of the moment.

Table 2.2 Good manners

Categories of cultural action	Anna	Beatrice's parents, partly reported by Beatrice
Statements about culture	'It is expected to arrange rooms, eat and make requests in a particular manner.'	'There are other ways of arranging rooms, eating and making requests.'
Global position and politics	Recognises a degree of chauvinism towards cultural conformity.	Conforming to 'standard' cultural norms is unworldly and lacks sophistication.
Cultural resources	The cultural practices of parents. Security in 'good manners'. Media examples.	More 'worldly' and 'sophisticated' cultural practices.
Personal trajectory		Her father's particular experience derived from his travel to the US.
Underlying universal processes	Seeking rules for behaviour and associating their identities with these rules.	

Being Successful

It could be argued that Anna was unable to succeed in any sense and therefore lacked the **underlying universal cultural processes** claimed above. Indeed, her knowledge of her own society does not particularly rescue her, and the most obvious code of manners does not work. However, after the event she *is* able to draw upon a scene from a classic film which helps her to make sense of Beatrice's father's behaviour, which would equip her to feel less threatened were such an occasion to arise again. This indicates that competence in such processes will accumulate over time as we move from one experience of small culture to another.

Even though she has problems even with the most familiar setting of 'family' within her own society, if she had to engage with her friend's family on more occasions, she *would* work out a way of dealing with them, even if it meant being in conflict with her friend's parents. We need to remember that success does not necessarily mean conformity. Sustained conflict situations can also work.

Global trajectory

The part played by **global position and politics** in the narrative is notably not to do with issues of the West, the non-West or globalisation which one might expect of this category. Instead it invokes the image of 'sophistication', worldliness or perhaps class – not necessarily in the sense of which class, but of how much class, or of having or not having class. The *Collins Dictionary* definition of class in this sense is 'excellence or elegance, especially in dress, design, or behaviour'. Here, Beatrice's father refers outside to a more international domain from which he can claim a greater sophistication and indeed mobility. The category thus plays the role of **cultural resources**. It is significant to note that he, like Anna, is in the process of constructing his identity through the **underlying universal cultural process** of constructing the cultural practice. At the same time he is able to impose what some may perceive to be a deviation from the cultural norm as the established norm of this particular cultural practice.

It also needs to be appreciated here that Beatrice's father is bringing his own **personal trajectory** to the dominant behaviour which he is imposing. He has had a particular history of life experience which leads him to impose and then reify this behaviour within the practice. Understanding this may enable Anna to imagine a personal angle which she also may bring to the practice in the event that she may wish to engage with it in the future, or to enable her to arrive at a better understanding of the complexity of any cultural practice in the future.

Dealing with being Othered

It might be argued that Anna is a victim of Beatrice and her family not being sufficiently open-minded, and Othering someone who they consider not one of them because she is too conformist. Othering can be defined as reducing a group of people to a negative stereotype. The occurrence here may seem relatively unimportant when compared, for example, to race or gender. However, as shall be demonstrated elsewhere, the beginnings of cultural prejudice are often in everyday incidents of this nature. On the other hand, Anna needs to learn how to deal with situations like this as she moves through her life and through her society.

Real complexity

Reconstruct an actual event in which you had to approach and make sense of a foreign cultural practice within your own society.

Try and submit yourself to the details of what actually happened rather than imagining what happened.

What were the unexpected features of the event which might not easily be explained by the expected cultural stereotype? Use the categories of cultural action to find other explanations.

Working out more foreign rules

Think of a time when you were able to make sense of a cultural practice in a foreign society by making use of experiences that you brought with you from home.

Dima and Christoff: future in-laws[3]

The following narrative[4] serves both to exemplify the points made so far about cultural practices and to delve more deeply into the issues connected with them, this time on an international level.

Christoff had known Dima's family for a long time, ever since he had worked in her country and been her father's colleague. When she came to do a summer course at a local language school they arranged to have coffee, and he was interested to hear about her recent engagement to Ehsan.

When she began to tell him about Ehsan's family coming to visit her family, he felt sufficiently familiar with the practice to ask her jokingly if she had served the tea. He knew very well that she wouldn't have because she was a professional woman in her early thirties and far from the stereotype. Dima took a moment to assess his comment, and then decided to follow the humour and not be offended. She replied that she had been so impressed when Ehsan had jumped up to help her mother serve the tea.

She explained that Ehsan's family had now been to visit a *second* time. The first time it was his parents and elder sister. This time, his sister's husband and their son had also come. It had been a great success. The two families had got on well. Ehsan's family had said that most of their relatives came from a provincial city in the south-east, and they were therefore free to get on with their affairs independently of them. They had agreed that it was okay for Dima and Ehsan to see each other, and that they would contribute equally to the expenses of the wedding and setting up home.

The visit had been scheduled for 5 until 7. This meant that Ehsan's family would not stay for dinner and Dima's family would be free afterwards to go to her other aunt for dinner. Christoff commented on how formal the timing was.

Christoff then expressed his ambivalence about the whole thing. He said that there was no tradition where he came from for such visits. With his own parents-in-law, the two families had agreed to meet for lunch some months before the wedding. (They lived quite far away, so the meeting had had to be carefully arranged in an equidistant location.) However, the meeting had in no sense been to approve the marriage. They had got on well, but if they hadn't it would not have stopped him and his fiancée from getting on with their relationship.

Then Dima surprised him by saying that it was just the same for her and Ehsan. They would have continued seeing each other even if their respective parents had not approved. She said that the two families would only ever meet occasionally, even though they lived in the same city – *perhaps* at the New Year. They were busy, modern people who had their own lives to get on with.

In the end Dima and Christoff agreed that each other's practices were strange but also familiar. Dima said that it was really a myth that some societies valued family life and loyalty to parents more than others. If you dig deep enough you will find that everyone finds some sort of way to be both loyal and independent. Nevertheless, she said that, for them, family support was a precious resource. Families would get together in formalmeetings to help married couples to resolve conflicts. But even then, she was careful to explain, this practice was probably far more varied and complex than people might imagine.

Then there was another angle which bothered Christoff. When Dima mentioned that she and Ehsan had both written on their Facebook sites that they were 'in a relationship', he asked her how she felt about having to use this language. He wanted to know if Dima thought that this meant they were being influenced by a Western globalisation that was putting phrases in their mouths and taking them away from their traditions. Dima said that such an idea was nonsense – that there was no way that they were being manipulated by Facebook – that she and Ehsan were making it their own, playing with it and claiming the power to take ownership of international trends.

While both Dima and Christoff are either describing or thinking about their own cultural practices, there is a form of intercultural interaction taking place because they are making sense of each other across what is at least potentially quite a large cultural divide, both in terms of geography and differences in expectation. Their exchange is to do with how the family relates to the individual and is therefore at the core of cultural identity. The application of the categories of cultural action in Table 2.3 helps to make sense of what is going on between them.

The **statements about culture** row shows Christoff beginning to feel that the practices which Dima describes are not as alien as he first imagined. Dima is able to explain to him that things are more complex and flexible than he expected. The **underlying universal cultural processes** row shows that both of them are trying to get to the bottom of things in a similar manner.

A significant detail in the narrative is that when Dima's and Ehsan's families meet they agree to share the cost of the wedding. This might be interpreted as a break from tradition, which might connect with Ehsan's parents' family being far away and therefore leaving them to construct their own tradition. On the other hand, it can be argued that this co-construction of culture is a theme that recurs in a number of settings reported in this book.

Table 2.3 Family vs. personal freedom

Categories of cultural action	Dima	Christoff
Statements about culture	'The families of a couple who are entering into a serious relationship meet to give their approval and discuss arrangements. 'However, this is a flexible practice and does not prevent the couple from getting on with their relationship. 'Also, after the wedding the two families would not have to see each other that often.'	'In my culture families do not meet to approve marriages. 'However, on reflection, families often do meet to give support to their children's relationships.'
Global position and politics	Facebook, though an American site, can be made use of, played with and owned by people outside the West (implying bottom-up globalisation).	Associates Facebook with Western-led (top-down) globalisation which erodes the non-Western culture. An initial suspicion that the practice 'in Dima's culture' inhibits personal freedom.
Cultural resources	A tradition of family support for married couples. Family-based traditions do not have to be in conflict with personal freedom. The ability to take ownership of global resources such as Facebook. A keen sense of modernity.	His society supports personal freedom and is less formal regarding couples in relationships.
Underlying universal processes	Speaking to each other about cultural practices and discussing the issues underpinning them. Differentiating, after reflection, between surface practice (family approval vs. no family approval) and more hidden meanings (family approval in dialogue with personal freedom).	

Dima and Christoff: the issue with Facebook

However, the **global position and politics** row, supported by the **cultural resources** row, shows that the Facebook issue pulls Dima and Christoff apart again and the discussion moves to a different level. It invokes the image of globalisation, which Christoff and Dima have very different views about.

- Christoff subscribes to what might be called a top-down globalisation, where the world is dominated by Western products and images of civilisation, and where any adoption by non-Western cultures would result in a loss of those cultures.
- Dima's view is very different. She claims what might be termed a bottom-up globalisation, where anybody can take ownership, on entirely their own terms, of products and practices wherever they come from.

Indeed, Christoff's view could be considered patronising, because it assumes that people from outside the West are not capable of colonising from the other direction and making Facebook their own. This confidence to take ownership on the part of Dima provides an extra cultural resource of modernity, which stands in some explicit defiance to what is in effect Christoff's more traditional notion that personal freedom is the domain of his own cultural background.

It is once again Christoff who has the most to learn, as this annex to the narrative describes.

Dima reflected quietly to herself how patronising Christoff was to imagine that she and Ehsan, and probably their entire nation, would be somehow corrupted by Facebook. She didn't say anything because it would be just too difficult to explain, and she didn't have time for it. Also, Christoff would think that it was just another topic for critical discussion – just like the silly activities in her English classes, where the teacher seemed to think that foreigners didn't know how to discuss. That's all it was for him. However, for people like Ehsan and her, Facebook and technologies like it represented a sustained struggle against government restrictions.

Yes, it *was* Western. That's where it came from. But so did football and the telephone. But how many scientists, engineers, technical people, inventors and so on came from places like she did; and how many of them would be making these things in their own countries if they had the opportunity? When things like Facebook arrived on the scene her people took to them like fish to water and knew exactly what to do. She looked at the carpet on the floor, which was produced by an Eastern country. No-one ever asked Westerners if it was safe to take on these Eastern ideas.

She also remembered the surprise on Christoff's face when she mentioned the precise timing of the visit. Did he really think that they couldn't organise things on time? It might not be such a high priority for them to think about absolutely *everything* in terms of time like these people did – always looking at their watches – but when it was something as important as the visit of the family of a potential husband, of course the timing was absolutely crucial. Anyway, it was all a myth, this thing about time in the West. Especially the young people seemed far more civilised about it. They were all looking at phones instead of watches!

One might disagree with Dima's statement about 'Eastern ideas' if one thinks about how members of the older generations might have rejected the rush of Eastern philosophies into Western societies in the 1960s. Nevertheless, she is saying more about the nature of bottom-up globalisation, which is represented in Table 2.4. However, this needs to be read as the product of Dima's own perception.

Two important terms arise out of Dima's statement. Being or feeling on the Periphery can be defined as lacking power and being defined politically, economically and culturally by others. In contrast, the Centre can be defined as having the global power to be able to define the rest of the world. These are not strictly geographical entities; though in recent times the Centre has equated with the West.

Table 2.4 Statement of bottom-up globalisation

Categories of cultural action	Dima's image of her countrypeople	Dima's image of Christoff
Statements about culture	'We are worldly and capable of taking ownership of and contributing to Western products. 'We don't let time-keeping dominate our lives but are careful of it when it is important.'	'They think we are unable to cope with Western products without being dominated by them. 'They think we can't deal with time-keeping.'
Global position and politics	A Periphery position means that there is a constant struggle for recognition. Government restrictions. Too difficult for the West to understand. The West presents a Centre perception of the world.	It's all just a matter of discussion.
Cultural resources	Success and contribution when given the opportunity, e.g. when working in the West.	Western products are produced entirely by Western society.
Underlying universal processes	Finding a way to align herself with the views of others.	

The issue of time-keeping, which is a common theme in the way in which national cultures have often been defined, is also raised. This has already been referred to in Table 2.1. Dima makes the important observation that, rather than being a matter of cultural ability, as is often thought, it is a matter of priority. Hence, a further factor in the choices of cultural practice, to those listed above, might be: What actions or events are most highly prioritised for attention to time-keeping?

Assessment

How far do you agree with Dima's analysis of Christoff and the West?

Remember and recount an event when you found yourself in either Dima's or Christoff's position.

Why might it be that, despite Christoff's initial understanding of commonality with Dima's cultural reality, it is the issue of Facebook which pulls them apart again? What is so deep in Christoff's cultural makeup which drives this?

What is Dima getting at when she comments on Christoff reducing the Facebook issue to 'just another topic for critical discussion', and connects this with her English classes?

Look again at Dima's observation about people looking at their phones instead of their watches. Does this mean that they are giving a higher priority to relationships rather than time-keeping? Could this be something new, or can new technologies reveal things that have previously been there but out of sight?

Misunderstanding and Othering

Dima and Christoff's discussions about in-laws and Facebook show that there is a huge potential for misunderstandings. We are often tempted to over-, under- or misinterpret what we see. One reason for this is the prejudices we all carry with us, and the surface, seductive easy answers which pass as evidence to support them. Table 2.5 presents two examples of such misunderstanding in particular domestic circumstances. As with Anna's experience of her friend's family, above, focusing on the family next door is familiar to everyone but also an excellent example of what can happen further afield.

The whole centre and right-hand section of Table 2.5 are placed under the heading of **underlying universal cultural processes** and **small culture formation**, not just because almost everything can be traced to this domain, but to show that both solutions and dangers reside there – both positive and negative types of understanding.

Table 2.5 Misunderstanding the people next door

	Produced by underlying universal cultural processes in small culture formation		
Observation	*Prejudice*	*Easy answer*	*Missed complexity of small culture formation*
Children address their parents by given name and no title.	'They are less polite than we are.'	'They don't use a respectful form of address.' 'We value politeness; they don't.'	There are a large variety of possible ways of showing respect. Within this cultural environment using given names is approved by parents and does carry respect.
Children are expected to keep quiet at meal times unless spoken to.	'They are more formal than we are.'	'They don't encourage open, critical discussion.' 'We value critical discussion; they don't.'	In every cultural arrangement there are rules of formality. Within this cultural environment they are expressed in a particular way. There may be other times and places where open, critical discussion is encouraged.

Negative understanding: prejudice and easy answers

The second and third columns indicate prejudice and easy answers, or superficial responses to difference. This is where what might seem to be a fairly innocent misunderstanding turns into a more sinister Othering. This can be directed at any group of people, but it is most often associated with race, ethnicity, foreigners or minority groups. There is the development of an accusatory tone as 'they' are compared with 'we'; and the easy answers are couched as 'they don't'. In such cases the easy answers which imply some form of deficiency can become so established that they are very hard to undo.

The problem with 'values'

Values play a significant role in this politics. They are used to heighten the moral element of what 'we do', or 'have', and 'they don't'. The *Collins English Dictionary* defines values as 'the moral principles and beliefs or accepted standards of a person or social group'. Everyone has values of one type or another. Values that sometimes come into discussion within the context of intercultural difference are to do with where loyalties lie – to our parents, to the family or to the individual. There are, however, both positive and negative sides to values:

- On the positive side, they represent us at our best and help us to adhere to 'good' principles. For example, we should strive for deeper understandings which counter prejudice. Such values may well transcend particular cultural realities.
- On the negative side, they can employ essentialist stereotypes to demarcate culturally superior from inferior behaviour. For example, when we characterise putting the individual and self-determination before family, parents and even work groups as the exclusive mark of Western society. This is problematic when such values are perceived as exclusive to a particular 'culture'.

The negative side clearly lends itself to the way in which rhetorics of war and notions of race, gender and cultural deficiency have been built around imagined values. Here it is important to note that values should not be allowed to become instrumental in Othering. They should not be allowed to represent uncrossable barriers that force us into an 'us–them' psychology.

On the positive side there is also the danger that universal values could be imposed in a top-down manner by a particular cultural or ideological stance. This has somehow to be resolved.

Seductive statements about culture

Closely connected to the values issue is another aspect of **particular cultural products** in the bottom-right of the grammar, that of **statements about culture**. The problem here is that when people say 'we value politeness' or 'we value critical discussion', as in Table 2.5, implying 'in our culture', it is easily taken as true, because, after all, they should know, they are the insiders, they know their own culture.

However, as is revealed in Table 2.5, such statements are easy answers. Such **statements about culture** are also **particular cultural products** because they are created as the outward show of a particular cultural reality, just as a piece of music or fine art. They are also stated as though they are exclusive to the culture of the people who state them, whereas in effect 'we value critical discussion' is more likely to be a universal. **Statements about culture** are particularly powerful aspects of **small culture formation**. They are the first on the list of categories of cultural action in the analyses of all the ethnographic narratives in this book because they set a powerful scene for what is going on between the various characters involved.

Positive understanding: appreciating complexity

The solution to the prejudice and easy answers is through understanding the full complexity of how the family operates in the right-hand column of Table 2.5. I say 'missed complexity' to describe this because the easy answers lead us to miss the opportunity of a deeper and more fruitful understanding. The complexity reveals that the differences between the two small family cultures are not as imagined. In fact 'they' *do* what we thought they could not; and the family next door may well share our values, but not in the ways we might expect.

As with Anna and her friend's family, above, it is necessary to find the commonalities in the various **small culture formations** one has experienced. Whereas the particular details of cultural practices will be different in different cultural environments, the mechanics of how they are formed can be very similar.

While the two practices in Table 2.5 are very different, they both represent rules for showing respect to older people. In both cases the family members will have adopted these rules either from tradition or through a process of negotiation about how such behaviour should be carried out, especially if the parents come from different family traditions. Using the given name and no title may seem less formal, but there may be more formality than one might think in the thoughtful manner in which people are addressed when there is a break from tradition.

Easy answers and Othering

Remember a time when you visited another family, another department at work, another sports team or any other social group to which you did not belong.

- What prejudices did you construct in this process?
- Recall the evidence for these prejudices. What role did easy answers, values and **statements about culture** play in this process?
- Reconsider the evidence and try to see a greater complexity of who they are which will serve to undo the prejudices.

Connect this experience with the Othering of a particular group of people with which you are familiar.

Recall examples when values have been used to project inferiority and superiority within a process of Othering.

Working things out

How might an increased intercultural awareness have helped Anna to be less intimidated by Beatrice's family, and Christoff to understand better Dima's position regarding Facebook? The following might help. Indeed, especially in the case of Christoff making connections between his and Dima's relationship with in-laws, these things are already happening:

- Understanding that people can be modern and complex – the engaged couple and their families, Beatrice's father.
- Understanding that personal feelings about how things should be may not be enough – that British families do not necessarily have more freedom, that good manners might not be sufficient.

- Being prepared to expand and adapt initial beliefs about how things are; to be more successful in interacting with the people in question; becoming more worldly.
- Engagement and interaction rather than just understanding difference: being able to share common experiences with Dima; learning to be more strategic with good manners.
- Building on common cultural understanding and ability to relate across boundaries – in all of the above.

The important point to make here is that what has been revealed in the two narratives by no means represents uncrossable cultural boundaries. The ability to relate across boundaries is demonstrated in the following example, from fiction, of finding resonances across societies. Indian Babo, witnessing a family party with his wife's relations in Wales in the early 1970s, observes the following in this humorous account:

> It reminded Babo strangely of one of [his father] Prem Kumar's Sunday card-playing sessions.… There was something very similar here, except in this Welsh-chintz version of the sideboard was heaving with devilled eggs instead of dhoklas. And instead of the sizeable paunches and behinds that middle-aged Jungjjus succumbed to, these men and women were powerfully stocky, more uniform in their roundness. But there was the same parochial pride and failings on display. The same aunts berating an unmarried girl to hurry up and get on with it. The same know-all uncle complaining that a son was spending money like a man with no arms.
>
> (Doshi 2010: 104–5)

Cultural practices need to be taken very seriously. They can be observed and described; but they must not be taken at face value. They need to be interpreted deeply.

Interviews

Interview four people and ask them:

- to describe a cultural practice which they first found strange and then found common ground with;
- to explain what happened to help them cross boundaries;
- what they were able to do as a result of this engagement;
- if this helped them to re-assess more familiar cultural practices;
- what they learnt about the people who owned the unfamiliar practice which they did not know before.

Share your findings with another investigator and find common factors.

Are people generally aware?

How far can you see these ideas about artefacts and small cultures working in the ethnographic narratives in this chapter?

Do the characters realise how many of these processes they may be sharing?

How far are they getting on with playing their roles so much that they do not realise what these roles entail?

Think of cases where you have avoided conciliation in an argument or another conflict situation because you have not stepped back to think how much you and the other people are in fact doing the same things.

Summary

- Differences in cultural practice can be due to a wide number of factors, only some of which derive from national structures, and many of which we will be familiar with from our own experience.
- Reading and negotiating culture begins in what might be considered domestic events, where all the categories of cultural action are active.
- The **cultural resources** we make use of will vary depending on the difficulties we face in a particular cultural event.
- **Cultural resources** may derive from small culture experience, depending on particular **personal trajectories**, as well as from national cultures.
- **Global positioning and politics** may relate to notions of class and sophistication, as well as to international alignments.
- We form small cultures around us all the time as we engage and interact with others. We thus carry the experience of **small culture formation** from one event to another.
- While much understanding may be gained through sharing experiences of cultural practices which may at first appear very foreign, there are deeper prejudices regarding difference, which are rooted in **global position and politics**, which can be very hard to acknowledge and shift.
- The **underlying universal cultural processes**, which we all share, provide the potential for us to see beyond prejudice by reading the complexity across cultural boundaries.
- However, the same shared processes also generate easy answers as a way of making sense of cultural strangeness under pressure, and lead to cultural prejudice and Othering.
- 'Values' are problematic when they are constructed as easy answers in the process of Othering.
- Cultural boundaries are not uncrossable.

Notes

1 A mug is a tall cup without a saucer, used mainly for hot drinks, often individually decorated with a coloured pattern or motif.
2 This is based on a personal experience of visiting a friend's family, a personal arrogance regarding eating like Americans, conversations with a number of people about their attitudes towards their children's friends.
3 In-laws are the parents, children or siblings of the spouse.
4 This is based on a conversation with a family visitor who recounted this event, conversations with a young couple about their marriage arrangements, a documentary about an Iranian local divorce court (Longinotto and Mir-Hosseini 1999), experience of wedding

arrangements in a variety of settings, discussions with a number of people about Facebook, being a user of Facebook, discussions with specialist researchers regarding the role of Facebook in Middle Eastern politics, and the recent experience of my daughter's wedding.

Further reference

YouTube Extract from Northanger Abbey: http://www.youtube.com/watch?v=1uA32oe QPg0&feature=related
   — In this extract from a 2007 television dramatisation of Jane Austen's book, first published in the early nineteenth century, Catherine, who has been a welcomed guest, finds herself being told off by one of her hosts. In a sequence after this extract she is ordered to leave suddenly in the middle of the night.
   — What can be learnt from this about breaking the rules of cultural practices when normal politeness is suddenly broken?
   — In the second half of the film clip, Catherine's friend Isabella is in serious trouble because of another instance of rule breaking. Can you work out what mistake she has made with regard to another dominant cultural practice of the day?

Honarbin-Holliday, M. (2008). *Becoming visible in Iran: women in contemporary Iranian society.* London: I.B. Tauris.
   — Pages 55 onwards provide a detailed description of the complex cultural practices of women's clothing in modern urban Iran.
   — What is surprising about the complexity? What does this surprise tell you about how far you reply in easy answers? How does the complexity help you to find something familiar and accessible in the practices?
   — See also the discussion of these descriptions in Holliday (2011a: 128–46).

Roberts, C. (2009). Cultures of organisations meet ethno-linguistic cultures: narratives in job interviews. In Feng, A., Byram, M. and Fleming, M. (eds), *Education and training: becoming interculturally competent.* Clevedon: Multilingual Matters: 15–31.
   — This chapter describes how interviews for jobs in large organisations are intercultural encounters which require a high degree of conformity within the established politics of the organisations.
   — Recall cultural practices which you have had to master, both 'at home' and 'abroad', under difficult circumstances in order to survive and succeed. What experience have you brought into these events which have helped you, and what important learning have you taken from them?

Lankshear, C., Gee, J.P., Knobel, M. and Searle, C. (1997). *Changing literacies.* Buckingham: Open University Press.
   — Chapter 1 describes the everyday processes of engaging with the complexities of cultural practices and the complexities of **small culture formation**.
   — It is argued that this is a normal part of everyday life as we all move through different phases in our lives, from home, to school, to new jobs, to the various social groups that we belong to.

Chapter 3

Investigating culture

This chapter builds on the work on cultural practices in Chapter 2 to develop strategies and disciplines for approaching and making sense of the culturally strange. In so doing, it capitalises on the everyday complexity of cultural practices as something we all have an understanding of, and through which we might find a route to the unfamiliar.

Approaching the unfamiliar and foreign

Though the point has already been made that the boundaries between the familiar and unfamiliar are blurred, it is useful first to attempt a comparison between approaching one and the other. There is indeed an advantage when approaching new cultural practices within our own society, no matter how strange. We already know something about the people and the situations involved. There are histories and traditions with which we are familiar. When we travel to other societies the cultural practices we encounter will be less familiar, and all of the issues of understanding become magnified.

Against understanding

The following factors may inhibit understanding when encountering unfamiliar cultural environments:

- Possibly unfamiliar institutions (e.g. political, educational, family, religious and legal), language, history, economy, politics, community structures and traditions. In terms of the grammar, the people we meet may be relying on different **cultural resources** and displaying different **particular cultural products**.
- A stronger temptation to Other because of prejudices and imagined differences in values which are rooted in our traditional images of the societies in question, which are derived from our **global position and politics**.
- The culture shock of being alone in an alien society.

The differences between societies implicit in these factors cannot be denied. However, the temptation to make too much of these differences needs to be somehow put aside. It is what we are able to understand once the culture shock has subsided that we need to build upon. We may imagine that we know less that we really do.

In favour of understanding

In this respect, there will be other factors which act in favour of understanding:

- Shared knowledge of how institutions (e.g. political, educational, family, religious and legal), language, history, economy, politics, community structures and traditions work everywhere, through the experience we gain of **small culture formation** through our **personal trajectories**.

These factors are within the domain of **underlying universal cultural processes**. However, it is a further complexity of the task of understanding that there are also negative elements in these processes which lead to Othering. Even at the basic level of visiting the family next door, the prejudices, easy answers and the negative 'us–them' side of values which inhibit understanding all derive from the same **underlying universal cultural processes**. They are also to do with trying to make sense of strange practices through comparison with the familiar, by making judgements, which are a normal way of aligning Self with Other. Saying superficial things about other people to make 'them' look bad and 'us' look good is a very basic part of behaviour and identity construction, which is central to **small culture formation**.

This chapter will therefore explore how the positive side of **underlying universal cultural processes** can be used to counter and undo the negative side.

Francisca, Gita and Hande: looking for an intercultural methodology

The way in which we all struggle with these different types of understanding, and how this can result in different methods for approaching culture, is demonstrated in the following narrative[1] in which three friends compare their experiences of either being recipients or users of such methods:

Francisca and Gita both had new jobs in the capital and tried to meet once a week for coffee to share experiences. They were both working for large organisations with international workforces where there were initiatives to learn how to work with cultural diversity.

Francisca was excited about some intercultural training sessions she had been to. She said that it had been really useful because they were given cultural profile information about different nationalities. Gita was immediately sceptical and said that she had heard about these profiles and advised Francisca not to be seduced by them. Francisca replied that she was aware of the dangers and that in fact their trainer had made a big point about how there were lots of exceptions, and that the profiles were to be considered as useful starting points. Gita said that she was really worried about this idea of 'useful starting points'. Francisca knew what was coming, because she felt that Gita was far too sensitive about issues of 'difference'. She wasn't surprised when Gita said that saying cultural profiles were useful starting points was like saying that race and gender stereotypes were useful starting points and that the very fact that the profiles were there at all encouraged discrimination. Gita went on to point out that saying there were exceptions just added to the seduction by implying that the profiles were inclusive even though they were not.

Francisca thought a lot about Gita's attack. She thought that Gita was being unfair because there was absolutely no evidence of any sort of discrimination in the way in which the intercultural trainer talked about things. Indeed, the trainer emphasised all the time that the profiles were completely neutral and, far from discriminating *against* people from other cultures, allowed them a safe space where they could be themselves. For Francisca, this meant that her own values would be respected and she wouldn't have to feel under pressure to be like people from other cultures. Also, there seemed to be so much careful research behind the profiles, which had been developed by serious academics over a long period of time. When Francisca tried to explain this, Gita got very angry indeed, and started going on about how patronising all of this was. Gita said that this business of 'safe space' had been the justification for Apartheid in South Africa, and for saying that women should 'stay at home' – to somehow 'give them' power to 'be themselves' in a domain which belonged to them, but which was in effect completely restricted.

Gita could see that Francisca wasn't taking her seriously. No-one ever did. She was just trying to work things out in her own terms; and sometimes she had to make extreme statements to get heard. She thought about Francisca talking about protecting her values. This was so important. She didn't want to give Francisca the impression that they didn't count. She found something of a resolution when she discussed her dilemma with another friend, Hande.

Hande was doing a course in anthropology and said that the approach to investigating culture which she had learnt about was very different to what Francisca had been describing. Instead of trying to define who people were from the outset, they were taught to watch how people behaved and to listen to what they said, and to try and work things out from there. She said it wasn't really a matter of whether Francisca was right or wrong, but that what she said, how she expressed what she believed, and what went on in her intercultural training sessions, was all stuff to be observed, and that *that* was the culture.

This made Gita think that her own anger was therefore also something to be observed, and that that was part of *her* culture. Well, what it *did* seem to mean was that the cultural profiling that Francisca had been talking about was also an observable part of the culture of the people who made them.

The next time Gita and Francisca had coffee, Gita decided to try out what Hande had been talking about. She asked Francisca to look around at the people in the café and try to work out what they were thinking and doing. But when she suggested forgetting about cultural profiles, Francisca said that it was impossible. They talked about this and agreed that it was actually quite hard to try and think about people without imagining how they fitted into ideas they already had about which culture they came from. Two men and a woman in a headscarf, who were speaking a foreign language that neither Gita nor Francisca recognised were most likely, they thought, to be from the Middle East, and this invoked media images of women being mistreated. Gita found herself thinking exactly the same thing about them as Francisca, and was quite shocked about this. Well, she thought, Francisca looked quite Mediterranean, so she asked her how she would feel if other people in the café just presumed that she always took long siestas in the afternoon and was always late for meetings.

When Francisca was horrified at this they began to talk about where these 'theories', which were in fact very inaccurate stereotypes, came from – well, from the media, from childhood, from the people they hung out with. It certainly was the case that they were very hard to shake off. So they tried to put the Middle East thing out of their heads; and there was absolutely no evidence, from the body language of the two men and the woman, or from their tone of voice, that the woman was being treated as they might expect, even if they were Middle Eastern. Both Francisca and Gita agreed that they did in fact know, from people they knew, that it was a myth anyway that Middle Eastern women were oppressed. How shocking, that even though they knew it was a myth, it still came so strongly into their minds.

When Francisca went to another training session she was thinking again about the experience in the café. She found it so hard to believe that all the scientific research that stood behind the cultural profiles could just be discounted. Of course, the people who carried them out must be influenced by the same prejudices that she and Gita had when they were in the café; but surely they wouldn't have allowed that to get in the way because they were carrying out objective research. Also, everyone in the training session clearly thought that the profiles were useful; and if what the trainer said was true there might be less pressure in the company to behave like Americans and British people. She knew that Gita would say that they weren't objective at all.

Table 3.1, employing the categories of cultural action, presents the basic position of each of the three characters as far as they are revealed in the narrative. I have added the category espoused methodology because it is of special interest here. The three approaches to methodology can be characterised as:

- Francisca – top-down, beginning with profiles or stereotypes;
- Gita – being wary of the prejudices which underpin these profiles or stereotypes;
- Hande – bottom-up, learning from direct observation.

Top-down here means beginning with large assumptions, whereas bottom-up means beginning with detail.

The rest of the table indicates some of the background to these approaches. The **cultural resources** row is not to do with national structures, but with the small cultures of Francisca's training group and the ethos it represents, and of Hande's academic programme. These represent the professional and academic influences on intercultural method. The **underlying universal cultural processes** are shared; but what is particularly noticeable in the narrative is the way in which Gita and Francisca struggle with their particular views of the world. They both learn how hard it is to shake off the prejudices which they have internalised about other people. But it is important to look here at how it gets in the way of how we see culture. This reminds me of a recent experience:

Table 3.1 Francisca, Gita and Hande

Categories of cultural action	Francisca	Gita	Hande
Statements about culture	'My values are different to people from other cultures.'	'I cannot be defined by cultural profiles.'	
Global position and politics	There is a need to be protected from Western culture by means of definitions of cultural difference.	Perceptions of cultural difference are underpinned by race and gender prejudice.	
Cultural resources	A professional culture which values cultural profiling to solve intercultural issues. Apparent consensus within her training group.	Knowledge of race and gender discrimination.	An academic culture.
Espoused methodology	Using cultural profiles (stereotypes) as helpful starting points to predict and explain behaviour, and to allow space for culture-specific values.	Not using cultural profiles because they are similar to discriminatory race or gender profiles.	Observing behaviour as it emerges.
Underlying universal processes	Struggling hard to make sense of perceptions of difference within professional and academic contexts.		

I met with a group of students to talk about stereotypes. They were mainly Eastern European and they talked about how they disliked how people made assumptions about what people imagined about them because of where they came from. One of them had been refused employment when it became clear what her nationality was. Then, when they talked about East Asian students, all the standard stereotypes began to flow in.

There is little information about Hande in the narrative; and one wonders what her struggles might be. One wonders what prejudices she brought to her research and how she would deal with them.

A critical qualitative approach

The methodology which I am going to propose for investigating culture is the one suggested by Hande – the *bottom-up* observation of behaviour – combined with Gita's wariness of prejudice, which relate to **global position and politics**. It applies disciplines which derive from more critical types of qualitative research and ethnography:

- making the familiar strange and putting aside easy answers;
- opening up to complexity;
- asking ethnographic questions;
- finding previous experience to aid cultural understanding;
- critical reading of global position and politics.

These will be described below as they emerge. It is important to note that these disciplines do not come in any particular order, and will be dealt with as they emerge within the context of the narrative. However, the final discipline, critical reading, will be the topic of Chapter 6. These disciplines are implicit in the methodology for writing ethnographic narratives throughout the book. It is important first, though, to look at the alternative.

The use of the term 'bottom-up' for an approach to investigation resonates with bottom-up globalisation. Both imply an acknowledgement of cultural phenomena which will be hidden by top-down cultural profiling.

The problem with stereotypes and a top-down approach

This choice of a critical qualitative method is in stark contrast with the top-down approach witnessed by Francisca in the narrative, and as such goes against a long-standing dominant tradition.

The top-down approach can be associated with stereotyping or, in academic circles, national cultural profiling. This involves working down from theories about culture X or culture Y and is considered by many to be a valid method. It is claimed that it employs a natural or scientific method which is neutral and objective. While it is recognised that stereotypes and cultural profiles are prone to over-generalisation, it is thought that they are nevertheless 'a good place to begin'.

As Gita points out, while stereotyping and profiling are indeed natural, and do represent a type of science, they are infected by prejudiced images of Self and Other which lead to unnecessarily divisive thinking. Because they begin with theories of what 'a culture' is like, the investigator is driven to notice examples of difference or similarities which confirm that the foreign Other is 'like us' or 'not like us' in limiting ways which are inevitably built on the 'us–them' discourses which are deep in the **global position and politics** that we are brought up with. Moreover, the strong objectivist claims lead to a denial of the influence of these discourses. At a domestic level, this top-down approach falls into the same easy answers as those concerning the family next door in Table 2.5.

There is, however, another point which has to be made. At the end of her discussions with Gita and Hande, Francisca comments that the theories of difference, if they are true, will protect her and her colleagues from having to adopt American and British behaviour. This is reflected in the **global position and politics** row in Table 3.1. This is a complex issue and must be set against Gita's statements about discrimination. Also, adhering to stereotypes of the Self to oppose the Other can be interpreted as Self-Othering if the stereotypes are negative.

Finding a different way of looking

Watch small groups of people in a public place.

- What prejudices do you have about them because of their appearance and where you imagine they come from?
- Where do these prejudices come from? To what degree might they derive from professional, academic, work or other small cultural groups, as well as from the media or wider-ranging narratives?

- What different things do you notice when you try and put these prejudices aside?
- How easy is it to put the prejudices aside?

Evaluate the arguments put forward by Francisca, Gita and Hande and my resulting choice of a bottom-up methodology

What are your reasons for supporting or rejecting each argument? Put your ideas to other members of your group.

Look up the concept of positivism and see how it relates to the top-down methodology.

Look at Chapters 6 and 7 and see what all this has to do with ideology.

Will top-down definitions of cultural difference protect or endanger Francisca's cultural identity against British and American influence in her company?

- What are the arguments for and against, considering what Gita has to say about prejudice?
- What experiences have you had which help you to answer this?

Making the familiar strange and putting aside easy answers

This concerns putting aside all the things which first spring to mind about cultural difference and trying to see what is really going on instead. As has been suggested throughout, these things will be:

- the stereotypes with which we are brought up and which we are constantly fed through our media;
- the familiar ways in which we are used to thinking about the culturally strange.

Ivonne preparing to go abroad

The following is a narrative[2] of the processes someone might go through in trying to apply this discipline.

Ivonne was invited to speak at a conference in Ex. In preparation she had been on a course in intercultural awareness, and she had to say that she didn't wholly approve of the approach. She didn't like being told by a rather self-righteous trainer that *everyone* in the West was prejudiced about people from the non-West to the verge of racism. She found this insulting. She didn't associate herself at all with a colonial past and thought of herself as politically Left and a feminist, who had fought for human rights all her life. She also thought that this concept of 'the West' was not really defined. She had also travelled widely, and always felt that she was open and prepared to learn from other cultures, though never to the Far East. She was also annoyed when the trainer said she shouldn't say 'other cultures' because it implied essentialist packaging. Well, she knew all about what it was like to be 'packaged', but she felt strongly that 'other cultures' did have their own values and ways of doing things and needed to be respected as such. She knew there were issues with Exian students in their universities and that stereotypes were really not helpful. One of her colleagues who had had Exian students had said to her recently that the stereotype didn't work as well as it used to because the younger generation weren't as hard working as their parents. Nevertheless, she was anxious about this trip and was going to give some of the advice she got on the course a fair try.

The first incident was dealing with the conference organisers to arrange the visit. They were less than what she expected in terms of efficiency. First they seemed over-formal, with too many titles. Then, at what seemed to her the very last minute, with just weeks to go, they started making demands first for an unreasonably long abstract, and then for scans of her passport, only explaining at the very last minute that the format she had sent it in wasn't the right one. Then, two nights before leaving she still wasn't sure who was going to meet her. They seemed to have no consideration whatsoever for how busy she might be, and how much she might need to plan ahead. The formality didn't allow for the basic politeness that might show at least that she understood her position.

Her inclination was to say that all this was to do with the collectivist stereotype, whereby people followed traditions of politeness, expressed through subservience and titles, but were just not able to think about the individual. Then she read one of the principles from her course notes – *try and put aside the most obvious explanations for cultural behaviour you find problematic, e.g. a particular cultural stereotype*. Ivonne remembered that this meant she should think of the people she was emailing as conference administrators instead of 'Exian' conference administrators, *because* the Exian stereotype was so strong in her mind, and, indeed, when she thought about it, quite negative.

When Ivonne tried to look at her communication with the conference organisers without thinking of them as Exian, her annoyance was still there, but tempered by remembering how hard it had been for one of the administrators in her office to find a way to address an important foreign visitor, and then pulling her hair out because she didn't realise until the last minute that she had forgotten to get some important information. Like many other people she felt constantly beleaguered by incompetence of one sort or another. To think of Exian administrators in the same way made her reflect on her annoyance regarding the intercultural communication course. Was it right to think of the Exian administrators by what must be the same measures of competence, when their culture must have different sets of standards? However, another way of looking at it was that she would meet them with the same underlying view she had of the people she knew – that they were basically nice people who were genuinely trying their best despite their mistakes.

Table 3.2 indicates a transition in Ivonne's views towards a different type of understanding. She begins to see the Exian administrators in similar ways to those she knows at home. The extra domain of 'familiar to strange' has been added to the categories of cultural action to indicate that this association between foreign and home behaviour is where the 'strange'resides. This does not mean that cultural difference is being ignored, but that cultural bridges are being considered instead of an uncrossable cultural line. Indeed, this journey into unfamiliar thinking leads Ivonne to reflect considerably, to moderate her annoyance, and to appreciate the Exian administrator's genuine desire to help.

Table 3.2 Ivonne putting aside easy answers

Categories of cultural action	Easy answers	New understanding
Statements about culture	'Exian culture is collectivist. 'Therefore the Exian administrators do not appreciate the needs of the individual.'	'The Exian administrators may be trying to solve similar problems to other administrators.'
Global position and politics	Foreign cultures need to have their own space and values. Denial of 'blanket' Western prejudice towards the non-West.	
Cultural resources	Background in feminism and human rights. Knowledge of what it is like to be 'packaged'. World travel, experience of other cultures.	Experience with administrators dealing with foreign visitors, who are nice people, trying their best, but who make mistakes.
Underlying universal processes	Making sense of annoying foreign behaviour through reference to negative stereotypes.	Making sense of annoying foreign behaviour through reference to similar behaviour in other professional contexts.
Familiar to strange	Familiar collectivist stereotype. Familiar mode of making sense of the Exian Other.	Strange experience of the possibility that Exian administrators might share behaviour and values with administrators at home.

Unresolved issues

Ivonne does nevertheless have issues with finding elements of the familiar in the foreign. Corresponding with Francisca's fears at the end of her discussions with Gita and Hande, she worries that leaving behind the notion of different cultures with different values will somehow leave less respect for difference. A contributing factor here may well be that the trainer on her intercultural awareness course might indeed be presenting the strategy in an inappropriate manner. It might be mentioned here, however, that Gita, and Dima in Chapter 2, might say that it is none of Ivonne's business, and might even be patronising to defend the territory of someone else's domain. And this in turn might have something to do with by whom and for what reason stereotypes are formed.

The following extracts come from Chimamanda Ngozi Adichie's novel about 1960s Nigeria. It can be argued that they represent stereotypes; and they raise the question of whether A is more Othering because it is constructed by British foreigners, and whether B is less Othering (or self-Othering) because it is constructed by a Nigerian speaking about her own family:

A) A long-standing expatriate explaining about Nigerians to a newcomer

She spoke with authority about Nigeria and Nigerians. When they drove past the noisy markets with music blaring from shops, the haphazard stalls of the streetside hawkers, the gutters thick with mouldy water, she said, 'They have a marvellous energy, really, but very little sense of hygiene, I'm afraid'. She told him the Hausa in the North were a dignified lot, the Igbo were surly and money-loving, and the Yoruba were rather jolly, even if they were first-rate lickspittles. On Saturday evenings, when she pointed at the crowds of brightly dressed people dancing in front of lit-up canopies on the streets, she said, 'There you go. The Yoruba get into huge debt just to throw these parties.'

(Adichie 2007: 69–70)

B) Views within a Nigerian family

Olana [visiting her aunt in the North] sat on a stool and carefully avoided looking at the cockroach eggs, smooth black capsules, lodged in all corners of the table.

(Adichie 2007: 51)

'I know you will marry Odenigbo, Sister, but honestly I am not sure you want to marry a man from Abba. Men from Abba are so ugly, ka!' … 'Men from Abba are not ugly.' Aunty Ifeka said. 'My people are from there, after all.'

(Adichie 2007: 52)

Their thinly veiled condescension, their false validations irritated her … that familiar superiority of English people who thought they understood Africans better than Africans understood themselves.

(Adichie 2007: 44)

Possible responses to the question are far from straightforward. There are many factors to consider:

- To the British foreigners their stereotypes of Nigerians might seem fairly innocuous, and perhaps not far from what Nigerians say about themselves.
- The 'thinly-veiled condescension' (or patronising attitude, superiority, disdain, haughtiness, loftiness, superciliousness, lordliness – *Collins English Dictionary*) of the British *may* be unconscious and even playful, perhaps even the result of a humour lost on the Nigerians.
- Olana's irrepressible views about sections of her own family may be no better, except that she *seems* to be more aware of her prejudice, which is certainly contextualised within playful banter in the second extract.
- There are complexities of race, class, religion, region and pending civil war between Nigerians which we cannot begin to see in these extracts.

- There is nevertheless another contextualising factor which all readers should certainly be at least made aware of – that of the recent history of Nigeria as a British colony.
- There is the question which Ivonne herself asked when these accounts were presented during her training session – that (a) this colonial history is a thing of the past, (b) people of her political persuasion are actively opposed to any form of neo-colonial policy in the present, or neo-colonial tendencies in tourism, immigration, globalisation and so on.
- The stereotypes described in these extracts are not based on scientific study in the same way as the collectivist and individualist profiles and therefore cannot possibly claim to be as serious as the one employed by Ivonne in her preparation for going to Ex or experienced by Francisca in her intercultural training sessions above.

These discussions around stereotypes are the very issues which novels like those of Adichie are all about; and such novels succeed splendidly in entering fully into the complexities which are important in the quest for intercultural awareness.

Returning to Ivonne, it does nevertheless seem to be the case that she is denying Western prejudice. On the one hand, she may feel that she is distancing herself from the West and therefore free of prejudice. On the other hand, she may be more deeply implicated than she can imagine.

The struggle with stereotypes

In a crowded public place, note the stereotypes which come to mind as you observe particular people.

- Write down the details of each stereotype.
- Looking closely at the language which is used, test the notion that it is not neutral but based on a negative or positive image.
- Trace the origins of the image.
- Watch the same people again, but this time (a) try hard to put aside the stereotype and the image it carries, and (b) try to link their behaviour with that of other people within your 'own group', whatever that is.
- How differently do they appear?

Opening up to complexity

This discipline searches for profound interconnections through what has been called thick description. This can be defined as interconnecting different facets of a social phenomenon to arrive at a deeper complexity of meanings. Thick description is arrived at by being open to what is going on in the wider vicinity of the events one is directly involved in. It is related to putting aside easy answers and making the familiar strange in that one must not be complacent about what the answers and solutions may be, and always be prepared to look further and wider. This also requires a preparedness to understand what is going on and what may be connected to what, even in a culturally unfamiliar setting. This in turn requires a cultural belief that there *are* details in the complexity of things which can be understood.

Ivonne, Jung and Lan: using previous experience

Thick description is closely related to the belief that there *are* connections within the complexity of things which make it possible to find links to previous experience. There is already an example of this in Ivonne finding she is able to link the behaviour of the Exian administrators to that of administrators in her own country with whom she is familiar. The following continuation of Ivonne's story illustrates how such links with prior experience grow out of thick description:

When Ivonne arrived at the airport she still had doubts in her mind that she would be met. It *had* happened to her once before, arriving at an international airport and there being no-one there to meet her. However, she was pleased when she came out and Jung was holding up a card showing her name. They greeted warmly and a driver appeared to take her suitcase and take her straight to a waiting minibus.

Jung politely explained that they had to go to another terminal before going to the hotel because they were also meeting two Exian delegates. He told her he was feeling quite anxious. This was only the second conference he had been involved in organising, and he was still gaining experience. He said it was quite hard to get people together on these particular dates, and he was aware that a number of mistakes had been made.

Ivonne then talked to Lan, one of the Exian delegates, during their journey to the hotel. Lan told Ivonne she had read some of her work and was really pleased to meet her, and that she had been assigned to look after her. When Lan presented her business card Ivonne had to explain that hers were in her luggage. Lan said that she knew exactly what that was like. She had lived in the US for three years, but this was really her home town.

Ivonne was pleased that the conference was held in the excellent five-star hotel in which she was staying. The welcome, programme and facilities were very much like in any international conference she had been to. What she really enjoyed was the large hotel foyer where delegates could sit, drink coffee and meet. On a number of occasions she sat there with Lan watching the conference go by and sharing notes.

Ivonne was particularly interested in Dr Wang, who was the person who had invited her and was the head of the conference organising committee. She thought to herself that Dr Wang was playing the Exian authority figure, with a huge amount of 'obedience' from other members of the committee. She seemed to be mostly engaged in walking around the foyer greeting and being greeted by people. However, Ivonne was now cautious of the stereotype issue and she resisted slipping into the easy notion of 'hierarchical Exian culture'. She suggested to Lan that Dr Wang must be very pleased with 'her' conference. Then she was surprised when Lan explained that things weren't as smoothly running as they looked and that they should try and rescue Dr Wang from 'all these people'. Ivonne was astonished to see her sending Wang a text. Within moments Wang looked at her phone, looked over, said something to the group she was talking to and came over. Wang smiled and sat down with them, and apologised to Ivonne for not coming over earlier – but there were so many disgruntled people to speak to.

Wang explained that the person on the committee who was responsible for booking local hotels for delegates had simply decided not to bother, the outcome being that lots of delegates from the provinces, who couldn't afford to stay five star, hadn't been able to come to the conference. This revelation for some reason made Ivonne feel far more relaxed – noting that things didn't get done, just like at home. It also became clear to her that the reason for Wang to be talking to so many people in the foyer was to apologise.

When Ivonne shared her surprise with Lan, she said something which made Ivonne feel a bit stupid for not having appreciated it before – that Ex was indeed a very authoritarian society, but that just like everywhere else, at the detailed local level this was acted out in a complex manner. Lan said that during her time in the US it had taken her quite a while to see the immense power under the surface in apparently very informal meetings.

When Ivonne gave her presentation Lan had to admit that she didn't know who to ask about setting up the PowerPoint. However, the Exian presenter who was following her worked with her to solve the problem of how to link their laptops to the data system in the auditorium. Ivonne felt they formed an efficient team. They talked about their nervousness about presenting, and she enjoyed a surprising camaraderie.

Figure 3.1 presents the elements of the thick description which Ivonne puts together in the narrative. Thick descriptions have to be of something. Within ethnography they would be of the community under study, and in qualitative research projects they would respond to the research questions. In Ivonne's case the thick description is of the cultural realities she encounters. It is important to note that this thick description is not in any way for the purpose of 'solving the problem' of how to deal with 'Exian culture', because that would be to return to making stereotypes or profiles the starting point. It is instead to help find the normal and ordinary in the complexity of what is going on. What is described in the narrative is not in any way exotic or indeed surprising.

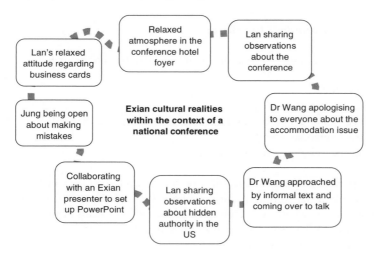

Figure 3.1 Developing a thick description

Becoming 'normal'

Consider the proposition that once you become involved in the detail of culturally foreign places you stop thinking of them as foreign.

- Within your group are there any instances, no matter how brief, when this has happened? What were the specific factors which allowed this to happen?
- What are the gains and losses of becoming considered 'normal' rather than 'foreign'?

Thick description

Think of a novel you have read where intercultural relations are described, but where stereotypes are avoided.

- What role does thick description play in the narrative?
- Construct a version of Figure 3.1 which captures the elements of the thick description.

What impact can this exercise have on your own circumstances?

Asking ethnographic questions

The third discipline is asking basic questions which a newcomer would need to know in order to operate within a cultural environment. Such questions are ethnographic questions. They are central to the bottom-up qualitative approach in that they begin with observation of the detail of what is there:

- What is going on?
- What are the rules for how to behave?

They thus concern the basic information for appropriate behaviour such as:

- how to be polite;
- how to show respect;
- rules for acceptable behaviour and lines which must not be crossed;
- how to assert personal agendas;
- when to speak and when to keep quiet.

There is an important difference here with the top-down questions which have been more traditional in intercultural communication studies – i.e. beginning with and therefore led by the notion that there *is* 'a culture' which can be described by means of a profile or stereotype (What is the culture? What is the stereotype? How is it different to my culture? What behaviour will I therefore need to deal with?).

Such encounters with new cultural practices, employing ethnographic questions, therefore require a lot of observation of behaviour and working out what is going on. Here is an example from my own experience:

> I first encountered my colleagues as a group in the common room at coffee time. Although they were my compatriots, with similar class and educational background, and although I had worked in similar institutions before, there were cultural features peculiar to this particular setting which I needed to observe. For example, colleagues came and went without greetings or leave-taking. It seemed understood on leaving that there was a pressing work engagement which needed no explanation. Also, talk about work had to be announced first. Much of this could not be learnt just by watching. It was necessary to watch for clues, form hypotheses – calculated guesses – about appropriate behaviour, then try things out, observe the result, then confirm, adapt or reject the hypothesis.
>
> (Holliday 2007: 10)

Here is another example, which suggests a very similar process from a very different society:

> A young Egyptian woman was living in the capital for the first time. She had never been to a restaurant before. In order to work out how to do this she first watched customers coming and going from across the street. As she gained confidence she went and stood just inside the door of the restaurant, which was sufficiently large and crowded for her not to be noticed. Here she watched and listened to how customers sat down and ordered. Eventually she learnt enough to sit down and order herself – to try out the hypotheses she had formulated as a result of her observations.
>
> (Holliday 2007: 11)

In both of these cases the newcomers gradually worked out what to do to become part of the cultural practice they were observing. In this sense they were carrying out the same sort of social research which ethnographers do – hence the reference to forming a hypothesis in the first example. In the second example the Egyptian woman approaches slowly, picking her position from which to observe carefully. In the conference, Ivonne has a very good ready-made place to position herself by sitting in the foyer of the conference hotel. In the first example above, I did not have the luxury which she had to approach the new practice at my leisure.

This process of working out the rules might be thought of as *reading culture*, which is a key aspect of **small culture formation**. We are all, under normal circumstances, able to read culture because we already have experience of culture from elsewhere in our life experience. Something will already have happened to the Egyptian student to enable her to make sense of what she observes in the restaurant. Somewhere else in her life she will have experienced forms of politeness, professionalism, customer relations, fine balances between deference and authority, managing personal spaces, which will help her to make sense. She may well also have heard about restaurants or seen them on television or even the internet.

Ivonne and Lan: complex views about eating

This continuation of Ivonne's experience in Ex demonstrates how she forms hypotheses on the basis not only of bottom-up observation of the situation she is in, but also prior experience.

In the evenings during the conference the delegates had dinner together. Ivonne had learnt as a student how to use chopsticks. So she did not find it too difficult to manage in the normal hurly-burly of these events where there were several sittings and people ate quickly from the dishes that were placed before them and passed by on the large revolving centre-pieces of each table. Apart from this detail and the nature of the food itself, a version of which she was familiar with from restaurants at home, these events were quite similar to conference meals in many places she had been before. There was the issue of how to use the various plates and bowls, but she managed to find out the *rules for acceptable behaviour and lines which must not be crossed* quickly from observation. She was also helped by usually being just one among several foreigners, which made her feel more anonymous. Nobody was using fingers, picking up or moving the central dishes or reaching across the table. To balance this, there seemed to be considerable variation in what sorts of food to put on which type of crockery, whether to use the spoons provided or chopsticks to get the food, and the amounts of food to put on their bowls or plates before eating.

On the third evening, the stakes were raised. Ivonne was invited to a formal 'banquet' in a private room with Dr Wang, senior members of the conference committee and other keynote speakers, all of whom were Exian. Ivonne was therefore less prepared to experiment. What she learnt in the less formal occasions now took the form of hypotheses. She also had hypotheses from what she had learnt more generally in the conference about the sort of rapport she could have with Dr Wang, Lan and others she had had conversations with.

The dinner began in a fairly formal manner, with Wang ordering dishes. Ivonne was interested to note how Wang was interrupted by other guests making alternative suggestions. Much of this was in English, so she could sense the sorts of preferences people had, some of which were to do with what the restaurant was well-known for and what was best in this particular season.

When Ivonne didn't begin to help herself to food, Lan asked why she wasn't starting. Ivonne explained that she preferred to wait and see how other people helped themselves before she began. Then Wang explained that they wanted her to start first because, since the flu epidemic of a couple of years before there had been a lot of anxiety about hygiene and a lot of discussion within families and in the media about whether or not it was good to take food straight from the shared dishes with chopsticks that you then put in your mouth. Therefore, the reason why they always now waited for guests to eat first was to see what their preferences were – to use chopsticks or to serve themselves with a spoon. One of the others then asked her which she preferred. When she said she didn't mind everyone seemed pleased and started helping themselves with their chopsticks.

> Someone commented on how well Ivonne used her chopsticks, and this set off a discussion in English around the table about how to use chopsticks. Ivonne was interested to note that several of them said that they didn't feel they had been properly taught as children.

As noted above, the purpose of this narrative is not to demonstrate the discovery of particular details about 'Exian culture', but to show how deeper levels of interaction can be arrived at. Here are some further disciplines which help:

- Be aware of the influence of theories, profiles and stereotypes and try to put them aside.
- Begin with a feeling of acceptance.
- Try to imagine oneself in the shoes of the person or people one is engaging with, acknowledging that it is possible to feel like them.
- Be prepared to engage with complexity that cannot be explained easily.

Working out the rules

Think of a time when you encountered a new cultural practice within your own society, e.g. while growing up, forming new relationships or during your career.

- What did you have to do to work out how to behave? What hypotheses did you form, and how did you confirm or adapt them?
- Which of the common elements of cultural practices listed above did you have to deal with, and how?
- Modify the list, adding other elements which you encountered.
- What had you experienced before which enabled you to read the new cultural practice?

Learning about culture

Recall an encounter in which you felt you were learning about an unfamiliar cultural reality.

- Describe the event in detail.
- Pinpoint places where you felt the disciplines described in this chapter were employed.
- Considering the contents of this chapter, how successful would you say the encounter was? What are the bases for your judgement?
- Employ the views of the people you are working with in this task. How do they differ and for what reasons?

Ethnographic narrative writing

The disciplines described in this chapter underpin my own writing of the ethnographic narratives around which most of the chapters in this book are written. They are ways to engage with intercultural scenarios; and they are based on observed events and people. If done well they take on a life of their own and lead the writer into places and understandings which might not have been expected at the outset. The following guideline is generic and can be applied to the themes arising out of any chapter in the book.

Guidelines for writing an ethnographic narrative

1   Recall an intercultural encounter.
2   Two or more of you need to work together, with one being the informant and the other(s) asking questions to build content for the narrative.
3   The narrative can be fictional, but based on real experience. The characters may be constructed from more than one person. The events and locations may also be constructed from more than one experience.
4   Make the narrative as neutral and objective as you can. It will help if you (a) work with someone from a different cultural background, (b) use the third person, (c) put opinions and impressions only into the thoughts or words of the characters, (d) place a minimum of adjectives and adverbs, and (e) do not judge the characters.
5   Use the categories of cultural action to analyse the narrative. You can add more categories from the grammar.
6   Note what emerges as unexpected from this process.
7   What were your prejudices during (a) the engagement with the practice and (b) while preparing the narrative?

Summary

- A bottom-up approach to investigating culture is advised because it begins with direct observation of the complexity of cultural behaviour.
- This needs to be accompanied by the disciplines of making the familiar strange and putting aside easy answers, and by opening up to complexity and asking ethnographic questions.
- The more traditional, top-down method of beginning with cultural profiles or stereotypes is not advised because focusing on the differences between distinct 'cultures' can lead to the same prejudiced thinking as 'everyday' theories about people.
- Making the familiar strange and putting aside easy answers entails putting aside familiar stereotypes and familiar ways of thinking about the culturally strange, and considering that there could be shared behaviour and values.
- Opening up to complexity requires seeking profound interconnections through thick description.
- Asking ethnographic questions will provide us with the basics about how to survive.
- Applying these disciplines can take us into new territories in which we enter into a deeper level of intercultural interaction, and where the complexities of individual people are engaged with.

Notes

1 This is based on a number of conversations with students and colleagues from different cultural backgrounds, visits to South Africa in the early 1990s and India in the mid-1990s, and discussions there with colleagues.

2 This is based on experiences of being an invited speaker at conferences in a wide variety of international locations, more recently a number of times in various locations in China, Mexico, Singapore, Nepal and South Korea, of conversations with Chinese and Mexican conference organisers, and of being an experienced conference organiser in Egypt and Britain.

Further reference

YouTube Extract from *Dances with Wolves*. http://www.youtube.com/watch?v=jbd1trNz 9bY&feature=related_

— This extract from the 1990 feature film depicts what might be interpreted to be a confrontation with a newcomer over a nineteenth-century Native American cultural practice concerning ownership.

— What elements of complexity are evident, and how do these contribute to opportunities for negotiation? How do subtitles help us understand this complexity? Is there evidence that everyone present is in the process of working things out, and that personalities can make even the most traditional practices problematic?

— From the expression on his face, what sort of ethnographic questions is the newcomer asking himself to work out the limits of how he is able to behave? Looking at the expressions on the faces of others who are present, is he the only one asking ethnographic questions? If not, what questions could the others be asking about their own cultural environment?

Holliday, A.R. (2011). *Intercultural communication & ideology*. London: Sage.

— Chapter 2 deals with the methodologies for critical cultural awareness.

— Pages 61–6 present another narrative about visiting Ex which may be compared with Ivonne's experience in this chapter.

Holliday, A.R., Hyde, M. and Kullman, J. (2010). *Intercultural communication: an advanced resource book for students*. 2nd edition. London: Routledge.

— Pages 57–9 present disciplines for intercultural communication.

— Page 232 provides a conceptual model for intercultural research.

Holliday, A.R. (2007). *Doing and writing qualitative research*. 2nd edition. London: Sage.

— Provides a practical account of how to write qualitative research. Chapter 4 deals with the basic qualitative disciplines described in this chapter.

Kumaravadivelu, B. (2007). *Cultural globalisation and language education*. New Haven, CT: Yale University Press.

— While focusing on English-language education, this book provides a full and excellent survey of the key literature which is concerned with a critical view of intercultural issues.

— From pages 170 onwards it explores how to put these ideas into practice for English language students to explore culture in the classroom.

Byram, M. (2008). *From foreign language education to education for intercultural citizenship: essays and reflections*. Clevedon: Multilingual Matters.
— Pages 162–3 deal with how British school children learning new languages need to apply ethnographic skills to cross cultural boundaries and to place their own and other's societies within a critical perspective.

Guilherme, M. (2007). English as a global language and education for cosmopolitan citizenship. *Language & Intercultural Communication* 7/1: 72–90.
— This article presents the principles required for a critical intercultural speaker within a West-non-West perspective.

Spradley, J.P. (1980). *Participant observation*. New York: Holt, Rinehart & Winston.
— The whole book is an excellent manual for anyone starting out on qualitative research. Pages 33 onwards explain how to approach new settings gradually.

Schutz, A. (1964). The stranger. *Collected papers, Volume 2*. The Hague: Martinus Nijhoff: 91–5.
— This describes how a person who is carrying out social research is like a stranger who is approaching a social setting for the first time.

Baumann, G. (1996). *Contesting culture*. Cambridge: Cambridge University Press.
— This is an ethnography of cultural complexity in the London borough of Southall. In chapter 1 it describes the need to put aside easy answers about the people being researched.

Geertz, C. (1993). *The interpretation of cultures*. London: Fontana.
— From page 6 onwards there is the classic example of thick description.

Chapter 4

Constructing culture

Putting aside easy answers and appreciating complexity, which are at the core of the disciplines introduced in Chapter 3, requires seeing the detail of what goes on in the construction of culture everywhere. Seeing this in the familiar at home can develop a sense of the less familiar abroad. This chapter therefore demonstrates that much of what we do when approaching the culturally unfamiliar begins with the everyday task of constructing culture. It looks at this process within **small culture formation** within the broader domain of **underlying universal cultural processes**.

I look more closely at some of the mechanisms of **small culture formation** – reading and making culture, constructing rules and meanings, imagining Self and Other. I shall begin with the observation made in Chapter 2, that when Anna visited her friend's family, even though the 'small culture' was most obviously the family she was visiting, she was creating her own small culture around her during the process and engaging in **small culture formation** on the run.

The constant process of forming culture

Very occasionally it is possible to see the making of culture laid bare. In drama and literature we see it in accounts of groups of people cast far away from their normal social environments as the result of shipwrecks or air crashes. Good examples are schoolboys forming a new and vicious tribal life in the *Lord of the Flies* novel (1954), and a disparate group of people constructing complex interrelationships in the *Lost* television series (2005).

Abi and Tomos making a cultural event

The following narrative[1] demonstrates the complexity of cultural creativity within a single event:

> Abi and Tomos announced to their family and friends that on 9 July there was going to be a special day for their daughter, Sarah, at nine months old. They had discussed this a lot before the final decision and announcement. They were not religious and therefore did not want to have a Christening, the Christian event for naming the baby; but wanted to celebrate their daughter's birth and entry into a community. Their two families were far away and with very different cultural traditions. A four-hour drive away, Tomos' parents

and brothers and their girlfriends were Welsh, and the parents had a strong religious background. A six-hour drive away, Abi's Iranian mother and English father had secular Muslim and Christian heritages. Abi had experienced a similar event for one of her friends' baby and had been inspired by it having been said that by attending she was joining the baby's community.

Despite Abi's secular upbringing, her family had adopted the notion of godparents. Her parents noted that godparents were taken more seriously than among their generation. There was little tradition of godparents in Iran, but her mother liked the tradition and Abi did have a Syrian godmother and American godfather, whose roles they and Abi took seriously. Her father was a godfather of two of his cousins; but nothing had ever been made of it. He wasn't really aware who his godparents were. So Sarah had two godmothers, Abi's English friend from university and Tomos' Welsh school friend, both of whom had husbands and young children between four and five hours' drive away.

As well as these family members and godparents, Abi and Tomos decided to invite people from their community. They were new to Plymouth, where they lived. Apart from colleagues, their core community comprised a Norwegian and Spanish couple with their young daughter, and four young English 'yoga mums', whom Abi had met at a yoga class for pregnant women, who had babies who were Sarah's age, along with their respective partners.[2] The grandparents and godparents and their families would stay in the town in hotels. Tomos' brothers and girlfriends would stay at the house.

It was not until fairly late that Abi and Tomos decided exactly what was going to happen during the day. During the morning the brothers were heard to say that they didn't really know what was going to happen, but got on with helping. There would be a buffet lunch, and then a sit-down dinner in the evening for the close family and godmothers. A major event in the afternoon was the time for the babies of the 'yoga mums' to eat. They shared a very new practice, called 'baby-led weaning', in which the babies were presented with an array of pieces of food at the table in the kitchen and allowed to help themselves. This was intended to help them to feel confident about eating and was believed to work well. The rest of the time the babies, some crawling, some sitting, played together in the middle of the living room floor, mostly individually, sometimes interacting. Their territory was marked by the large cloth designed for them which was spread across the floor, while parents sat at the edge and monitored their behaviour carefully. None of the grandparents had seen this sort of baby and parent behaviour before and were a bit mystified.

The overall ambiance of the day was very informal. Abi's father, who wore a smart jacket, felt a bit out of place until the Spanish friend arrived; and though he was much younger, he felt comfortable that he was more formally dressed. He felt that he, too, was expecting a more formal occasion. One of the godparents was heard to refer to how the event was in character with Abi and Tomos' wedding, which many of the guests felt was different, breaking with normal tradition, and intimate. Abi's parents heard this comment and mentioned it later.

Before the 'yoga mums' and their babies left at the end of the afternoon, Tomos made a short speech; and it was clear that the tradition for this in terms of timing and content was not established. It seemed that there had been some discussion beforehand about whether this was necessary or not. There was no mention of the baby's name, which took the event a long way from the traditional Christening, in which there would have been a 'naming' by a priest in a church with the godparents standing by. In the speech Tomos introduced the godmothers, thanked them for coming and also thanked the 'yoga mums' for their support.

In the evening just one set of godparents remained for the sit-down dinner. The other couple had to leave early because they had to get back home that evening for a work meeting the following day. Abi's parents were surprised because there was a lot of present giving by Tomos' family and his godmother school friend. They had brought presents but given them to Abi on arrival, unwrapped. It had not occurred to them that this would be a formal present-giving occasion. There was, however, no embarrassment because the whole spirit of the occasion was one of recognised cultural innovation. Abi's mother commented on this to her husband later, and noted that there never had been a tradition of formal wrapped present giving in Iranian families. She was so pleased that her daughter was engaging with the life of her husband's extended family because this was also important in her own background.

The following day all the members of the two families went out for lunch. Everyone paid for themselves, which became a sustained tradition on future occasions. This tradition was established by Abi and Tomos.

Collaboration in small culture formation

Table 4.1 presents an analysis of the narrative using the categories of cultural action. What is significant here is that creating Sarah day was not just a matter of planning and carrying out an event. At one level everyone is making sense of the event as it unfolds, including its architects. In doing this they are developing rules for how to behave. The importance of the day means that all parties are buying into it; and this desire to make it work automatically means that they are employing **underlying universal cultural processes** of reading culture as it develops and collaborating in its formation. In the **global position and politics** and **cultural resources** bands there is evidence that the two families have either cultural experiences or degrees of openness which support this process. The other people present at the day are not included in the table; but their preparedness to take part and the experiences they bring also make important contributions. Indeed, they are the core of the community that Abi and Tomos wish to build.

Cultural travel and building

At another level, Abi and Tomos have the explicit aim to create a cultural event with a major purpose being to build a community around them. As a young couple moving to a new city, with a new baby, as well as celebrating her birth, they are in the serious business of

Table 4.1 Elements of culture formation

Categories of cultural action	Abi and Tomos	Tomos' family	Abi's family
Statements about culture	'We want to mark Sarah's birth with a special event and engage with a community.'		'We don't give wrapped presents.'
Global position and politics	Resistance towards established religious norms.	Prepared to adapt to secular norms.	Appreciating commonalities between background and newcomer cultural practices.
Cultural resources	Local support group of 'yoga mums'. School and university friends. Experience of cultural diversity and travel (between them lived in seven countries and speak six languages). Abi's experience of a similar event.	Tradition of Christenings. Tradition of giving wrapped presents.	Mother's tradition of involvement with an extended family. Tradition of cultural creativity and diversity with regard to godparents. Expectation of dressing up for events like this. Tradition of Abi and Tomos' wedding, which was creatively different and intimate.
Underlying universal processes	Establishing a community Routinising the practices of feeding Sarah and managing spaces for playing. Routinising the practice of restaurant meals with family.	Making sense of and learning to play prescribed roles for Sarah day and visiting Abi and Tomos.	

designing, planning and implementing **small culture formation**. The consciousness with which they do this may be informed by their extensive experience of cultural travel, which provides core cultural expertise.

Sarah day is significant in its bringing together of distant cultural realities, between Britain and Iran, if not between England and Wales. This particular example has been chosen because of these obvious differences in cultural background. However, I wish to emphasise that very similar processes would take place if the participants came simply from different families, classes, cities or neighbourhoods.

Making things up

Consider an important traditional cultural event, either in the family or in another domain such as work, leisure or sports group, or community.

• Which parts of the planning and carrying out of the event were set out by tradition and which were 'made up' or creatively constructed?
• What were the reasons why some parts of it were 'made up' or creatively constructed?
• What therefore did the people involved have to learn?

Further afield

Consider a traditional cultural event you have witnessed in which people from more distant cultural backgrounds came together.

*   What were the differences and similarities with the case described in the first part of this activity?

Routinisation

A significant aspect of the construction of the naming day event, as indicated in the **underlying universal cultural processes** row in Table 4.1, was the process of routinisation, or establishing routines. This is a process whereby a piece of behaviour is established to the degree that it becomes a normal part of thinking-as-usual, or part of the everyday institutional processes of an organisation. The terms 'normalising' and 'embedding' are also used.

Tomos and Abi can therefore be said to be routinising the tradition of the naming day. They may only have one child and never do this again; but others in their community, peers or siblings may learn this tradition, or variations of it, and carry it on. Their parents are learning how to behave in this new culture of visiting their children. Indeed, on other occasions in which the two sets of parents visit together, such as the baby's birthday, they now have a tradition to build on, and do not have to solve the problem of whether or not they should pay for each other in restaurants. The informality which they experience here allows them to relax expectations. Present-wrapping and giving or not is no longer an issue. Indeed, there is already some history to build on. Abi and Tomos' wedding was also a creative cultural construction in which Welsh and Iranian traditions and expectations were mixed within a very informal and 'small', intimate event, all taking place in one building of a small hotel. It is significant that a reference was made to this by the godparents and others who were there. This played the role of contributing to a sense of heritage and history, which are important in establishing an event as normal. Histories are very important in this process and draw attention to the fact that all cultural events of this nature are deeply interconnected with what has gone before.

Another significant aspect of the event in the narrative, as indicated in the **underlying universal cultural processes** row in Table 4.1, was the learning of roles within this spirit of forming tradition. It is a paramount part of the building of behavioural norms that people do not have to make decisions and solve problems for every move that they take.

These processes become visible whenever people find themselves in strange circumstances and, in a sense, need to develop a modus operandi. A classic, comic example of this is when there are newcomers to a household with scarce bathroom resources and fun is made of the father figure who tries to enforce a rota for who can use the bathroom, and when, and how long they should take. My family still laugh at the régime I established when we drove from Syria to Britain and camped on the way – getting up at 6:00 a.m., packing the tent and loading the car by 6:30 a.m., driving for two hours before having breakfast, and so on.

When encountering a very strange cultural event it will be such routines that a newcomer will need to recognise and learn.

Rituals

When the routines become more elaborate, and the elaborations take on a sense of the aesthetic or iconic, we move into the domain of ritual. Examples of these are best known in ceremonies and religious practices such as praying. A humorous but serious example of this is in the following description[3] of the breakfast ritual in a girls' Quaker[4] boarding school:[5]

> The rising bell went at seven; but the girls were not allowed to go to breakfast until the bedroom head was satisfied that each person had learnt the breakfast text off by heart. This would be a poem or a reading which delivered a moral message for the day. They then entered the dining hall in year groups. Each girl had an allotted seat; but every two weeks they would have to move to another place two seats further along to ensure that they eventually would sit in all parts of the dining hall. They then all stood to recite the text learnt in the bedroom. When they all sat down, the head of each table would say 'teas'. This was the signal for each girl to pass her request for tea, with or without milk, or for coffee or just hot water back down the table. The head of the table then served the drink and passed it back person by person. (It was the Quaker custom that no-one should ask for anything until it had been offered, and that the people who offered would always attend to the needs of others). The same procedure was carried out for the toast and cereal. Slices of bread were always eaten in quarters, and slices of toast were eaten in halves. Each term[6] one table was assigned to delivering the post. At eight there would be silence while the radio news was turned on. Then the table responsible would deliver the post while everyone listened to the news; and no-one was allowed to talk. After breakfast the girls left the dining hall table by table. Then each girl had to carry out her 'offices'. These were assigned duties such as cleaning baths, or polishing shoes. (This practice was stopped in recent years when it became illegal for children to do menial tasks). Each girl would know the rules because they were explained by her 'nutcracker', the older girl assigned to supervise her throughout her school career.

The person who described this ritual to me said that as a child she found it brought order, composure and a sense of security to her daily life. It will always be difficult for a newcomer to master rituals of this nature, especially when they are embedded within an institutional setting which has high interpersonal stakes, connected with hierarchies and issues of obedience and behavioural monitoring, which must be the case with a boarding school. When asked what she brought to the breakfast event which enabled her to make sense of it and find her place within it, my informant said that she had experience of rules from primary school.

There will also always be room for personal negotiation even in rigid rituals. In this respect my informant explained that some of the girls did not sit in the allotted seats, did not learn the morning texts and sometimes did not even attend the breakfast. Sooner or later, though, they did get caught and told off.

Learning the rules

Recall a time when you had to learn a ritual of this nature.

- What were the benefits for you; and how did these balance with a loss of freedom?
- What experiences did you bring to the ritual that helped you to manage it?

Think of a time when you had to learn new rules in a culturally unfamiliar environment.

- In what ways did your knowledge of rituals and how they work help you to learn what to do?
- What were you able to contribute to the ritual because of your knowledge?

Describe a ritual with which you are familiar. In what ways can you trace it to functions of cultural identity and certainty? How are its participants aware of these functions?

Engineering conformity in the workplace

Routines and even rituals (e.g. the ceremonies of marching and rallies) are at the core of military training, but with the purpose of imposing and instilling discipline. This takes us to a further level of **small culture formation**, where the intention is, in varying degrees, to enforce or control the behaviour of others so that it conforms to specific goals. The military is an excellent example of this, where training results in individuals conforming to routines in such a manner that they can perform unquestioningly in times of immense stress and danger, where success depends on this performance.

To lesser degrees this control function is also a feature of professional groups. It is common within professional literature, business manuals, studies of organisations and so on to find a discussion of the best strategies that can be employed to achieve high levels of regulated and accountable professional performance. This high-profile strategic area of behaviour management is at the core of culture formation, and of understanding how culture operates because it both explicitly employs **underlying universal cultural processes** and lays bare its workings.

Managing institutional change is a particular area in this respect. The following narrative is an example of this.[7]

> The task was to get staff to adopt and employ within their day-to-day office practice the concept of Smart Project Planning. There had already been a series of staff development meetings in which the concept had been introduced; but there was little evidence of uptake.

Project planning was not such a problem. This was a well-known concept which had been around for some time. The 'smart' element, however, made a significant difference in that it meant that they should be prepared to shift the course of the project, sometimes quite subtly, to meet changes in circumstances as and when they happened.

During the training sessions the staff had been presented with case studies and asked to work in groups to work out and plot how project objectives could be adapted to changing circumstances. They had managed to do this quite well; and we thought that the group-work element would be effective in instilling new team behaviour. However, it became clear after the sessions that the participants had not been convinced that what they had done was any different to what they did normally; and there was no particular change observed in their work styles. They could perform Smart Project Management when pushed in specially designed tasks, but they weren't responding in a sufficiently disciplined manner in the projects they were managing as part of their daily work.

We realised that successful uptake might take longer than initially anticipated and that we needed to influence workplace behaviour from another angle. The concept of Smart Project Management needed to become part of the deeper fabric of the workplace. A possible vehicle for this was the monthly project progress report which everyone had to write. We inserted 'Smart Project Management' as a new heading, with bulleted stages matching actions against new circumstances that had to be completed in tabular form. We also planted these headings in the agenda forms that managers had to use for staff appraisals. This meant that 'Smart Project Management' as a term would be read and used in evaluative actions in two key professional events. We also placed a brief manual on the key steps in Smart Project Management on the office web pages for quick reference; and we made the phrase prominent in the 'key targets' section of flyers that staff would show to clients.

Within six months Smart Project Management had become an often-heard phrase in conversations around the workplace, and appeared on meeting agendas. Cynics might suggest that it was all talk and no real change in action. However, the key factor was the online manual, which was sufficiently succinct and catching to invite a lot of hits and to be cited convincingly in day-to-day decision-making.

Reification

What is described in this narrative is the process of reification, or making real something which is not initially seen to be so. If the innovation is as effective as the narrator claims, then the concept of Smart Project Management has been made so real to the employees of the organisation that they use it as a matter of fact in their daily work. This is a form of routinisation, but with the added feature of turning a concept from something insubstantial in the way people think about it into something substantial. The implication in the last paragraph of the narrative is that Smart Project Management has become a real part of the normal, thinking-as-usual world. Another term which is often used for this process within institutional settings is 'institutionalisation', the process of becoming a real, normal and routine part of everyday institutional life.

Dualities

It certainly must not be missed that the desired change might not have been successful and that people ended up *playing* with the new practice and even finding ways to resist. All sorts of dualities can accompany the presence of cultural norms, both in the workplace and in other cultural arenas. It is important to note that the narrative is written in a deadpan manner as though Smart Project Management is a serious and important innovation in the first place. This is the voice of the management who may (1) be buying into it completely because they are more highly motivated by making the institution successful, or (2) are also pretending to believe in Smart Project Management because it is a means of establishing institutional cohesion.

In this sense, this process of reifying Smart Project Management also represents the development of a discourse, a way of using language which represents ideas about how things are. In this respect, the process of reification can be one of constructing illusions – ideas about ourselves and others which are not true at all, but which are important for cultural identity and cohesion – the glue that holds people together. This takes us smoothly to the next section.

Institutional culture

Recall a time at work when you found yourself using new terminologies.

- To what degree did this involve new or changed behaviour?
- Can you trace it to changed strategies within the institution?
- To what degrees were people aware, critical, resistant, cynical or appreciative of these events?

How far do you think management is really taken in by the innovations which they promote? How far may they be more likely to be taken in because they are close to the strategy required for implementing them?

Self and Other

The relationship between Self and Other is a basic mechanism in this construction of illusions and the creation of social glue which is implicit in **small culture formation**. For any social group to form, hold together and survive, it needs to construct for itself a sense that it is different to others. It needs to convince itself that it has practices, values and, especially in the case of professional groups, expertise which are special. These attributes make the group worth joining, attract the loyalty of its members, and also provide it with a standing in the eyes of others. Examples are demonstrated in Table 4.2.

While the types of group in Table 4.2 are very different, there are commonalities in the manner in which Self and Other are constructed. For example, in the second column, 'values', 'ethos', 'mission statement' and 'ideology' have very much the same function relative to the group. 'Ideology' may indeed be used as a cover term for the others. A useful definition of ideology in this regard is 'a set of ideas put to work in the justification and

Table 4.2 Self and Other

Group	Construction of Self	Purpose	Implications for Other
Family	Family values (e.g. care, respect, quality of dress, food, behaviour). Artefacts (e.g. upkeep and presentation of the home, social locations and relationships, children's schools).	Holding the family together, bringing up children, preserving marriages, distribution of resources, living together, support of members.	Other families have less attractive values. This is evident in their artefacts.
Sports group	Sporting ethos (e.g. honour, fairness, discipline, success record). Artefacts (e.g. insignia, kit colours, endorsements).	Maintaining standing in the sports world, morale, determination to succeed	Other groups can be beaten.
Professional group, institution	Mission statement (e.g. principles, expertise, exclusivity, membership standards, qualifications). Artefacts (e.g. building, dress code, flyers, letterheads, business cards).	Maintaining customer loyalty, faith in services and products, community confidence.	Competitors are less effective.
Political party	Ideology (e.g. manifesto, attitudes to participants, poverty and élites, membership rules, morality). Artefacts (e.g. leaders, anthem, rallies, headquarters).	Attracting political support and credibility. Instilling confidence in the ability to rule.	Other parties are less fitting to rule.
Nation	Ruling principles (e.g. constitution, laws, foreign policy, alliances). Artefacts (e.g. head of state, national anthem, flag, buildings, statues, military uniforms, food, dress, ceremonies).	Maintaining loyalty, stability and faith in institutions and the economy.	Other nations are less just.

maintenance of vested interests' (Spears 1999: 19). Well-known examples are political ideologies such as communism, socialism and capitalism; but all social groups, including the ones listed in Table 4.2, can have ideologies.

Idealisation and demonisation

Implicit in the examples in Table 4.2 is the notion that the Self is idealised and the Other is demonised, resulting in actual Othering. The degree to which the formation of a group results in the Othering of other groups will depend on a number of factors, examples of which may be:

- scarcity of resources and territory;
- degree of competition;
- what will be lost in the event of defeat or dissolution;
- the need for the broader community to conform – e.g. standards of appearance, alliances against a common enemy.

In the last case an example might be a neighbourhood in which a particular family does not maintain the appearance of their property to the standard expected by the rest of the neighbourhood. Other cases could be where a particular business does not practice in the manner expected by other companies, or where a nation has policies which are disapproved of by its neighbours.

However, the image of the Other may not be demonised in this manner. An idealisation of the Self may result in other relationships with the Other. While this may seem on the surface to be an appreciation or celebration, at a deeper level it is considered also to be a form of Othering. This is because the observer somehow takes ownership of the Other by turning it into an object which satisfies the imagination rather than representing its full complexity. A common example of this is where we treat foreigners and their imagined 'cultures' as objects to be collected and displayed as status symbols.

A Self–Other politics therefore results in different types of idealisation of the Self which is supported by an Other which is constructed to suit and strengthen the idealisation

- as superior, in contrast with an inferior Other;
- as understanding and accommodating, in contrast with an exotic Other.

Other possibilities are:

- as vulnerable, in contrast with a superior Other;
- as attractive, in contrast with an appreciative Other;
- as high status, by being in the company of a high-status Other.

The last three possibilities may lead people to say that Self–Other politics may not always lead to negative Othering. The point to note, however, is that even if the image of the Other is positive, and indeed superior to the Self, it is nevertheless an image which is constructed, imagined and owned by the Self for the promotion of the Self's agenda.

Commonalities

Find terms or phrases in the third and fourth columns of Table 4.2 which are parallel in the same way as the examples given for the second column. Which term might be a cover term for the others?

Use these cover terms to write a continuation of the table for a group with which you are familiar.

Narratives

How do the examples and principles described in this section so far relate to each of the two ethnographic narratives earlier in the chapter?

Degrees of Othering

In what ways does loyal membership of this group require the Othering of another group?

How far do the other possibilities of Self and Other politics mentioned at the end of the chapter result in Othering?

Small culture formation on the run

While in Abi and Tomos' creation of Sarah day and in the institution change narrative above there are intentions to create culture, it is no more than we all do in the everyday business of engaging with and creating culture. On a daily basis we invent and perform routines and even invent small rituals as we engage, plan, solve problems, get used to things, move from one group to another. Table 4.3 attempts to plot such navigation of events in the process of daily construction of culture. As with many things discussed in this book, so much can pass by without notice. In the first column are a selection of things which I remember, at which I paused to think about. In the second column is a description of the **small culture forma-tion** which is taking place, plus other categories of cultural action.

Table 4.3 A day out

Event	Small culture formation – finding common ground for authentic, respectful interaction; exploring rules for mutual respect; learning how to communicate across cultural boundaries
I talked to the taxi driver who took me to the station. He had a nearly new large black Mercedes and we talked about why it was a good car to have because of the inexpensive parts and durability, and also because he could make money by doing high-class chauffeuring and get work that other taxi drivers didn't think of.	**Cultural resources**: Interest in cars, Sat Nav and lateral thinking about being successful. A strong class narrative in British society. **Global position and politics**: Awareness of potential prejudice across class cultural divides, and the importance of not patronising by imitating observed behaviour. **Statements about culture**: Implicit in global position and politics – 'my class is different to yours'. **Personal trajectory**: Experience of hitch hiking and working as a hospital porter when a student, bringing me into context with people from different backgrounds, and also of dealing with car mechanics in Iran, Syria and Egypt.
I noticed two colleagues speaking to each other on the train. My attention was attracted by the way the woman greeted the man sitting in front of me as she got on and walked down the aisle. I then watched them by the door before they got off as he told her about the difficult aspects of his work he had to deal with. I noted her supportive body language, tone of voice and expressions.	**Small culture formation**: Developing experience in professional comradeship; recognising and confirming rules for supportive collegial behaviour. **Statements about culture**: 'I am like them.' Cultural resources: Experience of similar interaction with own colleagues. **Personal trajectory**: History of forming strong collegial relationships with women colleagues and mature women students who work in other but similar organisations.

Event	Small culture formation – finding common ground for authentic, respectful interaction; exploring rules for mutual respect; learning how to communicate across cultural boundaries
On arrival at the seminar I found a long-standing British colleague from another university sitting behind the registration desk. I asked him about the lack of information about the programme. He told me that another colleague, who I also knew, had the programme but hadn't arrived yet. I then found a Korean colleague waiting in the seminar room, complaining about having arrived too early because she had expected that the event would start on time.	**Small culture formation**: Developing rules for acceptable criticism by simultaneously showing respect and collegiality. **Statements about culture**: 'I am like my British colleague; and we are not like foreigners might imagine us to be.' **Cultural resources**: A camaraderie regarding how difficult it often is to negotiate the exigencies of daily life to get things done. An acceptance that mistakes can be made in professional life. An annoyed resignation to daily incompetence. Knowledge that professional events of this type begin with coffee, with relaxed time-keeping. **Personal trajectory**: A professional history with an in-group of colleagues. Experience of involvement in the organising of events in a wide, international range of locations. **Global position and politics**: Appreciating that Western organisations are very often as disorganised as everywhere else.
I texted an Indian friend to see if she would be able to meet for coffee after the meeting. She replied to say she was working.	**Small culture formation**: Continuing to try out rules for when it is appropriate to text during professional events. **Statements about culture**: 'Texting is cosmopolitan and crosses cultural boundaries.' **Cultural resources**: Observation of lots of people texting in a wide variety of situations. Knowledge of how people can be annoyed by this behaviour. **Personal trajectory**: Experience of using texting as a major source of communication with Turkish colleagues while visiting a university in Istanbul, and with Syrian friends while visiting them in Damascus.

Cultural travel

There are several things to note about the contents of Table 4.3, which really is feeling its way in a very exploratory manner. In a number of cases I am bringing experience from distant cultural locations. It is certainly the case that there is a large element of cultural learning taking place, even with quite familiar events, and that this learning can stretch across 'home' cultural boundaries, which are themselves highly relative. There is a strong sense here of cultural learning through cultural travel.

What we imagine

In the taxi driver event it should be noted that **global position and politics** does not relate to relations between the East and West or global entities such as these, but to class divides. It should also be noted that these divides are imagined, hence the **statements about culture** which is implicit in this. Indeed, within the details of the known complexities of 'home' culture, it is very evident that 'class differences' have a great deal of imagination attached to them, albeit mediated by the powerful historical narratives present in the **cultural resources** which I deploy. This very clear ambivalence needs to be remembered when dealing with 'foreign' cultural difference. Connected with this is the reference to my Korean colleague in the meeting, where I 'expect' her to be surprised at the casual and creative time-keeping, and in the texting incident, where I derive some pleasure and indeed status in the notion that it is a cosmopolitan activity. There is so much incidence of playing with images; and it is the degree that this might be converted into cultural prejudice that we should be aware of.

Views about other people can easily be sparked off by such incidental things. These might include a person's name, a song or piece of music, a picture, object, artefact, costume, style of dress, type of food, or fragment of behaviour, which evoke particular images of foreign-ness, especially where they are associated with common stereotypes. An example which springs to mind is the film music in Hollywood Westerns which accompanies long-shots of groups of American Indians. Dolls or tourist pictures of Spanish flamenco dancers might be another evocative image.

Making culture on the run

Recall examples where you have yourself constructed or witnessed other people construct culture in the ways described in this chapter. This could include:

- large events or small day-to-day events;
- fine-tuning traditional behaviour or creating new traditions;
- establishing routines for you and other people to follow;
- learning new roles.

Recall examples where you have consciously tried to construct culture. Describe your purposes, the cultural group within which this happened, the strategies you used and the outcomes.

More specifically, evaluate Table 4.3. How far do the examples and analysis fit what you would expect? Would a table of this nature be useful in the above activities?

Unguarded processes

Do a talk-through of what happens in your unguarded head when encountering a 'foreign' person.

- Analyse the images and references which instigate the process or come into play as it develops.

Summary

- At one level, **small culture formation** involves making sense of events as they develop in whatever circumstances one finds oneself. At another level, it takes place during the conscious building of a community. The strategies involved will vary from conscious to unconscious.
- The processes of routinisation (making behaviour routine), reification (making unreal things appear real) and the development of rituals are important in establishing behavioural norms in **small culture formation**. They are implicit, consciously or unconsciously, in everyday processes from community building and making sense of events, to instilling conformity.
- These are the processes of reassurance and normality which we need to find when engaging with the culturally unfamiliar. They are also the processes of making sense of and engaging with the culturally unfamiliar, whether near home or abroad.
- The idealisation of Self and demonisation of the foreign Other are central to **small culture formation** and can take different forms in different circumstances. Even where the image of the foreign Other is not negative, it is still an imaginary product of the agenda of the Self.
- **Small culture formation** takes place all the time as we negotiate our relationship with events during the course of everyday life. This involves continuous learning of culture which transcends boundaries and is carried from place to place.
- **Small culture formation** in everyday circumstances at home is a powerful resource for learning to engage with unfamiliar cultural practices.

Notes

1 This is based on a personal family experience.
2 A generic term used for people in established sexual relationships who may not be married.
3 This is based on an interview with an ex-boarding-school pupil.
4 The Quakers are a Protestant Christian group who are known for being egalitarian and passivist.
5 A boarding school is a residential school where the majority of pupils would live, or 'board', throughout the school year.
6 Terms are the three-part divisions of the academic year.
7 This is based on extensive professional experience as a curriculum developer and experience of being 'developed' in several large institutions.

Further reference

Laing, R.D. (1961). *Self and Others*. London: Tavistock Publications.
  — A classic text on Self and Other.

Water fight in a Tehran park: http://tehranlive.org/2011/07/29/water-guns-war-in-tehran
  — This is a website which provides details concerning an event for families and children in the middle of the hot summer in a park in Tehran, Iran. While it may seem normal

to most people, in Iran this event constituted a form of political resistance against a disapproving government, during which arrests were made.
— Look at this as an example of new cultural construction.

Pulp Fiction restaurant scene: http://www.youtube.com/watch?v=YujYTVQ4_S0& feature=related
— This extract from the 1994 feature film shows two professional killers, or hit men, talking about their life principles, indicating that even criminals have their tightly regulated cultural rules.

Chapter 5

Dialogue with structure

This chapter builds on the notion of creativity in cultural construction within the context of the individual's potential dialogue with the structures often associated with 'national cultures'. These potentials will be looked at realistically, given that they may often be inhibited by circumstances and feed dominant rumours of 'national culture' dominance.

The national structures with which the dialogue takes place are on the left of the grammar within the general domain of **particular social and political structures**, including **cultural resources** and **global position and politics**. They structure how we are brought up to look at the rest of the world and contribute to our sense of national identity.

Nevertheless, these structures do not confine who we are. The potential for dialogue which, with these structures, is expressed through **personal trajectories** which comprise people's individual journeys through life, and through the **underlying universal cultural processes** which we all share and which provide us with the potential to transcend the particularities of national structures.

Rumour vs. Observation

Unfortunately we are beset by rumours about 'other cultures' which have developed over time for a number of reasons. They are embedded in the **underlying universal cultural processes** of constructing Self and Other within **small culture formation** and also in the historical narratives connected with the **global position and politics** with which we are brought up, as described in Chapters 3 and 7. These rumours lead us to imagine things about how our cultural lives are constructed, which may not be true or which may be exaggerated. A simple example of this is:

- the *rumour* or *belief* that British people are always punctual;
- The real-life *observation* that people are often late for meetings and often do not leave their prior location until the time of the meeting. They also often decide to be late for social events to avoid being 'the first to arrive'.

Unexpected behaviour

Share your own examples of behaviours you have *observed* which are different to what you have been led to *believe*.

What similar examples can be found in Ivonne's experience in Chapter 4?

There are a number of reasons for the actual behaviour not conforming to what we believe or imagine:

- The rumours are indeed rumours and wrong.
- The rumours are right, but there are lots of exceptions to the rule.
- There is a partial truth in the rumours in that they may relate to a particular institution, ideology or ethos within the society, but these do not confine or explain everyone's behaviour.

The first two possibilities are too simplistic. The first does not hold because all rumours are based on something. The question here is what the nature of that something might be. The second is an easy rationalisation which has been a long-standing excuse of upholding stereotypes. It is the third possibility which I want to deal with here.

How this works with Protestantism

The particular ideology or ethos with which I am most familiar from my own upbringing is Protestantism, which was a sixteenth-century northern European rebellion against established Christianity. While not all people in Britain are Protestant, it has been argued that the ethos of this branch of religion has had a major impact on British life and, indeed, on Western capitalism. The arguments for this were set out in Max Weber's key text, *The Protestant Ethic and the Spirit of Capitalism* (1977), first published in 1905. The first three columns of Table 5.1 set out a summary of the influence of Protestantism as I have experienced it in my own life. The final column represents the factors against this influence.

There are a number of things to be noted in Table 5.1. The construction of the non-Protestant Other in the second column is negative and demonised. Corruption and duplicity are indicated through loyalties to the group and the family, and placed in conflict with the honesty of the individual. This invokes the positivist individualist versus negative collectivist distinction. This implies that a major function of the Protestant ethos is to construct a positive Self and serves a very basic psychological need. It therefore provides a powerful **cultural resource** for identity.

The realisation in the final column that the image of Protestantism is not all-encompassing comes from extended observation of everyday behaviour. However:

Table 5.1 Dialogue with Protestantism

My perceptions of Protestantism	The construction of a non-Protestant Other	Influences on attitudes and behaviour	Factors acting against this influence
No priest to stand between God and the individual. Each person can interpret things for her or himself and should make their own decisions. There is no need to accept the authority of others. The individual must take personal responsibility for working out right and wrong and for her or his actions. People must do what they say they do and say what they really do. Personal industry is important to make a good impression on God.	They are positioned within a hierarchy in which priests stand between the individual and God. They do not need to take personal responsibility. They do not do what they say they will do (i.e. duplicitous). They are allowed to be corrupt, extravagant and to waste time.	A successful life requires a steady climb up the rungs of a ladder. Your career should not show any gaps that do not contribute to this success. Never borrow any money or waste anything.	Discovery that lots of people who are supposed to be Protestant: ■ rely on others for interpretation and to be told what to do; ■ do not do what they say they do or say what they really do; ■ do not believe that personal industry is important.

- Whether these observations are considered exceptions, or the norm, or whether this 'non-Protestant' behaviour is noticed at all, will of course also depend on the beliefs of the observer, and also on the circumstances within which the observer looks at her or his own society.
- Everyday behaviour is complex and multi-faceted, with many possible interpretations, each of which will be driven by how we wish to present who we are – the Self – at a particular time within particular circumstances.
- At the same time, to varying degrees in different social settings and societies, interpretations of the Self will be thrust upon us for a possible variety of political, educational, institutional or other reasons generated by the group dynamics of which we are a part.

Influences and other options

Consider a major cultural influence in your own life, which may be Confucianism or Protestantism, or something similar.

- Construct your own version of Table 5.1 and work out what you can learn from what you write in each column and the way in which you write it.

Consider the three statements about rumours earlier in the chapter and state your reasons for which ones you support.

The case of Confucianism

In parallel to Protestantism, much has been said about the influence of Confucianism in East Asian societies such as China, Japan and Korea. It has often been presumed that this influence has led to cultures of obedience, group loyalty and hierarchy, which do not encourage personal autonomy and creativity. This image fits very closely with the non-Protestant image of collectivism in Table 5.1.

Although Confucius, a sixth-century BC Chinese social philosopher, was indeed a major influence, there has been much questioning of exactly how powerful Confucianism has been on daily life – that notions of the totality of Confucianism are based on only particular aspects of the philosophy, or that its effects are exaggerated.

It is nevertheless also a powerful **cultural resource**. This is especially the case where people have to carry out demanding tasks in a foreign country, such as when East Asian students face the concept of critical thinking in British universities. It is indeed a stated aim of British education to develop critical thinking; and the expectation is that students in the classroom will express opinions and critique ideas which are presented to them either in writing or in oral discussion. In contrast, a lot of East Asian students find this difficult. They often appear more comfortable with a less discursive format where they are expected to bow to the authority of teachers and to the content of the syllabus.

However, this is not as straightforward as it looks. The big question is whether this is:

- really because their national cultures do not allow them to think critically;
- because they are just not used to thinking critically in classrooms because of the particular educational experience they have had; or
- because critical thinking is falsely and over-simplistically constructed and reified as the core feature of Western society.

Jenna and Malee: critical thinking

This issue is addressed in the following narrative.[1]

Jenna felt that her overall progress in her Cultural Studies course at the university was good, but she was still feeling a block with one aspect. Every assignment she got back had the comment that she needed to express her own views about the topic she was writing about and not just report what she had found out about it. When she met her tutor he said that this was part of a bigger problem that she seemed to have with critical thinking. This phrase 'critical thinking' kept on coming up. In the student handbook, which she had studied very carefully, it was cited as an important learning objective for the programme. Her tutor said that in class she was expected to express her views orally about the topic of discussion. He said that her English was excellent, both in her writing, and, *when* she spoke, in her oral communication as well, but that this wasn't enough.

She wasn't alone in this issue. There were a number of students on the course who came from her part of the world, and even from much further afield, who seemed to face similar problems. There was a general feeling among these students that it was all to do with their various cultures, which were in conflict with the culture they found here. It was either to do with their religion or, in the case of students from East Asia, with Confucianism. Of course she knew all about Confucianism; and certainly it made sense when other students said that it was a pillar of their culture and meant that they were brought up to respect authority and that that was why it was so difficult to express opinions. This view about culture also seemed to be shared by their tutors, who referred to it quite often – explaining how careful they were to understand their culture. This felt right to Jenna. All through her education at home her teachers had never encouraged her to show any personal opinion. This view was also reinforced by what was going on here. She had heard that there had been a conference at the university about Confucianism and East Asian students.

All of this helped Jenna because it gave her something to say to her tutor – that it was not part of her culture to express her opinion. It helped her to understand the nature of her problem, so that at least she knew where to begin to do something about it.

Then she met Malee, an East Asian student who presented a very different story. She said that the image of Confucianism that everyone was describing was far too simplistic, and that, in its full complexity, Confucianism didn't inhibit critical thinking at all. She said that it was time that East Asian students stopped making excuses and began to realise that critical thinking was not alien to their cultures at all. She was also angry that they were giving Westerners a bad impression, and were being labelled as culturally deficient as a result, when in fact they had thousands of years of civilisation.

When Jenna told Malee about her experiences at high school, of never being encouraged to speak out, Malee said that this was probably her teachers' excuse for not being able to teach more creatively, and that she needed instead to think of all the other times in her life when she was critical.

Jenna discussed what Malee had said with one of her friends she had been at high school with when she next spoke to her on Skype. Her friend reminded her about how they had secretly criticised their parents' image of them, and, indeed, what was often written in the press about high-school students. They had a reputation for only being interested in studying for examinations; yet they knew that this was not true at all. They had a private world as teenagers which they kept to themselves, in which they shared a critique of their society. In class, out of the sight of their teachers, they went beyond the syllabus by reading widely and discussing issues in groups outside the classroom. Her friend also reminded her that there was a history of revolution in their country; and in their universities students had a tradition of opposing their teachers to the extent of voting them out of their positions – not very often, but with great effect when it did happen.

Jenna went back to Malee and said that she understood that she did have critical thinking inside her; but that she still couldn't think of anything to say in class or to express as criticism in her assignments. Malee said that it was probably because the topics were just not interesting, and that there was a huge difference between being critical of really important things in your life and having to be critical of boring classroom topics. She said that in one of her classes there was a student who refused to talk about texts on gender and homosexuality because they were 'not relevant to her culture'.

Table 5.2 presents an analysis of the narrative through the categories of cultural action. It shows the clear dialogue taking place between two perceptions of Jenna's cultural background.

Table 5.2 Critical thinking

Categories of cultural action	Jenna	Malee	Local tutors and institution	Jenna's friend
Statements about culture	'My national culture does not encourage critical thinking.' Later modifies this and agrees with Malee.	'There is no problem with critical thinking. 'Confucianism is an excuse for inaction and poor teaching at high school.'	'Critical thinking is important for education. 'You must think critically in the way and in the time and place which we define.'	
Global position and politics	Our culture is different, special and in conflict with Western culture.	We are giving the West a bad impression. We are as good as them if not better.	East Asian students are a problem. Their cultures have to be taken into consideration. The non-West needs to address issues such as homosexuality and gender.	
Cultural resources	Confucianism. Not being encouraged to speak out at school School friends.	Confucianism as a complex concept. Critical thinking is present in everyday life. Thousands of years of civilisation.	Critical thinking as an important educational objective. Critical discussions about homosexuality and gender.	A history of resistance against dominant views. Revolution. Student power.
Agendas	Maintaining a good self-image. Damaged by the knowledge of a national conference to solve the problem of students like them.		Maintaining high grades. Student satisfaction, especially for high-fee-paying 'international' students. A convincing mission statement for the university.	Student resistance.
Underlying universal processes			Institutionalising critical thinking within very specific pre-designed pedagogic events.	Drawing on histories for reassurance.
	Constructing cultural explanations to deal with high-stake conflict. Constructing discourses of critical thinking to suit agendas.			

There are two basic points of view expressed in the narrative. Jenna and her tutors, who follow the policy of the university, maintain the more essentialist view that critical thinking is in conflict with East Asian culture. However, Malee and Jenna's school friend present the different, non-essentialist view that this is not the case at all, by arguing that a more complex interpretation of critical thinking does indeed have forms which are indigenous to East Asian society. This conflicting view opens up the possibility that a limited view of critical thinking has been falsely reified as an exclusive feature of the university. It could indeed be argued that it is the tutors who are not being sufficiently critical by not realising this. Their positioning of critical thinking with discussions about gender and homosexuality which cannot be appreciated by East Asian culture implies a cultural deficiency in East Asian culture.

The added 'agendas' row indicates how the different characters use their particular interpretations of critical thinking to support their particular interests. It is clear here that the stakes are high. Maintaining a good self-image in opposition to being a 'problem' is important both to Jenna and Malee. Jenna's friend is proud of a cultural heritage. The connected Othering of foreign students serves educational institution identities.

The **underlying universal cultural processes** row therefore indicates that critical thinking is a contested concept which all parties are able to use in the Self and Other constructions necessary for **small culture formation**.

High stakes

Think of times when people's reaction to foreigners has been influenced by acute circumstances (e.g. competition, shortage of resources such as land or jobs, threats to normal life or to reputation, status or position, or a threat to your struggle to do things in a particular way).

Describe a particular set of circumstances when this has happened, and how the image of the foreigners became different to the details of their actual lives.

Reconstruct one of your own experiences of being Othered in this way. It may have been as a child, with friends, at school, in the workplace, or when travelling.

Essentialism

Malee notes that she and her fellow East Asian students are being labelled as culturally deficient and being reduced to an essentialist view of Confucianism. Essentialism is a key concept in making sense of cultural forces such as Confucianism and Protestantism, and as such falls within the **underlying universal cultural processes** of **small culture formation**. The following light-hearted example is a good way to explain it, though the consequences are not light-hearted at all:

A student from Country X is sitting in the classroom. Suddenly, she jumps up on the table, waves her arms around and shouts and sings loudly. After a few minutes she returns to her seat.

An essentialist explanation is that this behaviour is because of her national culture, and that all people from Country X will behave in this way. A non-essentialist view would not try to explain behaviour in terms of national culture, or of any other stereotypical idea, and would appreciate that the reasons for this behaviour may simply be personal, that the student may be just eccentric, and that even if she is not, she is too complex to be reduced to a demeaning stereotype. Essentialism is thus implicit in Othering. How this applies to Confucianism, Protestantism and critical thinking is rationalised in Table 5.3.

Table 5.3 Essentialism and non-essentialism

	Essentialist explanation	Non-essentialist explanation
Protestantism and Confucianism	They define and confine all behaviour in a particular national culture.	They are a powerful element of the societies where they reside. They influence behaviour; but they do not determine it.
Individual people	Their behaviour is confined by the major forces of their national culture, such as Protestantism or Confucianism. Any behaviour which does not conform to these forces is eccentric or an exception to the rule.	Depending on institutional, political and other circumstances, they have the capacity to behave differently and resist these forces.
Critical thinking	Whether or not this exists depends on the major forces of national culture. In Confucian cultures it does not exist. In Protestant cultures it does exist. It is a value that is not present in Confucian cultures.	Critical thinking is a natural part of human existence. While it might not be encouraged in some circumstances, this does not mean that people do not possess the ability.
Action	We should not expect people from Confucian cultures to value critical thinking.	It may be necessary to explain that it is appropriate to display critical thinking in circumstances where it has not previously been encouraged.

A key issue here is the difference between appearance and actuality. I recall these critical incidents from my own life.

A new teacher came to my school when I was 14 and introduced classroom discussion for the first time. When I was asked to speak out in such a discussion I persisted in remaining silent. I felt that my privacy was being invaded. The teacher responded by calling me 'passive'. This made me even more angry and more determined not to speak.

> While attending a management course, a tutor asked us to go off in groups and discuss what we had been learning. I really did think this was silly; and I knew that my fellow participants felt the same way. However, most likely out of politeness they went off and went through the motions. I resisted and told the tutor I didn't find it relevant. This act of defiance plunged both the tutor and I into a very uncomfortable no-persons' land; and I found myself reassuring her that everything was OK and that this was not a criticism of her. This seemed so ironic as she had said that she welcomed critical feedback on the course.

Therefore, in Table 5.3, the non-essentialist column recognises elements of critical thinking which remain hidden in the essentialist column. In the final row, the essentialist action presented there is considered culturally accommodating because it allows the foreign Other to be different and folds the issue into 'values', implying that *they don't value critical thinking; but we must understand them and not expect them to.* The non-essentialist action is very different because it does not exclude anyone from enjoying critical thinking.

Being misunderstood

Think of a time when you have been misunderstood because of the way behaviour has been categorised or institutionalised by others.

An example of this might be people saying you are naïve because you don't swear. They have defined people as being worldly when they swear. You feel you are worldly for other reasons which they don't recognise.

This sort of thing might apply to being good at your job, being assertive, taking control of your life, taking responsibility, being reliable and so on.

What are the reasons why people need to define or institutionalise behaviour in this way? Link this to discussions so far in the text related to Self and Other.

Critical thinking

Explore as many examples of critical thinking as you can think of, in as many cultural environments as you have knowledge of, and consider the viability of the statement: *Critical thinking is a universal which relates to all people regardless of culture.*

Jenna, Bekka and Malee: the problem with 'Westernisation'

These issues are taken up in this continuation of Jenna's engagement with the issue of critical thinking, which takes a significant turn which could be considered positive or sinister.

Jenna felt a sense of liberation after her discussions with Malee and her friend from school. She had found it hard to make friends with local students and was surprised when Bekka began to take notice of her and wanted to have coffee after class. She wondered if it had anything to do with her having joined in a classroom discussion and talked about how at home there was a tradition of voting out figures of authority in extreme circumstances.

When they had coffee Bekka said that she was interested in what Jenna had been talking about and very surprised because she had heard that her culture was very hierarchical and authoritarian. Jenna replied that she had heard so many things about the local culture which did not seem to be true, like people always being on time. She had noticed so many students turning up late. Bekka said that from what she had read this would be explained by Jenna's culture being collectivist while hers was individualist. This response puzzled Jenna because the point she was making was that there was room for variation in both cultures. Bekka explained that individualist cultures were different because they were based on valuing self-expression and determination and therefore there could be a lot more variation of behaviour and people were free to not be on time if they wished, and that that would be respected.

As time went on Jenna felt that her relationship with Bekka soured. The more Jenna felt she was coming out and asserting herself in front of local students and tutors, the more Bekka went on about how different their cultures were. Then, in one of their coffee sessions, Bekka announced that she had noticed a remarkable change in Jenna – that she really had become so Westernised. Jenna wasn't sure how to take this. She felt that Bekka was congratulating her; but Malee was horrified when she mentioned this to her and said that the people here just couldn't stand the idea that foreigners could be as expressive, independent and critical as they were without having learnt it from them and having become assimilated into their ways.

The narrative demonstrates a further layer of Othering, in which the Self of Bekka constructs itself as complex and diverse and the foreign Other as simple and monolithic. This simplifying of the Other is a common part of essentialism because the simpler we can imagine a foreign society to be, the easier it is to imagine that everyone in that society is the same. Then, when Jenna moves beyond the boundaries Bekka has constructed for her she explains it as assimilation. Being 'Westernised' might be intended as a positive and a compliment by Bekka. Jenna is unsure, and Malee sees it as a diminishing of who she is. This is indicated in Table 5.4 which continues from Table 5.2 by adding the voice of Bekka and Malee's response.

Again, despite their differences, in the final row Bekka and Malee are both constructing theories of culture to deal with the conflicts they are facing, but with different outcomes. What is at stake for each of the characters is their cultural identity. Because Jenna appears more successful in the domain Bekka has constructed for her, and to cross its borders, this threatens Bekka's definition of herself. The suggestion of Westernisation threatens the cultural identity of Jenna and Malee.

Table 5.4 Analysis continued

Categories of cultural action	Bekka	Malee
Statements about culture	'My culture is individualist and your culture is collectivist, authoritarian and hierarchical.'	'My culture cannot be defined and pinned down in this way.'
Global position and politics	Western culture values the right for individuals to be what they want. People from other cultures who have and practice these values must have become Westernised and be like us.	My culture also values the right for individuals to be what they want. We do not have to be Westernised or assimilated to have these values.
Cultural resources	The right to behave as one wishes. Knowledge of collectivism and individualism.	
Underlying universal processes	Constructing cultural explanations to deal with high-stake conflicts.	
	Imagining assimilation.	Resisting assimilation.

Despite Malee's anger, the principle of assimilation, where foreign communities become absorbed into the society in which they have arrived, is well thought of by many. However, Kumaravadivelu, an Indian academic living in the US, thinks just the opposite:

> The proponents of cultural assimilation would expect me to adopt the behaviours, values, beliefs, and lifestyles of the dominant cultural community and become absorbed in it, losing my own in the process ... to have metamorphosed into a somebody with a totally different cultural persona.
>
> (Kumaravadivelu 2007: 4)

He follows this with a statement about not needing to be assimilated because he is able to accommodate complexity:

> I believe I live in several cultural domains at the same time – jumping in and out of them, sometimes with ease and sometimes with unease.... In fact one does not even have to cross one's national borders to experience cultural complexity. If we, as we must, go beyond the traditional approach to culture that narrowly associated cultural identity with national identity ... then we easily realise that human communities are not monocultural cocoons but rather multicultural mosaics.
>
> (Kumaravadivelu 2007: 5)

Being Westernised is also a very common concept. It is used by many people who associate many of the things which can be found so easily and in such profusion in the West (e.g. technology, facilities, clothing, attitudes) only with the West. It is thus a **statement about**

culture about the relationship between Self and Other, and indeed derives from the **under-lying universal cultural process** of making sense of Self and Other.

It may indeed be true that much of our modern life can be traced to Western technology and attitudes. However, at the same time, social, technological and political phenomena can be traced to multiple influences and causes in a world that has been interconnected by trade and other forms of communication since long before the modern era. Bekka's use of 'Westernised' implies an ownership which, whether adequately rooted in history or not, concerns an imagined superiority.

Rumours again

Revisit the three statements about rumours near the beginning of this chapter and reconsider them in the light of Jenna's experience, and especially what Bekka thinks of her.

Westernisation

Consider an attitude, a piece of technology and a piece of clothing which are common in the West. Trace influences or causes for each one which come from outside the West. Of course, to do this you will need to assess exactly what 'the West' refers to.

Recall an incident when you have been called or you have called someone else Westernised.

- How did you feel about yourself and the other person during the incident – as equals or otherwise?
- Was it a compliment or an insult?
- If you felt it was a compliment, how do you feel about it now after reading the narrative?
- Do you think being Westernised is an achievement or not, and why?
- What does being Westernised celebrate, and what does it deny?
- Is it just a simple term without any ideology behind it?

Loss or development

The discussion in this chapter has moved on to the issue of Westernisation, which may seem far away from the theme of dialogue with national structures. Perceptions of Westernisation are, however, at the core of where we stand with regard to dialogue with national structures. The following distinction sheds light on this:

- *Cultural development*: non-essentialist; supports the possibility of dialogue. We are not bound by national structures even though we are influenced by them. We can be different things without losing who we are and within our own cultural terms. Culture by its nature changes and adapts. Cultural behaviour which happens to be found also in the

West can easily be accommodated and may well already exist in some form in our own cultural environment.

* *Culture loss*: essentialist. Westernisation implies that types of behaviour are limited to particular cultures which cannot accommodate change and dialogue within their structures. To indulge in behaviour which does not fit the stereotype of the culture amounts to selling out to another national structure. The culture of the nation, the community or the group is being lost.

Cultural loss is certainly not within the perception of Malee in the above narrative, who is offended by the notion that so-called individualist characteristics cannot be part of her own cultural makeup. Neither is it within the experience of Jenna, who begins to see all sorts of evidence that the so-called individualist versus collectivist attributes that are supposed to prevent her from being like Western people do not fit what she sees in real life.

Modernisation and globalisation

There needs nevertheless to be caution here. The optimism of the 'cultural development' notion may under-estimate the dangers of modernisation and globalisation. Just because they can be absorbed, become part of and be claimed by the culture, it must not be ignored that forces of change still *can* be, and very often *are*, imposed by stronger forces which may not be positive in their impact.

Instances of top-down globalisation which are damaging and destructive would be international corporations invading local communities and destroying all sense of cultural roots and practices. However, on the side of cultural development, bottom-up globalisation, on the other hand, can work, and have positive influence where politically oppressed or other marginal communities can use outside influences as a form of liberation. These marginalised communities take global flows and make them their own. An example of this which is often cited is youth communities making use of hip-hop and rap to express social and political resistance, or the use of Facebook to facilitate revolution.

Bekka, in the above narrative, may fear the change that foreigners might bring to her society, discovering that newcomers can be as good as she is at what she herself values, but at the same time changing it. This is a different type of top-down globalisation, coming from what might seem a massive and unstoppable wave of immigration. Malee, on the other hand, claims for herself the values which Bekka says she owns as a form of resistance to a top-down globalisation generated by Bekka's West, which is in danger of ignoring and obliterating the cultural competencies which Malee brings with her.

The essentialist view of culture may therefore in some circumstances be constructed as an ideological force to serve political resistance.

Modernity and globalisation

Consider various political movements (e.g. revolution, activists, causes).

- Is it possible to locate them in the descriptions of culture development and culture loss above?
- How are the various elements of the concepts of culture development and culture loss used by the parties concerned to serve their political needs?
- If an essentialist view of culture is used to serve a political need, does this mean it is false or real?

Moving on

With respect to the possibility of cultural development, think of an example of cultural change within your own community or sphere of experience.

- Describe the new and old practices.
- What are the positive features which have been carried from one to the other?
- For what reasons are these features to be so valued?
- What has been gained in the new practice? What is more modern about it?

Cultural traps

It is very easy to fall into essentialist traps when faced with examples of cultural development, as the following personal experiences indicate. In each case a valuable lesson was learnt.

In the 1970s I lived in southern Iran and had a particularly good relationship with my dentist. We became friends and I used to visit him in his surgery while he was working with a patient. In the mid-1990s I found him again, now working in the capital and was excited about going to his surgery to see him. I naïvely believed that it would be the same. When I told the receptionist that I was there he did indeed interrupt his consultation with a patient to come out and see me; but it was very clear that times had changed and I would not be able to go in while he was working. He was wearing a mask and surgical gloves, and his body language told me there was a profound professional barrier that was not there before.

During another visit to Iran in the 2000s, my wife and I visited a cousin of hers who had a carpet shop in the bazaar. We were looking for a particular type of carpet and had tea with him while he sent someone to enquire at other shops. I felt he and I developed a rapport, and I later met him again at his mother's home for a family lunch. I told my wife that I was looking forward to visiting him again in his shop to develop the friendship. She retorted that he would be far too busy to spend time drinking tea: his time was far too valuable. She herself had discovered that times had changed. People, even family members, no longer just visited each other when they felt like it. Everyone was too busy and now made appointments before visiting.

Both of these cases exemplify a gradual modernisation which is happening in all societies, as more traditional behaviour gives way to new.

Creative cultural behaviour

Dialogue with one's national structures may not only happen because of some form of cultural confrontation such as that between East Asian and British students at university. People may also choose to be creative with what they have been brought up with. Indeed, in the spirit of Kumaravadivelu's comment above, as both we and our communities are multicultural mosaics by nature, such creativity is part of the normal makeup of who we are. I will focus for a minute on what happens in the societies in which we were brought up as a form of dialogue with structure.

I can make the following list of creative cultural changes I have observed in Britain within my experience, some of it quite recent:

- No longer holding doors open for the people behind you because there are electronic buttons to press.
- Leaving space between you and the person in front of you in a queue for a cash machine to give them privacy while entering personal details.
- When there are a number of counters in shops or other locations, having only one queue, which stands back in equidistant space from all the counters, so that the next customer can go to the next available one. This is sometimes organised by the owners, with a 'wait here' sign; but customers are now also organising themselves in this way.
- Buying coffee to take out and walking with it in tall cardboard cups. This is brought about by a sudden proliferation of coffee shops.
- Looking at smartphone screens nearly all the time, while walking, standing, talking, sitting, meeting, and so on.
- New expressions which come with every technological innovation, such as 'Facebooking', 'texting', and 'windows'.

Duality

This sense of creativity can also lead to forms of duality in cultural practice, where people may believe or claim that they subscribe to a practice but behave in a very different manner. This is where what people say about their culture may not correspond with what they actually do, which is the domain of **statements about culture** in the grammar. The dentist or the carpet shop owner in the examples above may well say that in Iran hospitality is more important than professionalism or business. They may genuinely believe this, may mourn its loss in 'modern' life, and may certainly express it as a defining principle of who they are when speaking to foreigners; and it may have been true at some time in the past.

In the workplace conformity narrative in Chapter 4 there was a concerted attempt to change behaviour within an organisation. On the surface this was successful because of the use of terms and principles in meetings and report writing. It may well have been the case, however, that employees were simply going through the motions of compliance and, in effect, playing with them. People have the immense capacity to conform in some respects and resist in others. They can, for example, perform dual behaviour between private and public life. This is well-known in instances of political oppression and under extreme institutional régimes. In business it is well-known for people to manipulate the essentialist stereotypes which have been thrust upon them for the purpose of selling back to the purveyors of the stereotypes – hence powerful images of exotic people, locations, food and so on in tourist advertising.

People who are referred to as Westernised, even when the behaviour this relates to is not exclusively Western, can nevertheless buy into the concept for a number of reasons:

- They believe the West is superior and wish to be associated with this superiority, and therefore feel that they can gain status and prestige through being assimilated.
- It is too difficult to object to being called Westernised.
- They have an ulterior motive for complying with the image of Westernisation (e.g. business, political gain, career or generally gaining status or membership to a group from which they can benefit).

Kumaravadivelu considers all three of these motives to be selling out to a dominant agenda through a process of self-Othering or self-marginalisation, and has the following to say:

> Self-marginalisation refers to the way in which the periphery surrenders its voice and vision to the centre.... Knowingly or unknowingly, [they] legitimise the characteristics of inferiority attributed to them by the dominating group.
>
> (Kumaravadivelu 2006: 22)

Here, the Centre, often capitalised, refers to the source of power in the world which is able to define the rest of the world. The Periphery, often capitalised, refers to the victim of this power, which has to struggle for visibility and recognition.

Observing change

Make your own list of examples of creative cultural change and consider the causes. Are they really changes, or just normal responses to new technologies?

You might look particularly at some core areas of tradition such as schooling, engagement and weddings, family relations, sport, workplace relationships.

Playing with change

Under what circumstances have you claimed to subscribe to national cultural norms when in fact you don't really. What was it that you claimed? What were your reasons?

Self-marginalisation

Evaluate the three reasons listed for accepting the 'Westernised' label. Describe in detail one example of each one which you have experienced, either in yourself or in someone else.

Summary

- There are many dominant rumours about the power which major social forces such as Confucianism and Protestantism have over the individual. Direct observation of actual behaviour will often contradict these rumours.
- The rumours are promoted by the everyday Self and Other politics of **small culture formation**.
- When stakes are high people make use of powerful narratives of 'national culture', such as critical thinking, either consciously or unconsciously, to maintain their positions. The Othering of foreigners is a likely outcome.
- Essentialism positions non-Westerners who display cultural creativity as having learnt this from the West and therefore as having become Westernised and assimilated.
- Non-essentialism recognises that cultural creativity can cross boundaries independently of Western definitions and without assimilation.
- Cultural change, within a process of bottom-up globalisation, may be part of a process of taking ownership of modernisation.
- Creative cultural behaviour is a normal part of everyday life in all societies.
- An unexpected example of cultural creativity is where, for a wide variety of reasons, people appear to comply with but in effect resist dominant structures.

Note

1   This is based on a number of conversations with students and colleagues from a variety of backgrounds, and on research into the experiences of British and international students in British and Australian universities (Caruana and Spurling 2006; Clifford and Montgomery 2011; Grimshaw 2010b; Harrison and Peacock 2009; Jones 2009; Montgomery 2010; Ryan and Louie 2007; Ryan and Viete 2009).

Further reference

Egyptian revolution link – MENA Solidarity Network: http://menasolidaritynetwork.com/egyptwomen-2
— Sections of the women's pages of this site show text, photographs and video extracts in which women speak out against the system.

Iranian women and football: http://www.hurriyetdailynews.com/female-football-fans-may-return-to-iran-stadiums.aspx?pageID=238&nID=21519&NewsCatID=364
— This is a media extract on Iranian women football supporters resisting the ban on them attending football matches because of the sight of men's bodies.

A short story of academic oppression in Egypt: http://www.guardian.co.uk/commentis-free/libertycentral/2011/jun/29/academic-freedom-egypt
— This is a media extract on Egyptian students and lecturers demanding access to banned literature on lesbianism.

Moeran, B. (1996). The Orient strikes back: advertising and imagining in Japan. *Theory, Culture and Society* 13/3: 77–112.
— A discussion of Japanese business using the stereotypes constructed by the West to sell back to the West.

Grimshaw, T. (2007). Problematising the construct of 'the Chinese learner': insights from ethnographic research. *Educational Studies* 33: 299–311.
— A discussion of common misperceptions of Chinese students.

Honarbin-Holliday, M. (2008). *Becoming visible in Iran: women in contemporary Iranian society*. London: I.B. Tauris.
— Page 73 discusses the female chancellor of an Iranian university keeping the cafeteria open during the fasting month of Ramadan, and distributing more colourful headscarves for women students to wear.
— Pages 104–5 offer a narrative about women's resistance to not being allowed to attend football matches.
— Pages 109–10 cover the role of coffee shops in Iran as sites of political resistance.

Holliday, A.R. (2011). *Intercultural communication & ideology*. London: Sage.
— Pages 4 onwards offer a full discussion of essentialism and non-essentialism.
— Pages 102–3 discuss cafés as a transcultural phenomenon.

Andrić, I. (1995). *Bridge over the Drina*. Edwards, L.F., Trans. London: Harvill Press.
— Pages 135–42 are a detailed account of the modernisation of a small Muslim town in Serbia with the advent of Austro-Hungarian control in the nineteenth century.

Samy Alim, H. and Pennycook, A. (2007). Glocal linguistic flows: hip-hop culture(s), identities, and the politics of language education. *Journal of Language, Identity & Education* 6/2: 89–100.
— A discussion of hip-hop as a transcultural phenomenon.

Chapter 6

Historical narratives

Much of the focus in this book is on **small culture formation** – the immediacy of constructing culture on an everyday basis in the current moment. However, it needs to be acknowledged that constructing culture in the present can be influenced very much by the historical narratives which we bring to the situation. These are powerful narratives which are long-standing and implicit in the **particular social and political structures** of nation, religion and ideology, and the **global position and politics** that collect around them. We all draw on these historical narratives as **cultural resources**, and we carry them through our **personal trajectories** within everyday cultural engagement.

Ivonne, Chung and Ning: simple things about food

These historical narratives find their way into the simplest everyday interactions. This is another incident from Ivonne's trip to Ex, first introduced in Chapter 3.

Act 1: art complex

After the conference Ivonne was invited to give talks at two universities, and Chung, a research student at one of the universities, was appointed to look after her. Ivonne had now got over the fear of losing her privacy and free time. They had talked frankly about this and she felt that Chung was quite relieved not to have to take her places at every free moment. Chung had a programme of the normal tourist sites to take Ivonne to, and he was surprised when she asked instead to visit a modern art complex which she had seen advertised on television in the hotel.

This turned the tables a bit because it was Chung who found himself on foreign territory, as he had never been to such a place before. He was pleased that much of the exhibition was housed in an old factory building with artefacts from Ex's industrial past, and that there was a section of the exhibits related to the Great Revolution. He found himself being more proud than he had expected about these things from 'his world' as he explained them to Ivonne within what he perceived as 'her world' of modern art; and afterwards he wondered if it was this association that had led him to tell Ivonne all about his difficult upbringing and struggle to get to university. He also felt that all of this was a welcome break from always talking about Confucianism.

Afterwards they went to a café within the complex. Although going to cafés like this later became a normal part of Chung's routine, this was his first time. When they went in and joined the queue it was Chung who felt the foreigner again, never having been to a café like this before. While he paid the bill with his expenses allowance, he let Ivonne order coffee, a muffin for him and a piece of cake for herself after she had ascertained what he was prepared to try. When they sat down, Chung looked around at other people to get some clues about how to eat the muffin. Obviously Ivonne noticed this because she said that it was something that she herself had only encountered in cafés like this and that no one really knew how to eat them.

Chung found Ivonne very easy to talk to and he felt they were being quite open about the nature of this 'intercultural experience'. He felt relaxed enough to explain to her that he hadn't been out of Ex or had much experience with foreigners like her, and that he was learning on the spot what sort of English, with what level of formality, to use – what level of questioning was polite, and so on. He explained that he felt quite uneasy to be in a café like this, which was renowned for being 'international' and 'Western'. He found himself being sceptical when Ivonne tried to explain that these types of 'latte café', as she called them, were new to her too. He didn't really believe her when she said that many people in her country had reservations about how quickly they had taken over the high street and work places, and that she was annoyed by 'this new cultural phenomenon of people everywhere walking around with cardboard coffee cups in their hands'.

It did, however, make him think again when she countered his view that these cafés were simply Western by saying that the owner of the café they were in must be Exian and that this was just part of a cultural change that was happening everywhere, but with a particularly local ownership. He thought to himself that, yes, why shouldn't Exian people take ownership of this trend.

Act 2: restaurant

Ivonne was also pleased to make contact with Ning, an ex-research student from her department, who was now employed at a good university there. By means of texting and Skype she arranged to go out for dinner. Ivonne had a dilemma though. Chung would also be expecting to take her to a restaurant to eat. She didn't think that Chung and Ning knew each other and she didn't want to offend either of them by suggesting bringing the other along. She didn't know what would be appropriate in Ex under such circumstances. She knew she was probably worrying over nothing; but she imagined rivalries and status issues connected to their two universities, and perhaps even gender issues. She was beginning to learn that it was naïve to assume that all people from the same 'culture' would automatically get on with each other. However, when all three met, although Ivonne felt they looked a little uneasy with each other, it seemed okay and Ning led the way to a restaurant of her choice.

A very large menu arrived, and Ning seemed to Ivonne to take the lead in ordering what they should have. She checked with Ivonne what sorts of things she couldn't eat. However, when the prawns arrived Ivonne was unable to eat them because they were tiny and had to be eaten whole. She couldn't face eating the heads, eyes and legs.

Ivonne felt she had developed some rapport with Chung. So, even though Ivonne was much older and more senior in status, it was not too much of a shock when he accused her of being a 'spoilt' Englishwoman who had never experienced hardship. Chung explained that the reason why Exian people ate so many types of food was because poverty had driven them to eat whatever they could find.

It took Ivonne a few minutes to collect herself, and then she thought of a response to this attack. She explained that she was brought up with a tradition of thrift, borne out of a long history of living with few resources. This meant that it would be thought extravagant and wasteful to order more food than people could eat, as she had seen people do in Ex. This led to a heated discussion about cultural politics.

After the event, Ivonne thought more about what had happened. She felt that really she would not have thought about the tradition of thrift within her family and class if she had not been pushed to it by Chung. Nevertheless, she felt that the tradition *was* there; even though she wasn't religious at all, it was influenced by Protestantism. She also realised that the image of individualism which went with Protestantism actually had a lot to do with her initial fears about this so-called 'Exian culture'. She wondered what had driven Chung to criticise her squeamishness about eating whole prawns. Then she thought back to their trip to the art galleries and cafés and what she had learnt about him and his pride in the political struggle of his past.

This is a complex narrative in which both Ivonne and Chung express some ambivalence about the lines they are taking and the historical narratives they are referring to. What happens is also embedded within very particular circumstances. Yet, particular historical narratives do begin to persist. Table 6.1 places this complexity within the context of the categories of cultural action and locates the historical narratives within the **cultural resources** domain. They are therefore drawn upon to deal with social difficulty – in this case making sense of some difficult interaction. That both Chung and Ivonne need to do this is reflected in the **underlying universal cultural processes** domain.

A number of things are noticeable about the manner in which the historical narratives emerge:

- They are invoked quite consciously to help provide support in a difficult difference of opinion.
- Neither Chung nor Ivonne totally buy into them. Although the narratives have powerful presence in their lives, they treat them with ambivalence.
- The narratives are nevertheless sufficiently powerful to wash away any polite reservation.
- The narratives have a power beyond the individual, as though they have a life of their own and are waiting in the wings for individuals to subscribe to them in times of need.
- They relate to a huge amount of moralistic theorising about values, even in response to something as ordinary as eating habits.

Table 6.1 Contesting narratives

Categories of cultural action	Ivonne	Chung
Statements about culture	'There are aspects of my upbringing which are different to common expectations about the West.'	'Exian people have suffered huge hardships and succeeded. 'I don't always think about this.'
Global position and politics	The West is misunderstood.	Western people are spoilt and cannot understand hardship. A history of being Othered by the West.
Historical narratives as cultural resources	A family history that goes back to working class origins. A tradition of thrift and care for resources.	A family history that goes back to severe poverty. Food traditions which are connected with poverty. A history of economic and political struggle. Confucianism is not the only historical narrative Affluence and extravagance belong to the West.
Underlying universal processes	Both parties trying to make sense of their interaction and finding narratives from which to assert their positions.	

Invention

In the case of Chung and Ivonne, it may be argued quite convincingly that the historical narratives, once they have been put in their place, are indeed grounded in historical reality. However, 'historical reality' can be a very difficult thing to establish. Historical narratives can be so entrenched in the mists of history that it is really hard to pin them down. In almost all cases there will be embellishments, preferred interpretations, convenient forgetting of discordant aspects, and myth, so that things which might actually have happened take on a power in people's minds which is far beyond them. The following two reconstructed accounts demonstrate this point.

The A embassy in B had a huge cotton banner hanging across the entire front of the upper floor of the building. Written against a black background were the words 'Remember C'. C was the name of a battle that took place in the seventh century which represented an important religious schism which was still a major reason for wars and conflicts in the region. This battle also had considerable influence on how the régime of A positioned itself in the region, and was certainly an important factor in many people's national identity.

D was at war with E and consciously established a propaganda committee which would help bind its people together in a concerted war effort. The people responsible for this were very aware that they were constructing images and messages which would catch the imagination of the public. They employed advertising agencies to create slogans and images; and the press and television was leant upon to collaborate. They employed singers and song-writers, and entertaining the troops was a major part of the strategy. They needed a core narrative to underpin the whole strategy. There was already a historical event which had been present in national songs.

Historical narratives everywhere

The examples above and below are kept purposefully anonymous. How far do they resonate with your own experience?

Is it fair to say that the historical narratives are almost always inventions of some type?

Try to pinpoint historical narratives which have been at the centre of your own national identity.

- Trace them back to real historical events and then assess how completely true they really are.
- How do they impact on your perceptions of cultural difference with other nations?

The case of country D may seem extreme; but there is an uncanny connection with the narrative about engineering conformity in the workplace in Chapter 4. Note also the employment of advertising people.

- How far can the construction of historical narratives in D be defended on the basis of social morale and solidarity?
- What examples are there of historians drawing attention to the 'myths' underpinning these events? How successful are they in discrediting the historical narratives? If they are not, why not?
- What are the connections? How far are the processes described here common in structure to forms of control at every level of society? How far is it in our nature to be vulnerable to them?

Consider some of the current world conflicts. How far can you trace them back to historical narratives? An obvious case might be that of the US historical narrative of 'democracy'.

Powerful myths

Consider the historical narratives cited by Ivonne and Chung when talking about eating at the beginning of this chapter.

- Think of similar historical narratives within your own social context which you have drawn on to make points about your cultural identity.

- How far can you trace these historical narratives to specific historical events?
- Where might there have been exaggerations of some aspects and a playing down of other aspects which have helped you to make your point?
- How far did the historical narratives lead you to claim values which you presented as superior to those of other people involved?
- How far might you find yourself subscribing or not subscribing to these historical narratives depending on the situation you find yourself in?

It was recognised that there was much myth attached to it; but it was decided to make use of it and even to re-interpret some of the details in a positive manner.

The committee were fully aware of how far they were bending the truth; but they felt this fully justified if it would result in increasing morale and less loss of life through increased efficiency in civil and military action. Once the war was over, the historical narrative which had been created by the propaganda committee continued to be powerful into the present. A number of academics, journalists and film makers wrote about the false nature of the events upon which it was based, but they had limited impact and almost everyone continued to subscribe to it.

Stefan, Alicia and Roxana: 'it's what you wear'

The following narrative demonstrates how historical narratives can work under the surface in a destructive manner to cause us to invent negative images of the foreign Other.[1]

When Stefan first met his new colleague, Roxana, he was so pleased to see someone different around the place. She was also personable and friendly and clearly knew her job very well. He knew he had to be careful though, and that he mustn't just jump to conclusions that she was foreign. He had been through the company's online diversity training course and knew all about that. He had found the course a bit of a chore and had been quite cynical about it; but on meeting Roxana he began to see its relevance.

Roxana did announce that she was born and brought up in A, but that she had been living here since her late teens when her parents came. He imagined that therefore he could refer to her as 'foreign'. Indeed, once they got to know each other better, he found her very easy to talk to and her 'foreignness' became one of the topics of their banter.

Anyway, it was so clear to him that she *was* different. It was difficult to put one's finger on exactly what it was until one of the other women in the office said that she was 'flashy', 'extravagant', 'materialistic', and 'a bit of a show-off'. She certainly did come over as being quite exotic. Somebody said that she dressed as though she was going to a cocktail party rather than the office. He found this odd when he considered the expensive power dressing of some of his more senior colleagues. But then when he heard her talking about how she missed the servants they had in A and how it was so good when she and her family visited their friends who had a villa in the South of France and were able to retain some of their 'old lifestyle'. She actually had quite a lot to say and didn't seem to notice the stony silence that these comments were met with. She certainly wasn't the submissive image that everyone imagined of women from A.

On further reflection, Stefan wondered if Roxana's growing unpopularity had anything to do with her being foreign. Everyone knew someone who was annoying because they talked things up instead of the general preference here to talk things down. With Roxana it was something more.

He got an answer when he met with his friend, Alicia. When he told her about Roxana she said that it wasn't just a matter of her personality, and that there *was* an important factor connected with her being foreign, and even coming from a particular part of the world. Alicia said that she was from a part of Europe which meant that she herself had experienced at least part of what Roxana must be going through, and that when she started reading about postcolonial politics as part of her university course she could see how a lot of things began to connect. She explained that there were deep national historical narratives that traced themselves right back to things like the war between the Greeks and Persians in the fifth century BC, and even the story of David and Goliath,[2] which represented the small person defeating the powerful giant. She said that the idea of the clever, agile, self-directed, free-thinking small nation defeating the huge, corrupt, wealthy and depraved empire underpinned much of how people here pictured the rest of the world. She said that these narratives were all around them, whether it was endless references to defeating the 'Evil Empire' in games and movies, or government rhetoric about spreading 'democracy' across the world when what they are really interested in is oil money. Stefan said he understood all of this, but couldn't see what it had to do with Roxana. He knew that Alicia was going to go on and on about this; but he did want to get to the bottom of it.

Alicia said that it was all also connected with a Protestant religious thing which disapproved of anything materially wasteful or inefficient. Stefan said that this was surely something in the past because there was so much wastefulness and inefficiency. Alicia replied that this wasn't the point. It is what's in people's minds that's important. A conviction of functional superiority can exist quite well alongside waste and inefficiency. This is probably why people get so angry when they see blatant and open showiness in people like Roxana, when they themselves are so mixed up about it. They associate Roxana's whole demeanour – her dress and open expression of luxury – with the extravagant corruption of the 'Evil Empire'.

Stefan thought about the issue of functional superiority. He remembered that even though Roxana was very good at her job, people kept praising her as though it was unexpected, as though she had learnt it from them. Then Alicia began to go on about how she felt so intimidated by local people. She said they repeatedly talked down at her, refused to take her behaviour seriously, calling it 'theatrical'. She said that women seemed afraid of her stealing their men, as though she was some sort of siren. She said this was evident in the way these women shot possessive looks at their husbands if the latter got into any sort of conversation with her during social occasions. Then the husbands themselves seemed extremely cautious and uncomfortable saying anything to her at all if there were chance encounters when their wives were not present. Alicia hated how these so-called 'feminist' women referred to her as being nothing more than 'glamorous' and 'decorative'.

At this point Stefan had had enough and told Alicia that as much as he liked her she needed to stop taking all this too seriously. He really was surprised that someone with such a strong personality could feel so intimidated.

Later on, back in the office, Stefan's colleague, Jane, was talking about Roxana. She said that Roxana's behaviour could be explained in terms of her culture – that Roxana didn't realise, even after 'being here so long' that in the culture of the country she was living in people were critical of women being submissive regarding material gender roles. Stefan immediately remembered what Alicia said about feminism and felt even more confused.

This was a difficult narrative to write because, even more so than the others in the book, it is based on events which are very often unrecognised, are very complex and will rely even more than others on how far it resonates with people's experience. Because Roxana remains silent in the narrative, Table 6.2 only reports what we hear from Stefan, Alicia and Jane. It is highly interpretive as are all the other 'categories of cultural action' analyses; and the difference between what goes into the different cells is quite blurred.

There are several things to note about the analysis. I have separated the historical narratives and **cultural resources** domains because they emerge as different in the narrative, though interconnected. The major historical narrative of the small, clever country defeating evil empires is suggested by Alicia as dominating Stefan and Jane and their society; but it may be the case that Stefan and Jane are unaware of this. What is 'foreign' or 'not' foreign is a site for contestation, given that Roxana may well herself 'not' be 'foreign' by nationality, having lived and worked in the country since her teens – something about which Stefan is rightly cautious from the outset.

Feminism emerges as a **cultural resource** which is a major area of contestation between Jane on one side and Alicia on the other, with Stefan taking a confused medium position:

- Jane's perception that Roxana is submissive with respect to the materialistic roles of her culture.
- Alicia's claim that this so-called feminism is fired by an ideological position which falsely associates Roxana and women like her with the 'evil empire', and by claiming a misguided monopoly on teaching women not to be submissive.
- Stefan's observation that local women who are senior colleagues are also extravagant in their power dressing and that neither Roxana nor Alicia appear in any way to be submissive.

Stefan nevertheless domesticates the issues by withdrawing to the notion that it is all to do with misunderstanding and miscommunication. These contradictions might be clarified a little in the following two narratives.

Table 6.2 Digging deep

Categories of cultural action	Stefan	Jane	Alicia
Statements about culture	'We are open and welcoming to foreigners, and appreciate the diversity within our multicultural society. 'There is some annoyance with certain types of people, either because of where they come from or their personality.'	'Our culture is critical about women's roles. 'Their culture is materialistic and believes women should submit themselves to material roles and images.'	'The attitudes in this country to people like me are intimidating. They think of us only as 'theatrical' sex objects who are after their husbands.' Implying: 'We are more liberated than they are, despite them claiming to be feminists.'
Global position and politics	There are popular historical narratives which demonise foreigners; but their extent must not be exaggerated.	Roxana's culture is uncritical regarding women's roles.	These popular historical narratives are all-pervasive and extend to everyday demonisation of foreigners.
Cultural resources	Complexity and diversity in his society. Accusations of racism or sexism can be a result of misunderstanding.	*Suggested by Stefan:* Feminist tradition.	Postcolonial studies. Knowledge of historical narratives which demonise non-Western people.
Historical narratives	*Suggested by Alicia:* Small, clever, agile, self-directed, free-thinking, small nations defeating huge, corrupt, wealthy, extravagant and depraved empires.		
		Our society is a place where people come to learn about criticality.	
Underlying universal processes	Observing behaviour and asking questions. Critical assessment. Referring to what is 'normal'.	Referring to common theories of culture. Critical assessment.	Referring to global politics. Critical assessment.
	Trying to make sense of incidents in which there is conflict with particular types of behaviour.		

Goran came over as a highly critical and politically aware young person. He said that his parents had brought him up to be open and accommodating and had introduced him to a wide range of international literature and film at every opportunity. He accepted that coming from an affluent, middle-class family meant that he had experienced no threats in his life that nurtured prejudice. When the issue of a particular minority group in his country was mentioned, he became visibly uncomfortable and said that this was his weak spot. They had come to his country perhaps over 1,000 years ago and they were the subject of so many jokes. He had to admit that, deep down, he did believe that they were dirty and somehow lacked the proper moral principles.

Hyun was a human rights activist to the extent that she sometimes thought that her life was no longer her own. She was particularly angry about the way in which foreign aid was just a mechanism for maintaining power over the countries that received it by making them dependent on the over-paid foreign experts that came with the aid package. When a conflict in a particular country was mentioned, she said that the insurgents had to be supported, even if it led to military intervention. When it was pointed out that the insurgents wished to ban women from higher education, she said that she had to admit that even the most politically aware people just couldn't keep up with everything that was going on.

The implication here is that there can be blind spots, where normally critical and aware people do not sustain their criticality in every part of their lives. These blind spots are nevertheless facilitated by historical narratives.

Making sense of making sense

Evaluate the analysis of Table 6.2 with a close reading of the narrative.

Consider the experiences of Stefan, Roxana, Alicia and Jane.

- Compare your own experiences which resonate with any of these characters.
- Use the categories of cultural action to evaluate the different viewpoints in one of these experiences.
- 'Culture' is only referred to explicitly at the end of the narrative. However, in what ways are differing cultural realities implicated throughout?
- What is the connection between Jane thinking that Roxana needs to be taught to be less submissive, and the Western monopoly on teaching critical thinking described in Chapter 5?
- Is Alicia right in her depiction of the historical narrative of small, clever, agile, self-directed, free-thinking nations defeating huge, corrupt, wealthy, extravagant and depraved empires?

Evaluate Stefan's view that Alicia is exaggerating and should really not take things so seriously.

Blind spots

Evaluate the proposition, implicit in the experiences of Goran and Hyun, that being critical and even an activist in many areas of your life may not increase your awareness of what is happening in other areas, and may even reduce your awareness.

Kay and Pushpa: sociological blindness

The previous narrative demonstrates how Alicia, and possibly Roxana, feel Othered by the historical narratives which they feel are behind the way in which they are treated. The following narrative demonstrates how this can work in both directions and how historical narratives can actually prevent people from seeing the social realities which are going on around them.[3]

Kay and Pushpa were not getting on at all. They were colleagues in an aid project. Kay was the foreign consultant and Pushpa the local advisor. It wasn't just the use of the term 'local' which was getting in the way. Both felt that they were being gravely misunderstood by the other. Kay sensed there were issues the moment they first met. Pushpa was very polite and even careful to say that they would get on as colleagues, and that she was sure she was a professional and good at her job; but there was definitely tension. Then, Kay began to understand what Pushpa's problem with her was. Through small comments she realised that Pushpa thought that she was totally immoral and lacking any form of personal standards. It was something to do with her being away from home without her family and without a husband, and that she was being labelled as some sort of totally loose woman who had a different man every night.

Pushpa, actually, couldn't help liking Kay. She was aware that Kay had worked out what she thought of her. She felt bad about her negative thoughts about her; but she just couldn't get out of her mind that in Kay's culture – and this was confirmed by the media – women were always getting drunk, quite commonly had babies out of wedlock, or had abortions, went around in public places half-naked, and had casual liaisons with men. However, she didn't want Kay to imagine that she disapproved of her because she herself wasn't modern and independent. Indeed, Pushpa made a big thing of telling Kay that she had travelled abroad by herself, and *didn't* need the permission of her father or husband as everyone seemed to think. She could go where she wanted and do what she wanted. She was pleased when Kay made a special note of her having a glass of wine when they went out for an office dinner. Pushpa's point was that in *her* culture there was a proper moral code; and women had a huge amount of self-respect.

What made Kay particularly angry at all this was the fact that Pushpa just didn't seem to get the point that she, Kay, also had a proper moral code. Pushpa seemed to have no idea how much she and her friends cared about the rules for decent behaviour, how much they cared about their personal reputations and integrity, and that while they were free to choose who they had relationships with, this was certainly not just a free-for-all. She wished that Pushpa could understand what she was going through at the moment, resisting the attractions of a man she had met at work because of the loyalty she had to her boyfriend at home. It was ironic. She wanted Pushpa to know that just because she couldn't cite 'culture' and 'tradition', like Pushpa did, that this meant she had no rules and traditions. Yes, two of her friends had had children outside long-term relationships, and were now single mothers; but Pushpa had no idea how much integrity they had, and with how much care they brought up their children with sound moral principles. Of course, one big issue was Kay's country's media. Just about every television drama was about murder, drug abuse, broken families and illicit sex.

The other side to the conflict between them was their professionalism. Kay was very clear that she was in Pushpa's country to help people to organise themselves and get the job done. She was there to help local people to overcome the inability, which was so deep in their collectivist culture, to make personal decisions, and to become creative and autonomous in the workplace.

Pushpa was, of course, very aware of the aims of the project because she had read the documentation. She and so many of her colleagues put up with the arrogance of these foreign experts as the basic price to pay for the considerable resources they could gain from having the project. International contact was always a good thing. Kay was just like all the other people who came with the project. There was a huge amount of apparent willingness to 'listen and learn' (actually written into the documentation) without really being able to see a lot that was going on.

Pushpa felt that Kay didn't appreciate that they were all just getting through quite an extreme political crisis. It was still very much in the memory of all the 'local' staff how they had had to evacuate 25 schools and then get them up and running in new, safer locations. The need for education to continue and to keep the lives of the children as stable as possible had been paramount. Absolutely everyone – administrative staff, volunteer parents, teachers and cleaners – had worked together with amazing personal responsibility and ingenuity to make it happen, all within a matter of days. Pushpa remembered telling Kay all about this on a number of occasions; but it didn't prevent Kay from organising yet another round of national seminars on how to plan, organise and take the initiative in health and safety projects, and on how to carry out personal work planning, as though no-one knew anything about such things.

The conflict between Pushpa and Kay is summarised in Table 6.3. The term sociological blindness refers to the inability to see what is happening in front of you because you are preoccupied with a theoretical perspective that contradicts it. The result is mutual Othering, in the sense that both parties read the other according to historical narratives which serve to reduce them.

Table 6.3 Narratives and misunderstandings

	Pushpa	Kay
Personal morality	**Historical narrative** 'Kay's society is morally corrupt. Women indulge in illicit sex, have children out of marriage and are always drunk'.	**Social reality** Women have very high moral standards with a strict code of rules, self-respect and integrity regarding sexual relations and bringing up children.
Being decisive, autonomous and creative	**Social reality** She and her colleagues are very capable of making decisions and organising themselves in an autonomous and creative manner, sometimes in extreme circumstances.	**Historical narrative** 'In collectivist cultures people are not used to making decisions and organising themselves in an autonomous and creative manner'.

The social reality regarding Kay's rules of behaviour resonates with the hidden complexity of how the family next door (Table 2.5) possesses all the values which we had suspected to be lacking, but which were realised at the surface level in a different manner to what we might expect. Pushpa, instead of listening to what Kay has to say, draws on the **cultural resource** of the common views about Kay's culture with which she has been brought up.

Kay, in turn, does not recognise the experiences of Pushpa and her colleagues, and instead draws on the common cultural theory of collectivism. An important factor here is that this theory of collectivism also serves to satisfy the particular sense of professional expertise which brings her to Pushpa's country in the first place. The employment of historical narratives therefore operates in both personal and professional domains.

There is also the possibility that, as with Ivonne and Chung earlier, both Pushpa and Kay are being driven to subscribe to and perhaps exaggerate historical narratives which they would not normally think too much about, because of the difficulty they find in being confronted with each other. The problem will be that because of this particular confrontation, their subscription to these historical narratives may become routinised and radicalise their views of the world.

Not noticing immediate realities

Prepare a 'categories of cultural action' analysis for the Pushpa–Kay narrative.

Have a frank discussion with someone in your group about how historical narratives have prevented you from seeing key things about each other's behaviour and abilities. Use Table 6.3 as a template.

Consider examples where historical narratives, which have not previously been so important, or taken so seriously, have been strengthened and grown out of proportion because of confrontation.

Types and solutions

The narratives in this chapter so far have indicated that it is not just one historical narrative that might influence us at any one time, but that there can be a complex web of such influences that might affect us in complex and sometimes conflicting ways. While they are normal and irremovable parts of our everyday lives, they are often based on deceptions and exaggerations, and they can be a major cause of Othering the people we interact with. It is therefore important that we learn about their nature and what they can do, and learn to think through and around them, and to put them aside.

A useful start might be to attempt a catalogue of their characteristics and effects, which may be some or all of the items listed in Figure 6.1.

Characteristics	Effects
Memories of historical events	To support political agendas
Real	To build morale in times of crisis
Myths	To establish traditions of how things should be done
Purposefully constructed or invented	To underpin both positive and chauvinistic 'values'
Political	To refer to sometimes when in a difficult position
Popular	Unknowingly to influence what are believed to be rational views
Elaborated, re-packaged, sanitised, exaggerated over time	To catch you unawares and perhaps embarrass you
Established, known and dealt with critically or supported and believed	Relating to all sorts of social groups from nation to family and small social groups
	To exacerbate cultural contestation
	To radicalise opinions about the foreign Other in times of conflict

Figure 6.1 Multiple characteristics and effects

Characteristics and effects

The arrows in the centre of Figure 6.1 indicate that there are multiple relationships between the characteristics and effects.

• Improve the figure by showing more precisely how particular characteristics are linked to which effects in the various narratives in this chapter.

• Evaluate and edit the listings as you see how far they fit the narratives, and also your own experiences.

Alicia: critical reading

Appreciating and indeed uncovering the very often hidden nature of historical narratives, and the **global position and politics** which they carry with them may require the particular methodology of critical reading. This is the final discipline from Chapter 3, which I take from the work of Cathie Wallace (2003). Its primary use is for the reading of texts from the media. However, within the broader remit of critical discourse analysis it could involve a reading of any form of written or oral communication. When people from different cultural backgrounds collaborate, it is often those who are most foreign to the text who are able to see meanings which remain hidden to those closest to it.

An example of critical reading can be seen in the following narrative, in which Alicia, introduced earlier in the chapter, encounters an online newspaper article published in the British national press (Thorpe 2012). It is about the American actor Claire Danes, preparing for her part as a CIA agent in the television drama, *Homeland*. The full text can be found onlineathttp://www.guardian.co.uk/tv-and-radio/2012/mar/03/homeland-claire-danes-carrie-mathison?fb=native.

Alicia quite enjoyed the first part of the article. It located the CIA agent played by Danes in a tradition of fictional law enforcement and secret agent characters who had problems with drugs, were alcoholics, had problem or broken marriages, or had deep depression and other psychological problems, and so on. This was fine. She recognised that crime and spy dramas were opportunities to explore the dysfunctional lives of the main characters. It made sense that people with such high-pressure jobs, working long hours against impossible odds, might well either be or turn into the sort of dysfunctional 'loners' that the article described.

However, Alicia paused with concern towards the end of the article when she came to the description of how Danes researched her role by interviewing real CIA agents. She noted particularly the following quote from Danes about the role of 'gender and sex':

> It can be an asset and used to their [CIA agents'] advantage, but it can also be problematic, and then they have to be creative about how to resolve that. It's a real issue in Arab cultures, where men don't have relationships with women like we do here.

What struck Alicia about this were the following conflicts which implied an Othering of 'Arab culture' as deficient.

- Fifteen paragraphs of the article had been spent deconstructing the complexity of law and security enforcement and how it was dramatised in the media. Readers were invited to understand the profound ambivalence of how European law and security enforcement personnel could be extremely dysfunctional and still able to do their jobs. The overall message was a complex relationship between cultural deficiency and cultural proficiency.
- Then, in sharp contrast, 'Arab cultures' were dispensed with in two lines. Readers were left with an unexamined statement of 'issue' with 'Arab cultures'. The overall message was a simplistic impression of cultural deficiency.
- In the cited extract, 'gender and sex' related to 'their' with regard to the CIA agents, and implied no specific gender relationship.
- In contrast, the 'real issue' related to 'men' in 'Arab cultures', implying an unequal relationship with women.
- Despite all their social dysfunctionality, the Western CIA agents were able to be creative and to resolve the 'sex and gender' issues.
- In 'Arab culture' it remained an issue characterised by a definitive 'don't'.

Alicia was also concerned that, after having seen the first episode of *Homeland*, it was clear that not only were Arab terrorists major characters in the drama, but the story pivoted around an American character having been turned by them. It therefore seemed to her to be a shortcoming that the article had not balanced the complex imagery of law and security enforcement with the complexities of the imagery of terrorism in Western media. There was no attempt to problematise the easy perceptions about the relationship between

- a particular group of people which was actually very large and diverse;
- a religion, which by no means the whole group subscribed to, and which did not, on the whole, support the negative attitude to gender and sex implied by the article; and
- a particular attitude towards sex and gender, which was by no means subscribed to by the majority of the members of that group of people or restricted to that group of people.

Alicia's final thought was that there was a huge amount of sophistication in the article, which one expected from the Western media, but which suddenly became remarkably unsophisticated when it dealt with the non-West.

She was also very concerned that a lot of people she knew, a good example being Stefan, would just take the negative characterisation of so-called 'Arab cultures' at face value. Their criticality would somehow be satisfied by the relatively profound analysis in the rest of the article. They would have little experience with which to evaluate the 'Arab cultures' stereotype, which was promoted everywhere else in the media.

Alicia's critical reading therefore focuses on the contrast in the article between the author's focus on representations of a particular type of police officer or secret agent in Western society and what is said about 'Arab cultures' by an actor reporting the research she carries out to support her role. The basic point Alicia makes is that while the concept of socially and personally dysfunctional yet effective professionals under pressure are part of an intellectual-ised complexity within Western society, 'Arab culture' is confined to a simplistic negative stereotype.

This contrast can be linked to two Western historical narratives which Alicia herself describes to Stefan earlier in the chapter:

- The notion of dysfunctional yet successfully problem-solving professionals resonates with the ideal of small, clever, agile, self-directed, free-thinking, small Western nations defeating huge, corrupt, wealthy, extravagant and depraved empires.
- The mirror notion of the depraved empire resonates with the long-term Western associ-ation between terrorism, Islam and the male attitudes to women in 'Arab cultures' referred to in the article.

A brief 'categories of cultural action' analysis of the ideology which Alicia sees between the lines of the article similarly indicates the following:

- **Statements about culture**: 'In "Arab cultures" male attitudes to women are different to how they are here'. 'We are very complex, and can be both dysfunctional and good at our jobs'.

- **Global position and politics**: Arab cultures are particularly difficult to understand when compared to 'ours' in the West.
- **Historical narratives as cultural resources**: Even though 'we' in the West may have debilitating personal, health, family and anti-social problems, 'we' can solve problems. Women are the victims of the relationships men have with them in 'Arab cultures'.
- **Underlying universal processes**: Interpreting how a master actor makes sense of people from an unfamiliar cultural background who are part of a drama she is working in.

As with any critical reading, there does need to be a note of caution. The analysis represents Alicia's imagination of the author's ideology set against her own ideological stance and subjectivity. It needs to be appreciated that the article which Alicia has read is highly complex, with multiple possible interpretations. It is not possible to know exactly what the intentions of the author were, or indeed, and connected with this, the intentions of the newspaper in which the article appears. The quotation attributed to the actor, Claire Danes, cited by Alicia, plus others in the article, are actually the design of the writer of the whole piece, who has selected them and framed them in the way that she does. We do not know in what context Danes herself said these words, or how that context may have made them appear different.

Critical reading

Why is it the case that foreigners to a text may often be able to see historical narratives which others might not?

Read the whole of the text from which the above media extract is taken.

- Follow the links, for the author, the television programme, the television channel, the newspaper and so on, to get a broader context for what is written.
- Re-assess Alicia's analysis.

Look in a current newspaper or magazine.

- Search for examples of historical narratives and assess how frequently they appear in any given edition.
- Focus on one particular article or story and carry out a 'categories of cultural action' analysis.
- Further evaluate and possibly adapt the categories of cultural action for this purpose.

Further evaluate the proposition that historical narratives are present everywhere in views of our own and others' societies.

Taking stock

What this chapter has not tried to do is to list a series of specific historical narratives. Instead, examples of such narratives have been allowed to emerge from the characters in the narratives presented in the chapter. The reason for this is that historical narratives are not fixed entities, but emerge, grow, intermingle, adapt, change form and are invoked in different versions at different times, depending on all the circumstances so far discussed. Nevertheless, to prevent descent into confusion, and partly to illustrate this variability, Table 6.4 attempts to capture the particular historical narratives that have emerged in this way in this chapter. The names, descriptions and versions are, of course, shorthand labels for highly complex notions.

What might be noticed from the listing in Table 6.4 is that there are extensions to historical narratives which may not by themselves seem to be connected, but which do take on extra meanings when these connections are noticed. Some of these extensions – e.g. discussions about current morality and professional abilities in the Pushpa–Kay narrative – may be very recent extensions of older historical narratives.

Table 6.4 Emerging historical narratives

Name	Description and origin	Introduced by	Extension	Introduced by
Thrift	A family history that goes back to working class origins, with a strong tradition of thrift (undisclosed).	Ivonne, this chapter.		
Poverty	A family history that goes back to severe poverty, connected with a national history of economic and political struggle, affecting attitudes to food, and promoting the notion that affluence and extravagance belong to the West (Ex).	Chung, this chapter.		
Resisting depraved empires	Small, clever, agile, self-directed, free-thinking, small Western nations defeating huge, corrupt, wealthy, extravagant and depraved empires (the West).	Alicia, this chapter.	Spreading democracy and human rights.	Jane, this chapter.
Personal morality	The West is morally corrupt. Women indulge in illicit sex, have children out of marriage, and are always drunk. They don't notice what we (outside the West) can do.	Pushpa, this chapter.	Able to manage one's own morality and needs to educate non-Western people how to plan and organise.	Kay, this chapter.

Orientalism

Table 6.4 therefore emphasises that the historical narratives referred to throughout the chapter are difficult to define precisely, and may indeed be dependent on a complex of associations. A concept which pulls these associations together is that of Orientalism. This was defined by Edward Said's (1978) book of the same title. His thesis is that through literature, art and the popular media, the West has depicted an imagined, Othering, exotic picture of the East which is based more on Western preoccupations than with what is actually going on in the East. This falls precisely within the **global position and politics** domain of the grammar, in which an idealised Western Self is defined against a demonised non-Western Other. This imagery fits largely with the 'resisting depraved empires' narrative which is traced through several of the narratives in Table 6.4, and its extensions.

Figure 6.2 illustrates this collecting of the historical narrative of the clever West versus depraved empires around the theme of Orientalism, taking in the more recent narratives of 9/11 and Islamophobia.[4] Orientalism may be interpreted as an ideology, as may the driving forces of the inventions related to wars and national identities earlier in the chapter.

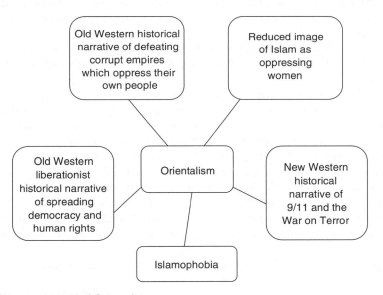

Figure 6.2 The associations of Orientalism

Further connections

Explore the connections in Figure 6.2 further.

*   How does the image of oppressed women in Islam connect with the 'corrupt empire' narrative and the liberationist Western narrative of democracy and human rights?
*   Refer to examples from the narratives in this and other chapters and the Claire Danes text in exploring this connection.

- In what sense is the image of oppressed women in Islam 'reduced'?
- How does this 'reduction' connect with Othering and Self and Other politics?
- How far is this Othering driven by historical narratives?
- What is the relationship between the Orientalist thesis and the relationship between Centre and Periphery with regard to bottom-up globalisation and Dima's defence of owning Facebook in Chapter 2, and the discussion of globalisation and modernity in Chapter 5.

Evaluate the connections which are implied in Table 6.4 and Figure 6.2. Are the suggested relationships being stretched too far to support the historical narrative idea?

Summary

- Historical narratives have a life of their own and can be drawn on as **cultural resources** in different ways at different times, when they are needed, in everyday **small culture formation**.
- There may be different historical narratives operating at the same time, even within the same person's view of things, which may be in conflict with each other to varying degrees.
- Historical narratives can lead to cultural contestation, through invoking partisan values, where normally people might be more respectful of each other's backgrounds.
- Historical narratives can be constructed and reconstructed by means of manipulating historical records for a wide range of political and social purposes, during times of crisis and for the purpose of building national or other identities.
- Historical narratives can be instrumental in the process of Othering, as they contribute to the construction of Self and Other images and theories of culture.
- People may be unaware of the way in which they are being influenced by historical narratives. They may be aware and critical of some historical narratives and unaware of how others inhibit their awareness and criticality – leading to partial sociological blindness.
- Historical narratives which have not previously been important or taken so seriously may be strengthened and routinised at times of confrontation.
- Historical narratives may be difficult to define precisely. They may be extended or mutate into new forms as they respond to current events, and may contribute to or be influenced by ideologies of the day.

Notes

1 This narrative is based on the reported experience of several women from the Middle East, the Indian subcontinent, South America and Southern Europe, observation of a large number of events in the workplace, experience of widespread imagery in the media and cinema, and experience of personal prejudice.

2 In an Old Testament story, David was a teenager armed only with a slingshot who killed the Philistine giant and champion, and later became king of Israel.

3 This narrative is based on extensive experience in aid projects and consultancy work in English-language education in Iran, Pakistan, Egypt, Syria, India, South Africa and the Czech Republic, research reports of institutional and personal innovation in China (Ge 2004; Grimshaw 2002), witnessing the organisation of a conference in Nepal in 2011, knowledge of a primary–secondary school which had to be moved for safety reasons within a period of a week in Damascus during the anti-government uprising in 2012, the narrative of living in a war zone in Biafra in Adichie (2007), personal experience of living in Iran during the 1979 revolution, and interviews with a young British woman about her moral integrity.

4 Islamophobia is a fairly recent Western narrative within which Islam is perceived as both a source of terrorism and easily angered. 9/11 is a prime motivator for the former, leading to the US 'War of Terror' and the invasions of Iraq and Afghanistan in 2003 and 2001. The Salman Rushdie affair is a leading example of the latter, in which, in 1989, the Supreme Leader of Iran, Ayatollah Khomeini, issued a decree calling for his execution because he had offended Islam in his novel *Satanic Verses*. The result is a widespread popular anxiety regarding Muslim people everywhere, regardless of their personal politics and religious dispositions.

Further reference

How to eat a muffin: http://www.wikihow.com/Eat-a-Muffin
— Instructions on how to eat a muffin. This relates to the experience of Chung going to the unfamiliar café with Ivonne and engaging with the task of eating a muffin.

Arundhati Roy – *The Day of the Jackals* (2003): http://www.youtube.com/watch?v=hu3D YOBjd0Q&feature=related
— Talking about the strongly held yet false narratives about weapons of mass destruction.

Wallace, C. (2003). *Critical reading in language education*. Basingstoke: Palgrave Macmillan.
— This provides an excellent account of a group of students from widely varying cultural backgrounds working together to apply critical reading to texts from the media. The mixture of newcomer and familiar viewpoints helps them to appreciate the ideologies implicit in intercultural relations.

Naghibi, N. (2007). *Rethinking global sisterhood: Western feminism and Iran*. Minneapolis, MN: University of Minnesota Press.

Osanloo, A. (2009). *The politics of women's rights in Iran*. Princeton, NJ: Princeton University Press.

Rostami-Povey, E. (2007). *Afghan women: identity and invasion*. London: Zed Books.
— Naghibi, page xxiii; Osanloo, page 201; Rostami-Povey, page 113 – these critique Western feminism as Othering women outside the West as culturally deficient.

Chatziefstathiou, D. and Henry, I. (2007). Hellenism and Olympism: Pierre de Coubertin and the Greek challenge to the early Olympic movement. *Sport in History* 27/1: 24–43.

— A critique of how an association between an idealised Anglo-Saxon heritage and an idealised ancient Greek Hellenism was forged to represent an 'advanced' 'Western' modernity with which to 'improve' the world through sport.

Things we forgot to remember about the Boston Tea Party: http://www.bbc.co.uk/programmes/b01724mf
— Radio programme about how the real events of the Boston Tea Party were far away from the idealisation of the event in American national narratives.

Wu Ming (2009). *Mantuana*. Whiteside, S., Trans. London: Verso.
— This historical novel concerns the political opposition to the American War of Independence carried out by the Native American Iroquois Confederacy on humanitarian grounds. It challenges two common historical narratives – that independence supported universal human rights, and that Native Americans in the eighteenth century did not have sophisticated government and education.

'Caucasians': http://en.wikipedia.org/wiki/Caucasian_race
— This is a reference to the Wikipedia page. The reliability of Wikipedia is often contested. However, this page does suggest that the term 'Caucasian' includes North Africa, the Horn of Africa, Western Asia, parts of Central Asia and South Asia. Readers are therefore invited to look at this proposition further through research in perhaps more reliable sources, and then place this against the common usage which relates to 'White' people.

Mernissi, F. (2001). *Scheherazade goes West: different cultures, different harems.* New York: Washington Square Press.
— A provocative discussion of images of the harem among Western men.

Holliday, A.R. (2011). *Intercultural communication & ideology.* London: Sage.
— Pages 33–6 describe examples of decentred critical reading of articles in the Western press which reveal hidden Western historical narratives.

Chapter 7

Discourses of culture

This is the first of two chapters which focus on the bottom right of the grammar, in the **statements about culture** domain. Whereas historical narratives, in Chapter 6, are part of the driving force for how we construct culture, derived from **global position and politics**, discourses are under the heading of **particular cultural products**. This chapter therefore explores discourses of culture as things that we construct in order to make sense of culture, but which then take on a life of their own and can easily begin to dominate what we think is real about culture.

Discourses

A discourse is a way of using language which represents ideas about how things are. Discourses which are specialised ways of talking and writing that belong to particular groups, such as technical, professional, academic and political discourses, can be a powerful means of establishing ideas and forms of behaviour. They draw people into the thinking which underpins them. In this sense, discourses are a central part of **small culture formation**, and are at the core of reification, as described in Chapter 4. We all have experience of being influenced by discourses in everyday life. Discourses also have a role in Self and Other politics in that they can create a specialist language which alienates outsiders and strengthens the prestige of insiders. Indeed, we most easily recognise discourses when we are outsiders to them. They relate to how **statements about culture** can easily become packaged in such a way that they are reified, and become considered the 'truth' about how things are. Looking at discourses will therefore enable an evaluation of major concepts which have entered our everyday thinking about culture in terms of how far they promote or inhibit our understanding.

We can also be drawn in – something like this:

1   A group of people is joined by a new member who has an endearing personality and who uses particularly Othering expressions about foreigners.
2   The group at first are unhappy about his attitude; but they do not want to reject him because they like his overall presence.
3   The newcomer also has an opinion about political correctness which resonates with the group – that there is a virtue in speaking one's mind and saying things as they are, and that there is no harm in a bit of banter and teasing.
4   Over time this attitude catches on in the group and they begin to use his language.

Encountering discourses

Recall a time when you found yourself with a group of people from a particular professional, sports, technical or other interest group, where, although they were speaking your language, you could not understand what they were talking about and felt excluded.

Examples of this could be being with a group of friends who are all teachers, lawyers, football fans, etc., or going to buy a computer and being lost in the technical references.

Gains, losses and power

Discourses can be strategically deployed for the purpose of influencing, changing or controlling behaviour. An example of this is the narrative about changing institutional behaviour in Chapter 4. 'Smart Project Management' was introduced by the management of an organisation in such a way that the phrase became commonly used in a wide range of everyday institutional events and influenced a change in behaviour. This is a recent observation from my own experience:

> In order to improve the ratings of the university in a time of financial crisis, the management launched a new concept – 'students as partners in learning and teaching'. This was a conscious break from a previous concept – 'students as customers' – which was not considered sufficiently in tune with the intrinsic value of education. The launch of the new concept was accompanied by concerns that the university was under-performing in the national survey of student satisfaction, especially in the area of students recognising and appreciating how far their evaluations were being addressed. There followed the launch of a campaign to increase student awareness. Individual departments responded with leaflets to be distributed among students, with the slogan, 'you say, we do'. In the new strategic plan, much was said about the university's 'values', within which 'partnership' was a recurring term, as it was within reports and department meetings.

Part of the context of this introduction of a new discourse is the placing of 'learning' before 'teaching', to place the student first, the previous term having been 'teaching and learning'. A member of the university is 'on message' when they are explicitly aware of the discourse and can reproduce it in public meetings and networking.

In a more domestic domain is the example of 'baby-led' weaning, referred to in Chapter 4. It is significant because of the relative newness of the term, promoted by the original research of Rapley and Murkett (2008). The phrase refers to a procedure for feeding babies in the months following weaning in which they can help themselves to accessible items of food which are spread out in front of them instead of being spoon-fed. One of many websites on the topic[1] presents a text which combines a useful acronym and reference to a medical authority:

Baby-led weaning
Approved by the BabyCentre Medical Advisory Board
Sponsored by Heinz
What is baby-led weaning?
How do I get BLW started?
What are the benefits of BLW?
Are there any down sides to BLW?
Won't my baby choke if we try BLW?
Is BLW suitable for breastfed and formula-fed babies?
Are there any reasons why I shouldn't try BLW?
Where can I find out more?

The hyperlink on 'Heinz' leads to the food company site on the same topic,[2] with the text 'We know that many mums are interested in baby led weaning but what is it and should you give it a try with your baby?' There are also books, magazine articles, scientific reports and expensive yet practical plastic cloths – to spread out in front of the baby, on which the small items of food will be spread. Altogether, this phenomenon might be called a technology because of the precise science, technique and terminology which it involves.

In both of the cases of 'partners in learning and teaching' and baby-led weaning there is an element of control and manipulation in that the views of the people concerned are being influenced and indeed formed by the adoption of language which is both seductive and convenient. However, at the same time, there are clear benefits. Table 7.1 expresses these gains and losses, and shows that the losses concern some lack of recognition resulting from the way in which the discourses impose a particular reality.

The final column implies that the discourse takes on a 'dominant' role in determining what is important – hence giving rise to the notion of dominant discourse as a powerful way of looking at things which marginalises competing ways of looking at things.

The power possessed by discourses to impose a particular reality gives them a central role in acts of chauvinism such as sexism and racism. Sustained negative constructions of a foreign or different Other require a particular language to support them. This language can be so powerful that it draws members in and becomes normalised behaviour.

Table 7.1 Discourses: gains and losses

Discourse	Promoters	Participants gain	Participants and others lose
'Partners in learning and teaching'	University management, to improve the ratings of the university.	Employees gaining morale and keeping their jobs; very likely an improved educational experience for students and teachers.	University employees and students lose some recognition that they were already in partnership; possible loss or loss of recognition for other practices.
'Baby-led weaning'	Health services; companies who sell related products such as food items and plastic sheets for spreading food items; media and authors.	Parents getting guidance and certainty of direction; very likely an improved experience for babies and parents.	Possible loss of more traditional practices and resulting conflicts.

Gains and losses

Use Table 7.1 or a variation of it to plot an institutional or domestic discourse you are involved with.

•   Evaluate the final column of the table.

Recall cases where you feel you have become victim to a dominant discourse.

•   What was the nature of the discourse?
•   Were you able to resist it? If so, how? If not, why not?
•   Was the dominant discourse created by a particular group for this purpose, or did it take on a life of its own and become out of control?

Being drawn in

Recall a time when you found yourself with a group of people who spoke about a particular topic in such a chauvinistic way that you had no choice but

•   to take part in their way of speaking about the topic, and conform to how they depicted it;
•   to keep quiet and withdraw; or
•   to resist and become unpopular.

The topic could be gender (i.e. a sexist discourse) or race (i.e. a racist discourse). How easy or difficult is it to resist the power of this dominant discourse and the temptation to conform?

Consider instances when you have heard people say 'I don't like this way of talking'. What were the circumstances and outcomes?

Agency and control

Considering what has been said about the power of discourses to change and control the ways in which we look at things, the following questions about discourses have often been raised in academic literature:

•   Are we totally controlled by one discourse or another?
•   Are we able to dialogue with and influence discourses?
•   Can we stand outside discourses?
•   If individuals are able to influence, change or make discourses, must it be from the position of another discourse?

These questions concern the nature of social construction, and how we answer them can be aligned to one of two paradigms:

- If we feel that everything and everyone are determined by discourses, we might be aligned by social constructionism.
- If we feel that we can stand outside discourses and see the true nature of the realities which they attempt to construct, we might be aligned to social constructivism.

This book tends towards the latter in that it maintains that there is a truth about the nature of culture which is often blurred by powerful discourses in the academy and in everyday life.

Discourses as social constructions

It needs to be remembered throughout this chapter and the book as a whole that discourses *are* social constructions – fictional labels for what are in fact fluid social phenomena which do not have hard, real boundaries or territories. Discourses are not really real things at all, but convenient labels for kinds of things. In this chapter a number of names for discourses will be used. It must never be forgotten that these are simply such conveniences. If one says that such and such discourses do or do not exist, it means that there is or there is not sufficient experience of that 'kind of thing' to make it worth noting and talking about. The term 'discourse' is an imposition, itself part of a particular discourse for describing society. In effect, as small cultures, categorising and describing them is an act of stereotyping and can fall into an essentialist trap.

We therefore need to be very careful. On the other hand, if we think of discourses as social forces rather than places, which can move, change, grow, shrink, and incorporate and be incorporated by others, a non-essentialist view, as encouraged for 'culture', may be approached. In this sense these discourses of culture are rather like historical narratives except that they may be less long-standing, particular to groups rather than nations and generally smaller. They will, however, contribute to these narratives, though not in a one-to-one manner. Indeed, because the most powerful historical narratives tend themselves to be ideologically marked, wherever they are located they might well be supported by the 'essentialist culture and language' discourse described below.

Agency or control

Consider the various discourses which govern aspects of your life.

- To what degree are you really controlled by them? How much agency do you have to change, resist or respond creatively to them? How far are you able to contribute to their formation?
- What are the factors which govern the degrees of agency or control which you possess?

Ramla, Ed and Jonathan: sticking to principles

The following narrative[3] indicates a particular complexity in the deployment and use of discourses of and about culture in the **statements about culture** domain of the grammar. Looking at this exchange in terms of discourses may serve to explain something of what is going on.

Ramla was taking part in an international project to develop a set of documents and guidelines for inducting new employees. There were new colleagues from a range of countries, and she felt it was a massive opportunity to be able to get together in this way and learn about new cultures. There were, however, a number of issues which were raising their heads, which she was finding quite hard to negotiate. The project leader was from a particular country which had for a long time been the most influential in the organisation. It was supposed to be fully international, but in effect she and a number of her colleagues from the South, as they labelled themselves, felt that they had often been side-lined when it came to promotions and opportunities. Now they were making the most of this opportunity to have their voices heard.

The issue of culture was very much on the agenda. At least Ramla was making sure that it was – to ensure a true inclusivity for people from diverse backgrounds. That morning they had spent several hours on a particular phrase, which was to do with being direct in expressing one's opinions to line managers. Ramla argued that this was not an acceptable norm in her own culture and in a number of other cultures with which she was familiar. This had resulted in a deadlock. Those who disagreed with Ramla maintained that the clause was important because it represented a sense of equality in the organisation which was the only way forward to encourage a diversity of backgrounds and interests, and also to ensure efficiency in communication. Ramla had caused a bit of a stir when she suggested that this was a particularly Western point of view and would alienate a lot of people who just did not feel comfortable being so direct.

When Ramla met with her friend Ed later and told him about this, he said that she was going too far, and that he didn't think that the proposed clause was Western at all. Jonathan, who was sitting with them in the canteen, was interested to know that Ramla and Ed came from the same country and wanted to know why they had different views. Ramla pointed out that their society was very complex, of course – this didn't even need to be pointed out – and that Ed was right to make her remember that, yes, not everyone had problems with being direct. Indeed, many of her countrypeople were well-known for their directness. So then Ed wanted to know why she was pushing it so much. He felt that it was really something that was important for their parents' generation, and that anyway it depended on what sort of family you came from, and, in the workplace, what sort of place it was, whether in the private or public sector, and that sort of thing. Ramla replied that sometimes you just had to make a stand. She knew that there were plenty of examples in their society of what she was complaining about, but that this wasn't really their culture. Being direct was very often just considered to be rude. She then went on to talk about how basic expressions of politeness in their language were being lost as a result of this cultural loss. Ed replied that the language changed, and that you only had to read their literature of the last century to see how different it was then to what she was talking about.

Jonathan joined in and said he knew what they were talking about. Where he came from, really nobody worried too much about people being direct anymore. All this business of beating about the bush, having to say 'no' three times before accepting an offer, was considered very out of date. Yes, there were some very traditional expressions that went with all of that, which no one used any more, which was sad in a way; but nowadays people just didn't have time for them. He said that he did, nevertheless, find it very disturbing when very young nurses spoke so directly to his 86-year-old father when he was in hospital. He therefore shared some of their anxieties even though he felt he was probably 'Western'. He said that he didn't mind at all being direct; but he really didn't think it was something that needed to be pushed as part of the company ethos about 'equality', which everyone knew didn't really exist at all. Jonathan was a little bit confused because all he had heard before this, from people from the same culture as Ramla and Ed, was that there was no way that they could be direct under any circumstances at all. He had, however, heard that Ramla had been very 'direct' in the meetings she was talking about.

The analysis in Table 7.2 adds a discourses domain to the categories of cultural action to highlight their presence. The discourses identified in this analysis have been present in a number of the narratives in previous chapters. This will be dealt with below. What is of particular interest is Ramla's apparent subscription to several different discourses. She may appear to be contradicting herself. This certainly seems to be what Ed and Jonathan are thinking.

The characteristics of the three discourses referred to in Table 7.2, plus those for the other narratives in the chapter, are presented in Table 7.3, which will be referred to throughout the chapter. The names I have given them are, of course, working labels, simply as a means of making my own sense of what is going on. In a sense, they are the products of the 'critical cosmopolitan' discourse, which represents the line taken by this book – this being the discourse which claims to stand outside and recognise the others as discourses. The Outcomes column tends therefore to be critical of all the other discourses. The Origins column indicates that the discourses both connect with schools of thought within the academy as well as with common attitudes in everyday life.

Table 7.2 Competing discourses

Categories of cultural action	Ramla (Country A)	Ed (Country A)	Jonathan (Country B)
Statements about culture	'In our culture we are not direct in the way we speak to each other. 'Our society is complex, and not everyone has problems with being direct. 'We are well-known for being direct. 'Being direct is not really part of our culture and results in the loss of expressions of politeness in their language. 'We are non-Western.'	'It is not particularly Western to be direct. 'Not being direct was an issue with the older generation; and language changes.'	'Where I come from people are no longer worried about being direct, even if there is a loss of traditional language. 'Being too direct is inappropriate for the older generation 'I am probably Western.'
Discourses	'West vs. the rest' 'Essentialist culture and language' 'Critical cosmopolitan.'	'Critical cosmopolitan'.	
Global position and politics	Resisting Western directness.	Does not perceive a conflict with the West.	
Cultural resources	Tradition of not being direct in her country. Knowledge that there are also direct people in her country. Experience of being marginalised at work.	Experience of complex relationships with directness.	
Underlying universal cultural processes	Making sense of cultural relations within an organisation. Taking action to manage marginalised cultural relationships within an organisation.	Making sense of the way in which a friend is taking action to manage cultural relations within her workplace.	

Table 7.3 Discourses of culture

Working label	Characteristics	Associations	Origins	Outcomes
West vs. the rest	The West is dominating the way culture is conceptualised and holds powerful notions of what is 'normal', 'desirable', 'proficient' and 'deficient'.	Centre vs. Periphery voices, where the Centre always defines and Periphery is always defined.	In the academy: critical sociology and cultural studies (e.g. Al Sheykh 1998; Bhabha 1994; Hall 1996; Said 1978). Popular resistance against Western hegemony.	Recognition of complexity, marginal realities, non-Western modernity and proficiency. Bottom-up globalisation. Exaggeration of non-Western cultural traits and values through recourse to the 'essentialist culture and language' discourse.
Essentialist culture and language	Cultures (e.g. national, religious) are separate entities, each with their particular characteristics which define the traits and values of the people within them. Language has a major defining role.	E.g. the differentiation between collectivist cultures (group oriented, hierarchical, indirect, traditional) and individualist cultures (self-direction, innovative, autonomy, direct, organising, planning ahead). Cultural relativism.	In the academy: national cultural profiling (e.g. Hofstede 2003; Triandis 1995) Cultural linguistics which associates particular languages with particular cultural values. Popular use of 'culture' as a place which can be visited.	Ability to describe, predict, differentiate and defend particular traits and values. Strong sense of cultural identity. Traits and values which do not fit are exceptions. Change and deviation is caused by external influence.
Critical cosmopolitan	Acknowledges the complexity of cultural realities.	The notion of 'culture' is negotiable, contestable, socially constructed, etc.	In the academy: postmodern, critical cosmopolitan sociology (e.g. Delanty et al. 2008b; Holliday 2011a; King 1991; Kumaravadivelu 2007) Unmarked experience of everyday life	Contesting the 'essentialist culture and language' discourse. Apparently not acknowledging stronger positions of cultural identity.

Table 7.3 continued

Working label	Characteristics	Associations	Origins	Outcomes
West as steward	Modernity and progress resides in the West.	Orientalism. The notion that non-Western cultures are deficient and lack characteristics which can only be learnt in the West.	Colonialism. 'War on terror'. Excuse for invading others so that they can be educated (e.g. Adichie 2007; Zimmerman 2006). In the academy: postcolonial studies (e.g. Said 1978; Sangari 1994).	Top-down globalisation.
Third space	There is a neutral domain in which people from different cultures can come together and be themselves.	Hybridity. Cultural values cannot really be totally shared. Strong relationship between culture and the first language.	In the academy (e.g. Bhabha 1994; Guilherme 2002; Kramsch 1993; Zhu 2008).	The maintenance of an uncrossable intercultural line.
Liberal multi-culturalism	We can best respect and understand other cultures through the expression of their defining characteristics.	Different cultures have defining characteristics which place them apart. These can be seen in popular products, e.g. festivals, food and costumes.	Political and social policies to encourage the expression and sharing of cultural artefacts, e.g. in education.	The maintenance of Othering exotic characteristics (Delanty *et al.* 2008b; Kubota 2004; Kumaravadivelu 2007: 104–6; Spears 1999).

Plotting and assessing the discourses

Locate the discourses listed in Table 7.3 in the narratives throughout the book by attaching them to individual characters.

Remember that individuals may employ more than one discourse at once and at different times.

Evaluating Table 7.3

See if you can improve on the listing by renaming the discourses or dividing them in different ways.

Critique the table with regard to the language used.

- How fair is the representation of the discourses?
- In what way does the final outcomes column represent the interests of the 'critical cosmopolitan' discourse?
- Is it possible to talk about discourses neutrally, without being influenced by a particular discourse?

Projecting strong essentialist statements

The reason for the conflict in Ramla's position in the above narrative may to some extent be explained in the final column of the 'West versus the rest' row and the final two columns of the 'critical cosmopolitan' row, which can be captured in the following points:

- Ramla has experience of her cultural background being marginalised by what she considers to be Western cultural norms. She therefore subscribes to the 'West versus the rest' discourse.
- To counter this Western view she needs to emphasise her own cultural norms by employing the 'essentialist culture and language' discourse.
- This is in fact in conflict with her everyday experience of her own cultural background to the extent that she is also able, when not explicitly resisting the Western views, to employ the 'critical cosmopolitan' discourse. This does not, however, sufficiently serve her anti-West resistance agenda; so she returns to the 'essentialist culture and language' discourse.

Projecting strong essentialist statements about one's culture in this way, even when they do not correspond with the complexities of everyday reality, is a common phenomenon. There may be a variety of reasons for people to do this. The following is a working list which may be developed further:

- They subscribe wholly to the 'essentialist culture and language' discourse and believe that traits and values which do not conform to it are exceptions.
- They are in circumstances which require them to make special efforts to present who they are by exaggerating.
- They are being asked to make quick responses to leading questions about their 'culture', and have not thought about it too much.

The last case could be a researcher presenting them with a ready-made theory of culture which they find convenient to go along with. It needs to be remembered here that a lot of people may not have thought too much about cultural identity before.

One might equally wonder why people listening to these statements take them at face value, when they should know from their own life experience that cultural realities are more complex. The following is another working list of possible reasons:

- They are seduced by the easy answers of the 'essentialist culture and language' discourse.
- These are, after all, statements that are made by insiders to 'the culture' who ought to know.

- They are caught up in Othering the group concerned, the process of which is supported by the resulting stereotype.
- They are under pressure to make quick sense as newcomers.
- They are attracted by exotic realities.
- They are carrying out research based on the theories which are associated with the 'essentialist culture and language' discourse.

Regarding the second point, note Jonathan's confusion in the narrative when two people 'from the same culture' give him very different accounts of what 'it' is like. Regarding the final point, a major error in the academic domain of the 'essentialist culture and language' discourse is that marked statements will appear as objective and scientific descriptions, when in effect they may be different types of responses to the pressures of interviews.

False leads

Recall instances when you have made exaggerated, marked statements about 'your culture'. What were the reasons for you doing this?

Recall instances when you have taken other people's statements about 'their culture' at face value.

- What has been your agenda for doing this? Has there been anything for you to gain from going along with such easy answers?
- Why do you not understand from your own experience of exaggerating why others might be doing this?

Edit and add to the above lists of reasons for subscribing to or being taken in by the 'essentialist culture and language' discourse.

Nada, Jahan and Osama: getting it wrong?

The discussion so far in this chapter gives the impression that it must be very hard for onlookers to know what to believe and what not to believe. Various discourses may be constructed for the purpose of diverse agendas; but they are always real for the people who employ them at their particular moments in time. The following narrative[4] addresses this issue.

Nada had to write an essay about cultural identity for her coursework. It had to be based on an interview with someone from a different cultural background to her own. She chose to interview Jahan because he was the most foreign person in her group, at least from her point of view, and he always seemed pleasant and friendly. She thought it would be an opportunity to get to know him better.

In a session to help them prepare for the interviews, their tutor said that they should avoid using the word 'culture' altogether because he said this would make the questions too 'leading' and take everyone off on predictable paths. Nada really couldn't understand this. If they were supposed to be talking about culture, why couldn't they just name it? She really believed that people would simply talk about what they believed, and that it was false and even patronising to use 'special devices' to make them talk in particular ways.

During the interview she found Jahan warm and expressive. He had a lot to say; and she didn't have to work hard at all to keep it going. One or two of her other classmates had told her that they had found it really difficult to keep the interview from drying up.

He began by saying that he was pleased that they were meeting in a public place because it was actually against his culture to mix with women outside his family. He went on to describe how difficult it was for people who came from his country to work in pairs in the classroom with people of the opposite sex and be expected to talk about quite personal things sometimes. He explained that talking to her was different because she was a professional woman who had introduced herself to him formally about the interview.

Nada was very impressed with Jahan for being prepared to stick to his cultural values in this way. She felt he had principles and traditions which she was afraid were not being taken seriously in the international setting of their programme. When she came to write the assignment she found some recent research which confirmed what Jahan had told her about his culture. Moreover, some of this literature explained why his culture and others like it were not compatible with the culture in which their programme was taking place. She had also read about Othering, and argued in her assignment that the aims and values of the programme they were on were Othering Jahan's culture by failing to recognise the cultural incompatibility and forcing people like him into inappropriate behaviour.

When Nada got a low grade for her assignment, with the comment that she was in effect Othering Jahan and his culture, and that she was not being sufficiently critical of the literature, she really couldn't understand where to turn. Her first reaction was to think that the person who marked it was being so insensitive about people like Jahan – other cultures generally – that he just couldn't see beyond his own cultural values, and actually proved the point that she was making in her assignment. She didn't, however, anticipate what happened next.

She was talking about the issue with a group of people when her friend, Osama, got quite angry and said that Nada was being really ignorant in taking people like Jahan seriously. Osama said that if Nada had heard that sort of thing from someone in her own so-called 'culture' she would have rejected him immediately for being sexist.

Osama did come from the same region as Jahan; but Nada wondered if she really knew his culture. Osama went on to say that Nada was being very naïve and needed to know that, just like everywhere else in the world, there were lots of political issues. He said that the problem with people like Jahan was that they claimed that they represented their entire society, whereas in fact they represented a particular religious group.

Osama said that Nada's tutor was right in saying that they needed to be more critical of the literature, much of which was only interested in confirming stereotypes. On the other hand, it was Jahan who was Othering himself by claiming that his entire society is confined within a narrow stereotype. Osama was also angry because people like Nada just jumped at every opportunity to find some exotic cultural practice to protect. Moreover, he wasn't entirely convinced that her tutor's liberal attitude wasn't also part of some sort of cultural superiority, to say how people should or should not talk about other people's cultural backgrounds.

Table 7.4 opposite attempts to make sense of the complex conflicts evident in this narrative. An overriding implication in the analysis is that Nada's programme and her tutor are Western, whereas Jahan and Osama are not Western. This is not stated in the narrative, and how far the issues are to do with Western and non-Western positions is always a matter of debate anyway. The implication is nevertheless there.

It is also evident that an individual cannot only employ more than one and also contradictory discourses, as noted with Ramla earlier in the chapter, but also that people on different sides of an argument can employ the same discourses as each other. Hence, although Osama is angry about Jahan's point of view, they both share the 'West versus the rest' discourse. The implication here is that discourses can be coupled with different discourses. At another-time, in other circumstances, when perhaps being anti-Western is the major concern, Osama and Jahan could indeed find themselves on the same side of the argument.

Suspicion towards well-wishing

Osama's ambivalence towards Nada's tutor's comments arises from his suspicion that, despite their disagreement with each other, both Nada and her tutor subscribe to the 'West as steward' discourse, in which they assume a role in caring for the cultural well-being of the non-Western Other. This discourse is related to the part of the Orientalist thesis which imagines the non-West to be culturally deficient or oppressed and in need of liberation, and that improvement can only be attained through educative contact with the West. This discourse has been evident in a number of narratives throughout the book.

There is some connection here with the tutor's instruction to ban the term 'culture' in the **cultural resources** row. This involves a political correctness strategy through which it is thought that a discourse can be undone by changing key aspects of its language. More shall be said about this strategy below. Here it is necessary to note that the strategy is met with suspicion by Osama, who feels that it is presumptuous and patronising for the tutor to think that she can defend his (Osama's) point of view.

Table 7.4 'Who is right?'

Categories of cultural action	Jahan	Nada	Academic literature read by Nada	Osama	Programme tutor
Statements about culture	'My culture has practices and values that are incompatible with those of the programme.'	'I agree with Jahan that his culture has practices and values which are incompatible with those of our programme.'	'Different cultures have traits and values which are not compatible with each other.'	'People like Jahan claim wrongly that they represent their entire society when in fact they are making sexist statements 'They are Othering themselves by subscribing to a limiting stereotype.'	'Using the term "culture" leads to essentialism. We should be critical of what is claimed by the literature.'
Discourses	'Essentialist culture and language.' 'West versus the rest.'	(According to Osama) 'West as steward.'		'Critical cosmopolitan.' 'West versus the rest.'	(According to Osama) 'West as steward.'
Global position and politics	Convinced of being Othered by the West.	Sensitivity to other cultures. Cultural relativism.		Cultural politics in her part of the world. Distrust of the West.	
Cultural resources	Cultural practice of gender segregation.		Objectivist tradition in cultural profiling.		Using certain terms, such as 'culture', can influence how you construct others.
Underlying universal cultural processes	Trying to make sense of conflicting statements about culture.				

Cultural resistance

Strong elements of cultural resistance are revealed in Table 7.4, with Jahan employing the 'essentialist culture and language' discourse and Osama employing the 'critical cosmopolitan' discourse. This alignment can also be seen with several characters in ethnographic narratives in earlier chapters, as indicated in Table 7.5.

Table 7.5 Discourses of resistance

		For 'different cultures, different values' *'Essentialist culture and language' discourse*	*Against 'different cultures, different values'* *'Critical cosmopolitan' discourse*
About 'us'		**Francisca**, agreeing with a methodology that emphasises essentialist cultural descriptions (Chapter 3). 'Emphasising different cultures with different characteristics protects us from having to behave like Americans and British.'	**Dima**, defending the right to use Facebook (Chapter 2). Bottom-up globalisation: 'We are able to claim Western cultural practices and make them our own on our own terms.' **Gita**, disagreeing with a methodology that emphasises essentialist cultural descriptions (Chapter 3). 'These cultural theories are invented by the Centre and discriminate against the Periphery in the same way as racist and sexist descriptions.'
About 'them'		**Christoff**, concerned that people in Dima's society use Facebook. Top-down globalisation: 'Western cultural practices may have a corrupting influence on non-Western cultures.' **Ivonne**, resisting a non-essentialist approach before going to Ex (Chapter 3). 'Other cultures need their own space to be themselves and to have their own values.'	

The objectivist myth

The heading 'Who is right?' is used for Table 7.4 because the narrative reveals that it is very hard to arrive at a straightforward conclusion about what Jahan has to say and about what Osama has to say about him. Not only is it difficult for Nada to assess what she is hearing from Jahan, but it is also very hard for her to assess the discoursal aspects of what she has read in the literature.

The 'essentialist culture and language' discourse is seductive not only because it claims logical and systematic insider knowledge, but also because it is present in an academic literature which claims objective knowledge. This is indicated in the **cultural resources** row. Moreover, by claiming objective knowledge, this academic literature does not acknowledge that it is making statements which are themselves socially and politically constructed within their own small cultures of knowledge which define how they think and operate. This process is described by Kuhn's revolutionary (1970) *The Structure of Scientific Revolutions*. It can be argued that groups of academics get into **small culture formation** with respect to the construction and reification of ideas, to give an outward impression of objective professionalism. What academic literature says about culture can therefore also be considered to represent discourses of and about culture within the **statements about culture** domain of the grammar.

Complex pictures

Think about your discussions or arguments with other people concerning issues of culture and identity.

- Which discourses do you employ?
- Can you indeed say that there is more than one? Do they contradict each other?
- Does this mean that you present yourself in different ways to different people or at different times?
- If you do, does this mean that (1) you are undecided, (2) you have a strategy to present different views to different people, or (3) there really is more than one way of looking at things, and even different truths?
- How far do you see all of this in the other people taking part in the discussions or arguments?
- Are people who employ conflicting discourses (1) liars, (2) unable to decide who they are, or (3) struggling to deal with complex reality?

A discourse of science

A reason for the sustained power of the 'essentialist culture and language' discourse is its roots in what many have called the structural-functional model of society, depicted in Figure 7.1. This can be traced back to the French sociologist Emile Durkheim (1858–1917). That he was a biologist by training is implicit in the organic nature of the model. Its success has to do with itsstraightforward nature. It is far easier to understand than the grammar of culture presented in this book, which is based on the alternative, social action model of the German sociologist Max Weber (1864–1920).

The structural-functional model presents national culture as neatly containing all other aspects of society within it, which in turn contain behaviour and values. This means that behaviour and values are (1) explainable and predictable by the characteristics of the national culture, and (2) essentially different to behaviour and values in another national culture.

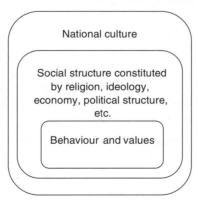

Figure 7.1 Structural-functional model

This picture of culture lends itself well to a positivist scientific enterprise. This promise of explanation and prediction is very seductive. An example of how a discourse is built around this promise, in the case of individualism and collectivism, is plotted in Figure 7.2.

The depiction in the figure is of course from the point of view of the 'critical cosmopolitan' discourse. Hence, the scientific theoretical premises of bubbles 1 and 2 are influenced by popular notions in 3 about a West–rest divide and a naïve, surface reading of **statements about culture** in 4. The positivist quest of finding examples to support the theory is in 5 and 7, with a convenient dispatching of exceptions in 6. The technical terms which grow out of science in 8 provides the language to build the discourse. Bubble 9 represents the driving force of the discourse, in which academics can build their careers on developing the intricacies of theory, and professionals the reliable training.

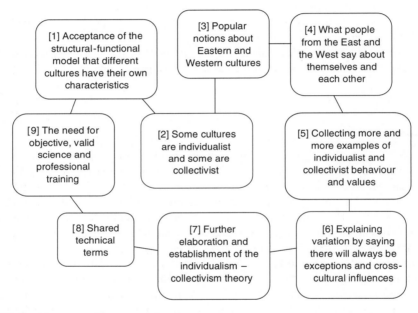

Figure 7.2 Development of an essentialist discourse

Neutrality in research

Assess the notion that research and academic views about the nature of culture fall into the same category of **statements about culture** in the grammar as what people say about themselves in everyday life.

Can you find examples of any of the processes represented in Figure 7.2?

Nada, Osama, Theobald and Jahan: 'shall we share our cultures?'

Two major and influential discourses have emerged out of the difficulty which Nada faces in the previous narrative in getting the whole culture issue right. These are the 'third space' discourse and the 'liberal multicultural' discourse. These, and their attendant issues, are demonstrated in the following continuation of the narrative[5] about Nada, Osama and Jahan:

Nada found Osama's attitude very difficult to understand, and she felt quite offended at being accused of being patronising. In her experience all the students were looking for opportunities for their cultures to be recognised and understood, if only a little. It seemed to her that they were delighted, on international evenings, to bring their national food, sing their national songs, and sometimes even display dancing and costumes. When there were national festivals, the organisers of the evenings distributed leaflets and sometimes organised special displays on the campus.

Jahan was one of the people who took part in these events; and he complained that in the university where he was previously there had been no such provision. Nada herself sometimes brought dishes that she felt belonged to her own cultural heritage. Her grandparents on both sides had migrated there when her parents were children. Being labelled 'Western' by implication by Osama also bothered her. She hadn't thought of herself in that way before.

What Nada found particularly meaningful from her programme was the notion of a 'third space'. This was a different tutor to the one who had set the assignment and banned the mention of 'culture'. The third space idea, as far as she could work it out, acknowledged cultural difference and that people had different values that might not always be compatible, but that they could meet and understand each other in some sort of intermediary place in which they could be themselves as well as getting on with other people. It seemed to her that that was what these international evenings were all about – as long as home studentsalso went to them. She knew, however, that that was often not the case. Perhaps her interviewing Jahan was a third space activity.

Nada dreaded meeting Osama again. When she did it wasn't good at all. He did however appeal to Nada's own cultural background when he said, 'You yourself must surely appreciate that we are all more than traditional food, songs, clothes and festivals'. Osama said that the best that these international evenings could do was to encourage people to withdraw into exaggerations of who they were and become some sort of exotic spectacle for those home students who did turn up. What was most alarming to Nada was that another student, Theobald, was there, who had actually been one of the organisers of the evenings, and he started saying that Nada probably didn't realise how so many of 'them' just put up with representing themselves with food and costumes because they had nowhere else to turn. He said that very few people would actually come out and say this because it was even more demeaning to admit it.

Nada then began to think that everyone was just clutching at straws.[6] She recalled how many of the home students said that the reasons why they didn't mix with international students was because they were so frightened to offend them. One of her friends had told her that he didn't dare talk about what he ate for breakfast because mention of eating bacon would be just too dangerous in case it offended someone's religion. He then said that really all this talk of culture was only relevant anyway to foreigners. When she told Osama this, the response was how patronising it was to imagine that people everywhere couldn't deal with diversity. He said that everyone came from societies which were sufficiently complex for them to have grown up with diversity, and that when people decided that they could not, this was the cause of ethnic conflict and civil wars. He said that thinking that only 'foreigners' had culture was a clear outcome of basing everything on festivals, food and costumes, and giving the impression that 'culture' means 'ethnic' – old-fashioned traditions.

Regarding the third space idea, Osama simply said that he was who he was and didn't want to be shoe-horned[7] into a convenient place where he wasn't considered to belong to anyone in particular. Nada responded that she was increasingly getting the impression, especially from Nada's friend, that people *were* finding it hard to belong anywhere. Osama retorted that this was because of the oppressive attitudes of the so-called 'home' people (she clearly thought this was a bit of a euphemism) and didn't mean at all that foreigners did not have the capacity to extend who they were into new places, if only they were allowed.

The two discourses emerging in this narrative are the 'liberal multiculturalism' and the 'third space' discourses, both listed in Table 7.3. These have become very powerful discourses which claim to go out to people from diverse cultural backgrounds and embrace the richness of who they are. The 'third space' discourse, particularly, has provided people who have felt marginalised by more dominant cultural realities of the places they have travelled to with a space to be themselves. Liberal multiculturalism, which has been criticised for being 'nice' and naïve, needs to be distinguished from a more hard-nosed critical multiculturalism which is more aligned to the 'critical cosmopolitan' discourse.

Table 7.6 attempts to make some sense of the various views expressed in this narrative with regard to the 'liberal multiculturalism' and 'third space' discourses. They initially provide Nada with a solution to 'who is right'. Nevertheless, she once again finds mixed views. Her original interviewee, Jahan, provides the most secure support. One of the attractions of these two discourses is that they run quite smoothly from the 'essentialist culture and language' discourse to which Jahan also subscribes; and this might subsequently explain why this discourse is also so popular and well-established. The firmness and apparent neutrality of the central idea that there are separate cultures with their own distinct and describable features is solid and supportive. Osama's total rejection of this is perhaps predictable and certainly expected by Nada. However, Theobald springs a surprise by saying that a lot of people put up with the convenience of the 'liberal multicultural' discourse out of desperation. Interestingly, in the middle of this discussion, Nada comes out and states her position regarding the West, and therefore finds some common ground with Theobald when prompted by Osama.

Table 7.6 Searching for space

	Responses to the discourses				
Discourses	*Jahan*	*Osama*	*Theobald*	*Nada*	*Nada's friend*
'Liberal multicultural' discourse	Subscribes. Needs the opportunity to express his culture in events.	Rejects. Encourages exaggerated distortion of who people are. Gives the impression that 'culture' means ethnicity, and ethnicity is only to do with the non-Western Other.	Ambivalent. People put up with presenting exaggerated distortions of their cultures because they have nowhere else to turn.	Subscribes. Doesn't feel any tension between 'the West' and international people expressing examples of their cultures.	Uncomfortable. Issues around culture are only relevant to foreigners.
'Third space' discourse	Subscribes by implication.	Rejects. Doesn't need to be shoe-horned into an intermediate place.	Still searching. Marginalised.	Subscribes. Opportunities to present one's own cultural artefacts.	Not relevant.

Festivals and food

However, Osama's relentless critique of both of these discourses is very real, and shared by a number of commentators, as evidenced in the bottom right cell of Table 7.3. The following extracts are from the influential Black sociologist Stuart Hall, speaking about his experience of moving from Jamaica to Britain, and about the implications for how we must look at culture:

> People think of Jamaica as a simple society. In fact, it had the most complicated colour stratification system in the world.... Compared with that, the normal class stratification [in Britain] is absolute child's play. But the word 'Black' was never uttered.
>
> (Hall 1991b: 53)

> In that moment, the enemy was ethnicity ... 'multi-culturalism' ... 'the exotic' ... the exotica of difference. Nobody would talk of racism but they were perfectly prepared to have 'International Evenings', when we would all come and cook our native dishes, sing our native songs, and appear in our own native costume.... I have been de-racinated for four hundred years. The last thing I am going to do is to dress up in some native Jamaican costume and appear in the spectacle of multi-culturalism.
>
> (Hall 1991b: 55–6)

These two extracts are about the complexity of cultural experience and about how people (in Britain, but perhaps everywhere else too) choose to look at it. Some people have referred to the phenomenon represented here as 'boutique' multiculturalism, in which the foreign Other is simplified as an attractive commodity – hence the reference to exotic. Exoticising can be defined as seeing something as having a strange or bizarre allure, beauty or quality.

Food and festivals

Interview recent and long-term newcomers to the country where you are about how they feel about how their cultural backgrounds are represented in the society where they now live.

Given how powerful the 'liberal multicultural' discourse might be, how might you encourage them to reveal deeper feelings? What sorts of questions will you ask?

Osama's anger about the 'third space' discourse is also mirrored in this account by an Indian academic living in the US, and connected with the notion of hybridity:

> Proponents of cultural hybridity would expect me to create a 'third culture', or a 'third space', without allowing either my inherited Indian culture or my learned American culture to fully determine my values and beliefs ... a state of ambivalence ... in-between-ness that is supposed to result when individuals ... displace themselves from one national/cultural context ... into another. I do not believe I am dangling in cultural limbo. Instead I believe I live in several cultural domains at the same time – jumping in and out of them, sometimes with ease and sometimes with unease.... In fact one does not even have to cross one's national borders to experience cultural complexity. If we, as we must, go beyond the traditional approach to culture that narrowly associated cultural identity with national identity ... then we easily realise that human communities are not monocultural cocoons but rather multicultural mosaics.
>
> (Kumaravadivelu 2007: 5)

Hybridity

The notion of being hybrid implies being mixed, or impure. Can this, however, be read in both positive and derogatory ways? Some people like the term because it opposes the essentialist notion of a 'pure' or even 'virgin' culture.

Consider the views of Kumaravadivelu above and Osama in the narrative earlier in this chapter.

- Does hybridity imply 'in-between', and an implied acceptance of essentialism, as they both seem to imply?
- … or does it imply complexity and a rejection of essentialism?

Managing and undoing discourses

There is a reference to political correctness in the Nada, Jahan and Osama narrative in this chapter, where Nada's tutor suggests that the students should not use the word 'culture' in their interviews. This is an attempt to undo the 'essentialist culture and language' discourse by constructing new behaviour around a different use of language.

This strategy connects with the narrative about engineering conformity in Chapter 4, where, by introducing a new technical phrase which employees then use in meetings and reports, new behaviour is introduced. The implication here is that discourses are at least partially built around particular items of language. Indeed, where it is the case that a major tenet of the 'essentialist culture and language' discourse is the notion of 'a culture' which has particular describable characteristics, not being able to use the term 'a culture' would force people to find other ways to express what they wish to talk about and perhaps lead them at least to talk less easily about cultural issues.

Such a strategy might not normally fall under the heading of political correctness unless it concerns undoing a prejudice. For supporters of the 'critical cosmopolitan' discourse, the 'essentialist culture and language' discourse *is* prejudicial due to the Othering which is considered to be at its heart. This would therefore be the thinking behind Nada's tutor enforcing the ban.

The following extract is taken from the end of the Clare Danes text in Chapter 6.

> To research the role of CIA agent Mathison for *Homeland*, she also visited real agents in their workplace and asked them about the part that gender and sex play in their work: 'It can be an asset and used to their advantage, but it can also be problematic, and then they have to be creative about how to resolve that. It's a real issue in Arab cultures, where men don't have relationships with women like we do here'.

It can be argued that the statement about 'Arab cultures' and 'relationships with women' is employing the 'essentialist culture and language' discourse. If the word 'Arab' was not used I feel that it would not be so easy to make the essentialist statement.

Playing with words

Collect examples of how particular nations, people or 'cultures' are described or referred to in the media and among people you know.

- What are the key words or phrases in the descriptions and references?
- What would be the effect of removing these words and phrases?
- What do people need to do when they are not able to avoid conversations in which these words and phrases are used?

Using 'culture' everywhere

It cannot be ignored that the term 'culture' is commonly used by everyone everywhere. Most of the characters in the ethnographic narratives in this book talk easily about their and other people's 'cultures', even when employing the 'critical cosmopolitan' discourse.

- What are your views about this?
- Would it really make any difference if any of the characters had to find other ways of talking about what they refer to as 'culture'?

Summary

- Discourses are central to the construction of reality and Self and Other politics within the domain of **small culture formation**.
- They can draw people into adopting and conforming to cultural practices. This can result in a loss of agency, hiding and cutting off other practices, or encouraging the adoption of beneficial practices.
- The concept of 'discourse' is used to make sense of complex social processes. How particular discourses are named and defined is a matter of debate.
- Individuals can have complex roles with respect to discourses – designing, complying with or being seduced by them, and with varying degrees of awareness of their power and control.
- People's different positions regarding the nature of culture can be traced to competing discourses.
- Discourses about culture can be traced both to everyday and academic traditions. In both domains they can give the impression of being neutral and reliable. They can contribute to professional and academic respectability and the building of careers.
- Individuals can reject or buy into particular or multiple conflicting discourses in different ways at different times for a variety of reasons.
- The celebration of difference can lead to 'cultures' being depicted as exotic commodities and can easily drive the complexity of people's natures to the margins.

Notes

1 http://www.babycentre.co.uk/baby/startingsolids/babyledweaning
2 http://www.heinzbaby.co.uk
3 This narrative is based on numerous comments from colleagues and acquaintances on cultural issues with institutional language, observation of the language of nurses with elderly patients in hospitals, research projects which have indicated that people interviewed display multiple and sometimes conflicting discourses (Armenta, in progress; Oral, in progress).
4 This narrative is based on the experience of students talking and writing about each other's cultural realities, and of a number of discussions following conferences and other presentations.

5 The development of the second part of this narrative draws from research carried out on home university student attitudes to international students (Montgomery 2010), and numerous conversations with newcomers and long-standing immigrants, and an interview with a British person about attitudes to foreigners.
6 'Clutching at straws' means turning to even hopeless solutions out of desperation.
7 A shoe horn is a spoon-like device to help get your foot into a tight-fitting shoe.

Further reference

Hall, S. (1991). The local and the global: globalization and ethnicity. *Culture, globalization and the world-system*. Minneapolis, MN: University of Minnesota Press: 19–39.
— A discussion of the broad ideological and discoursal nature of 'culture'.

Delanty, G., Wodak, R. and Jones, P. (eds). (2008). *Identity, belonging and migration*. Liverpool: Liverpool University Press.
— This deals with the dominant Western discourses of culture and race.

Fairclough, N. (2006). *Language and globalization*. London: Routledge.
— This deals with the conflicts between Centre and Periphery discourses of culture.

Baumann, G. (1996). *Contesting culture*. Cambridge: Cambridge University Press.
— The everyday constructions of diverse images of culture in the London Borough of Southall are discussed.

Lankshear, C., Gee, J.P., Knobel, M. and Searle, C. (1997). *Changing literacies*. Buckingham: Open University Press.
— An analysis of how we all travel through multiple discourses in everyday life.

Holliday, A.R. (2011). *Intercultural communication & ideology*. London: Sage.
— Pages 114–9 offer discourses of modernity, tradition and Westernisation.

Adichie, C.N. (2007). *Half of a yellow sun*. London: Harper Collins.
— While this is a novel about the Nigerian civil war in the late 1960s, it is also a study of a Nigerian family who struggle to maintain a modernist discourse of culture in the face of an Othering colonial past.

Zimmerman, A.L. (2006). *Innocents abroad*. Cambridge, MA: Harvard University Press.
— An anthropology of American Peace Corps workers at the beginning of the twentieth century, through letters home.
— This is an excellent telling of the 'West as steward' discourse.

Chapter 8

Prejudice

This chapter will look at how we can so easily fall into the trap of prejudice when encountering people from other cultural backgrounds. It will build on observations from Chapters 6 and 7, which deal with the sorts of constructs which lead us to prejudice.

Within the grammar, prejudice resides in a number of domains. **Statements about culture** seduce us with convincing but exaggerated versions of who we and others are. From **cultural resources** emerge easy answers about national structures. From **global positioning** emerge the all-pervasive Self and Other politics around the issues of identity and power which take centre place in **small culture formation**. Indeed, it has to be acknowledged that prejudice, which is connected with images built on prior formulae for Self and Other representation, is a very basic aspect of how we deal with each other. Ideology is also a central factor because of its ability to structure the large systems of ideas which then support prejudice.

Cultural prejudice and race

Cultural prejudice is closely associated with racism. Spears (1999: 11–12) defines neo-racism as any form of rationalising the subordination of a defined group of people on the basis of culture, even though race is not an explicit agenda in the minds of the people concerned. This is parallel to my own definition of cultural prejudice, or culturism: 'any thought or act' which reduces people to something less than what they are on the basis of an essentialist view of culture (Holliday 2005b: 17). Cultural prejudice might therefore be considered to be a form of neo-racism.

Innocent beginnings

The connection between culture and prejudice can be seen through the relationship between culture and discourses. Figure 8.1 groups the discourses which were introduced in Chapter 7 into two parts.

The discourses on the left are labelled 'innocent' because they derive from an objectivist tradition which takes for granted as fact a world which is divided into separate cultures, each with their separate defining characteristics. As such, these innocent discourses deny that the descriptions of 'other' cultures may be marked by ideology through the influence of **global position and politics**. This means that the possibility of prejudice in such descriptions is also denied. The discourses on the left also deny that they are discourses.

The discourses on the right of the figure are labelled 'ideological' because they are built on the premise that culture and ideology are deeply interconnected. They therefore recognise that they are discourses and ideologically motivated, with the potential for prejudice. At the same time, they accuse the innocent discourses on the left of being ideologically motivated, with the potential of prejudice. Therefore, implicit in ideological discourses is recognition of the need to continuously be wary of ideology and prejudice whenever **statements about culture** are made.

The differences between the discourses on the left and the right will create serious disagreements regarding whether or not prejudice is present in particular instances of cultural description. Take, for example, the case, which is implicit in several of the ethnographic narratives in this book:

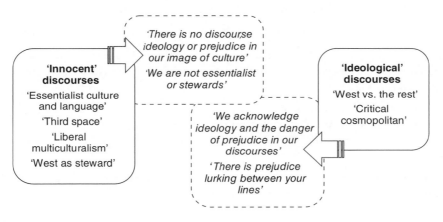

Figure 8.1 Innocence or ideology

- Bekka suggests that Jenna finds it difficult to have a critical discussion in the classroom because of her culture.
- **Interpretation A:** Bekka is being culturist because she is reducing Jenna to a stereotype which implies cultural deficiency. It is the same as saying she finds it difficult to have critical discussion in the classroom because of her race, or because of her gender.
- **Interpretation B:** This is simply a description of how things are based on what we know about cultural differences. It is evidenced by what people like Jenna often say about themselves and on extensive interview and questionnaire research. Bekka does not have any intention to be culturist and is in fact appreciating Jenna's different cultural origins.

I use the term 'culturist' because it indicates a parallel with 'racist' and 'sexist'. Interpretation A therefore makes the point that Bekka's statement is of the same order as racist or sexist statements. The strength of argument supporting interpretation B indicates how difficult a task it is to establish that there is prejudice embedded in cultural descriptions. The innocent discourses on the left of Figure 8.1 would claim no interest but that of science and understanding. In effect, they fall into the domain of easy answers and are therefore very difficult to shake.

There is a parallel here with establishing the occurrence of racism. People accused of being racist may say that they were just teasing and did not mean anything by it, and deny that they had any racist intentions. Victims of racism may also deny the racist intention. For this reason, since the Stephen Lawrence Inquiry[1] in 1999, it has become established that witnessing racism by a third party is sufficient evidence for its existence.

The paradox of prejudice

How might Figure 8.1 be adapted to represent incidences of bullying, racism or sexism?

Why are 'innocent', on the left, and 'ideological', on the right, in inverted commas?

Find examples of the relationships in Figure 8.1 in narratives throughout the book.

Reconstruct a case, which you have witnessed or been victim of, in which a culturist statement has been made, but in which the maker of the statement seemed unaware of its culturist content.

- What made the statement culturist?
- Why would the maker of the statement be unaware?
- How did the victim of the statement react? If it was you, how did you feel about it?

Evaluate the proposition that culturist statements often go unrecognised and unnoticed because they are perceived to be innocent.

Martha and Katya: meeting behaviour

The following narrative[2] demonstrates both the ease and the paradox surrounding cultural prejudice.

Act I

Martha noted a new member at the committee meeting, Katya. From her accent she imagined that she was a foreigner; and this was confirmed later. As part of Katya's role she had to make a short report on recent events in her department. Martha was horrified to see that she seemed to have several pages of notes and proceeded to read aloud from them in what was, in effect, a speech. The result was that she went on a lot longer than was required. Martha found herself thinking that this sort of behaviour in meetings came from Katya's culture and was just inappropriate.

Martha did think afterwards about why she felt so negative about Katya's behaviour. She talked about it to her colleague, Johannes. She explained that there definitely was a cultural stereotype which made it easy to label what happened. It was even attached to an image of a society in which there were issues with democracy and freedom – where people made long speeches and never listened to anyone else. Martha said she'd come across a lot of this sort of thing – people who just were not able to take part in a discussion among equals, like the image of children who weren't allowed to say anything at the dinner table until the father had died, and then they took over and assumed exactly the same role as the one they had despised for so many years. She pointed out that they would all be men – sons. It was only the sons who would get to inherit the right to speak.

Johannes listened to all of this. He knew exactly what Martha meant. But Martha was pleased when he suggested that she might be reading too much into Katya making a speech. Johannes said he knew Katya, and she was clearly a very bright young woman – definitely very *foreign*. Good heavens! They wondered if they were allowed even to talk about Katya in this way – all this political correctness.

The point Johannes wanted to make was that Katya probably just hadn't been to a committee meeting before and still had to work out how to behave. He was sure that by the third meeting she would be better at meeting behaviour than all of them. She had some very powerful points to make. Martha acknowledged all of this; but she made the point that the *type* of mistake Katya was making – the *type* of starting point – was very different to the starting point from which *she* – and she was sure Johannes too – had to learn about how to behave in committee meetings.

Martha then remembered an excellent example. She was at a conference presentation recently in a non-European location. When it came to time for questions some guy stood up and started giving a lecture. It was not just that it was a lecture rather than a question, it was also entirely off the topic. Martha then pointed out that it was a country with an oppressive régime, with absolutely no women's rights – and that actually she began to think that the people probably deserved what they got.

Act 2

It was some time later that Martha had more to do with Katya. They were in a number of the same meetings; and she also went to a presentation that she gave. She began to like and admire her, and thought how well she was coming on. Martha therefore decided to make friends. She felt that she had been a bit prejudiced and should try and appreciate Katya's culture. She was curious about the oral tradition that must be behind the practice of making speeches, and how she felt about the things she had had to leave behind to become successful here. Martha felt that she should try and appreciate her culture rather than seeing it as a negative force.

Katya was used to questions about 'her culture', but did not feel they were sincere because they did not really seem to be about her. They seemed to be about an image of who she was which was acceptable within her relationship with people like Martha. She answered them with the same degree of learnt discipline that she employed in responding to the rules of committee meetings – in order to maintain her position and gain what she wanted. Therefore, with Martha, it was convenient to tell her that, yes, in her culture they had a different type of respect for parents and people in positions of power, and that, yes, it was difficult to criticise authority. Somehow Katya felt that this was what Martha wanted to hear. Certainly, some of it was true; but there were many other things that got her here and enabled her to be successful.

At a deeper level, she could also see how all this stuff about authority was also true here. There were so many meetings that she went to where colleagues were complaining about not being heard. She felt, however, that it was just too complicated and difficult to tell Martha what she really felt. It didn't seem relevant to talk about how the media, arts and activist groups in her country were just as critical as they were here.

With the people she considered her friends here she knew that they thought she was a bit of a pain for always going on about those things. But, at the risk of overstating her case, she felt that she just had to push, push, push against the prevailing ethos of cultural superiority in this place. If there *was* such a thing as an overall cultural characteristic of a place, here it was this constant desire to show everyone that they were the only people in the world who were free.

Table 8.1 looks at the narrative through the categories of cultural action, focusing on Martha and Katya, with Katya in the second column because she is responding to Martha, and with an added layer for discourses.

Katya's account in Act 2 reveals the naivety in Martha's approach to her and her continued prejudice. While in the **underlying universal cultural processes** band both are trying to work out how to deal with the other, there is also a split:

- Martha begins to recognise her possible prejudice and tries to compensate by going out to Katya to learn more about her.
- Katya is very cautious about this because Martha is still working on the same simplistic stereotype within the same ideology.
- Martha is therefore still subscribing to the innocent 'essentialist culture and language' and 'liberal multicultural' discourses, working only with the imagined 'facts' of the stereotype and not understanding that they are ideological.
- Katya subscribes to the ideological 'critical cosmopolitan' discourse and therefore deals with Martha in a creative, political manner, which Martha will be unaware of.

Martha is employing an 'essentialist culture and language' discourse because she sees her relationship with Katya as representing two separate 'cultures' with separate practice and value systems. I am claiming that she is employing a 'liberal multicultural' discourse because she sees the solution to understanding to be in the domain of sharing these two separate entities.

Table 8.1 Prejudiced or not?

Categories of cultural action	Martha	Katya
Statements about culture	'We value democracy and listening to the views of others. 'We don't make long speeches which inhibit other people's freedom to express themselves.'	Stated to Martha: 'We have a respect for parents and people in power which makes criticising authority difficult.' In private and with friends: 'We are critical like everyone else, but not naïve about the presence of authority.'
Discourses	'Essentialist culture and language', 'liberal multicultural.'	'Critical cosmopolitan.'
Global position and politics	Belief that foreigners are less free and democratic.	Having to deal with being thought of as culturally inferior.
Cultural resources	Being superior to others. Having a democratic system for meetings and committees.	Critical media, arts and activist groups.
Underlying universal cultural processes	Trying to work out how to deal with a problematic cultural Other.	
	Appreciating possible prejudice and trying to go out to Katya and understand her culture.	Being cautious and disciplined in what she reveals. Employing different strategies at different times to best deal with a dominant ideology.

I am interpreting Martha's perceptions as cultural prejudice because she is applying judgements to a specific culture of people, and Katya sees this prejudice continuing between the lines of the questions she asks her.

Common theme

Evaluate the statement that there is a common theme of prejudice running through almost all the ethnographic narratives in the book.

To what extent is this a common theme in almost all cases of intercultural misunderstanding?

To what degree can it be said that prejudice is a common feature of intercultural misunderstanding?

Martha and Katya

Evaluate the assumption that Martha is denying the ideological underpinning to her prejudice, and continues to be prejudiced even when she tries to learn more about Katya.

Is Katya being unfair on Martha by assuming that she cannot be herself with her and that Martha would not understand who she really is?

Cultural prejudice

Search into your experience for examples of cultural prejudice similar to that which Katya feels.

Explore the degree to which there is denial of its existence, and what forms this denial takes.

What would be the consequences of speaking out against it?

- What might happen if Katya told Martha exactly what she thought?
- Is Katya right in thinking that Martha simply would not understand?
- In your experience and in narratives in this book, what are the different strategies that people use to save face while not speaking out?

Francisca, Hande and Gita: missing home, belief and disbelief

The implication so far in the chapter is that prejudice, and associated ideologies and discourses, is everywhere, between the lines of our everyday lives. The following narrative indicates the everyday dangers of falling into the trap of prejudice, especially when dealing with the strangeness of living away from home. While the conversation between the two friends, first introduced in Chapter 3, does not deal with explicit prejudice, it explores what some of the reasons for prejudice might be.

Gita and Hande talked about how they missed home. They both agreed that it was hard to find the ingredients they needed to cook the dishes they missed, and that there was just the temptation to rely on fast food and pizzas. They missed their families and the ambiance and the sounds of the streets in the medium-sized towns that they each came from.

Francisca asked Gita what she thought of these events which they both knew about where someone would cook their national food and invite friends round to taste it. Gita said it was great in many ways because other people would get some sort of idea where she came from. The problem was that people very quickly jumped to the conclusion that this was all she was. She described an occasion when friends had arrived and shown real surprise that she was playing what one of them referred to as 'Western' music. They very clearly thought that she had somehow learnt to like it since she had been here; good heavens – it was Bob Dylan, someone that her parents had played when she was a young child. Francisca laughed in recognition and asked Gita if she ever consciously exaggerated behaviour which she thought would be the opposite of what people expected, just to get the point across – like the woman they both knew who made a big thing about ordering a glass of wine whenever they were out together because everyone just took it for granted that alcohol was against her religion. Yes, like people thinking that all people from a particular culture had arranged marriages, or had to give all their earnings to the family.

This made Gita remember her discussion with Francisca about the people they had seen in the café and how they couldn't stop the standard 'culture' references rising up when they saw people with particular features or styles of clothing. And just as she had been about to ask Hande if she felt liberated being away from the pressures of family life.

They went back to things that they missed and talked about how it was very hard for other people who had not been away from home like they were to understand what it was like to wake up imagining for a moment being in one's own country, with familiar smells of breakfast and the smells and sounds, and the colour of the light that one had grown up with. It was so hard not to find the food one was used to. They agreed that they could eventually work out how they were supposed to behave, and that they could even get used to having to try so much harder to make friends.

Back to family life again, they began to talk about issues that they had in common – concerning boyfriends, family pressures for them to get married and so on; and there was a huge amount they had in common. They talked about this and decided that it was because these were fairly universal things – except perhaps for Western people. So what was the issue there? Was it in fact the case that the West *was* completely different to everywhere else? *Was* it after all the case that the world really was divided into individualist and collectivist cultures?

Hande said that she had heard on several occasions people from the East and the South, when they met each other, even for a short period of time, say 'you are like us'; and it had something to do with shared understandings about the nature of life, or something like that. Gita asked Hande if she thought it was to do with things like family loyalties and the issues that arose from that. Hande said she wasn't sure. Gita said she thought it might have something to do with a warmth that arose from all sorts of things that people had to deal with which meant they had to depend on each other more. Then she thought again and said that it might not be that at all, because she had heard Westerners talking about dealing with all those things. The problem was that Westerners didn't *think* that foreigners could be like them, perhaps because of all this stuff about food and festivals, and being traditional and religious; and so they just kept their distance.

Gita then thought about Francisca again. It could be argued that she was Western, though it was sometimes hard to work out who was and who wasn't. They talked a lot about cultural things and also seemed to share a lot of feelings about them. They talked about language a lot – about how in a new language it just wasn't possible to say certain things and that it could actually begin to change the way you thought. Gita always maintained that this was part of the bigger issue – back to food and smells again. She had once talked about sitting on her balcony to someone and been misunderstood. The other person thought she meant she had a private box at the theatre. Then she realised that no-one here *had* balconies at home – and that this cut out an entire human experience, a sensuality to do with inside–outside, the possibility of sleeping there, how people thought about bedrooms, beds, neighbours, privacy, sharing and so on.

Then Francisca had told her that when she was a student she had lived in a small apartment without any chairs, just cushions and rugs; and she had decided that even these differences were not final. It wasn't because her 'West' was at the borders with the East – they had talked and laughed about this a lot – because the other students had been very 'Northern'.

In the narrative the three friends explore together the complexities of cultural difference. Rather than looking at their different views, which are very much shared, Table 8.2 applies the categories of cultural action to the states of intercultural awareness that they experience, and indicates that there are at least three states operating simultaneously – prejudice, ambivalence and understanding.

Table 8.2 From prejudice to understanding

Categories of cultural action	Prejudice	Ambivalence	Understanding
Statements about culture	Experiences of food, domestic arrangements and language are very particular to our cultural background.		Food, domestic arrangements and language are important to all of us in different ways and can be the basis of cutting through difference and understanding each other.
Global position and politics	A lack of appreciation of these things by foreigners is created by a polarisation between the West and the non-West.	These particular things cannot be appreciated by foreigners.	Perceptions of global difference, e.g. between the West and non-West, can get in the way of understanding. We need to overcome mutual cultural disbelief.
Cultural resources	Either collectivist or individualist experiences.	Upbringing, memories, places, group loyalties.	Occasions when people from different cultural backgrounds have been able to share and appreciate each other's experiences.
Underlying universal processes	Struggling to make sense of who we are in terms of where we come from and our roots.		

Polarisation

Prejudice is certainly there; and the friends despair at its presence. It is evident, on the left of the table, that prejudice is associated with a lack of appreciation on one's cultural background which is associated with a cultural polarisation in the minds of others. The polarisation is brought about by cultural disbelief.

- Cultural disbelief – that while 'other cultures' have the right to be themselves they present a 'problem' because they are incompatible with an *imagined* Western world view.

On the right of the table there is an exploration of how understanding can overcome this polarisation and also that cultural disbelief can be mutual. Implicit in this understanding is therefore cultural belief.

- Cultural belief – that the cultural background of *any* person is rich and resourceful to the extent that it can be engaged with, learnt from and indeed expanded into.

An immediate word of caution is necessary here, however. Cultural belief does not imply a cultural relativism which allows for anything. It needs to be set against a need for contestation of cultural practices which may appear opposed to the human rights which underpin cultural belief.

The polarisation on the left of the table is a powerful barrier to cultural belief for similar but different reasons. It is both very real in how many people think about culture. However, it is the premise of this book that it is *imagined*, but in different ways.

The polarisation between Western and non-Western realities is imposed by **global position and politics**, and is rooted in the Centre position of the West in defining the rest of the world and pushing non-Western realities to the margins.

The polarisation between collectivism and individualism, in the **cultural resources** domain, has been very much promoted by the academic and training communities in intercultural communication, as well as having been the substance for bugle-calls of opposing identities across the world, within the domain of **statements about culture**.

Ambivalence and struggle

The centre part of Table 8.2 indicates that throughout the narrative the three friends are involved in an ambivalent struggle to make sense. This is also indicated in the **underlying universal cultural processes** which run across all the columns, where the friends all explore each other's experience, which helps to increase their understanding.

It is Gita's experience with Francisca, wherever she comes from, that we must work with – to overcome Gita's temptation to cross to the dark side and believe that there really is a collectivist–individualist divide. It may well be the case that Francisca and Gita can talk deeply because Francisca is somehow on the fringes of whatever this 'Western' domain is, and that people from the non-West *do* have more in common; but I prefer to follow the notion that there is sufficient ground for cultural belief to be attained.

Figure 8.2 shows that the ambivalence which the three friends experience extends into both prejudice and understanding, and that it is the struggle to make sense which enables movement between cultural disbelief and cultural belief. However, the struggle to make sense does move in *both directions*. As discussed in Chapter 4, this struggle, which is implicit in **underlying universal cultural processes** and the deep fabric of **small culture formation**, as well asleading to understanding, can also lead to prejudice through polarised stereotypes, such as individualism and collectivism. The struggle, through ambivalence, is therefore crucial, but must be guided in the right direction.

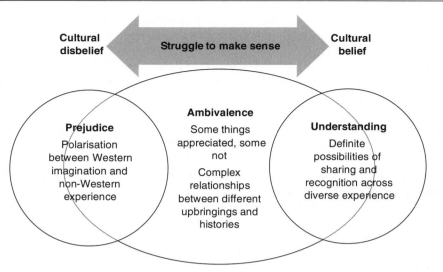

Figure 8.2 Complex struggle

Two principles thus emerge from the discussion between Gita, Hande and Francisca, as they are prepared to expand themselves into the experiences of others:

- The answers are really in front of our eyes if we only look.
- It depends on *where* we begin our gaze, and *what* questions we ask.

The second point relates to the disciplines and methodology employed, as discussed in Chapter 3.

Evaluate the analysis in Table 8.2. How might you write the table differently?

What to ask

Imagine you are making friends with Gita, Hande and Francisca. What sorts of things would you ask them after overhearing their conversation?

What sorts of things might you ask someone from another cultural background who (1) you know, or (2) you have just met?

What can you find from your own background that you might be able to share? Think about:

- family relationships;
- other relationships – self-image, being understood;
- what you like about your environment – sounds, smells, food;
- other things that might cut through to common issues in human experience.

Images of culture

What do you agree or disagree with in what they say? Think particularly about what they say about the West.

Consider examples in your own experience where:

* you have exaggerated something about your culture (what were your reasons?);
* you have found that because of this exaggeration people haven't seen you as you would like to be seen;
* there are things that people would not expect of you which you have exaggerated (what were your reasons?).

Making connections back

Look at the other narratives you have read so far and see what impact the **personal trajectories** of the characters has on what they do and think.

Are there any particular events in your own life which will affect your experience of cultural identity?

The feasibility of cultural belief

Evaluate the statement: 'Most people who struggle with cultural difference rely on stereotypes to help them make sense'.

Look again at the discussion of stereotypes in Chapter 3. Evaluate the statement made by this book that stereotypes encourage cultural disbelief.

Look critically at how you think about people from other cultural backgrounds. Try again the task in Chapter 3 (Watch small groups of people in a public place. What prejudices do you have about them because of their appearance and where you imagine they come from?).

* How often do you sink into cultural disbelief?
* In what circumstances?
* If you manage to rise to cultural belief, what do you learn which helps you to get there?

Alicia, Stefan and banter

Cultural disbelief is a major feature of cultural prejudice, if not the defining feature. Because of the ideology of culturism, it also underpins the innocent discourses of culture listed in Figure 8.1 and is therefore very often denied by those who practise it. The implication is therefore that cultural disbelief itself becomes unrecognised, and this can make it especially harmful for its victims, who have therefore to suffer in silence.

This lack of recognition has already been seen in a number of ethnographic narratives throughout the book. The following narrative[3] returns to Alicia and her experience of banter, first introduced in Chapter 6.

> Feeling attacked and marginalised had become an almost weekly experience for Alicia. It wasn't just what people said, but glances, body language, tone of voice and generally things that you had to think twice about – to be sure that it actually had happened at all, because it was so unbelievable. It was what people referred to as 'banter' – a clever way of making fun of people. It amounted to lots of comments which normally seemed to centre on her coming from an extended family and therefore not having the freedom to do what she wanted.
>
> > 'Oh, I bet if someone came to *your* house they'd have to get through all your aunts and uncles before they could even *speak* to you'.
>
> A lot of it seemed to come from movies and TV dramas – exaggerated images.
> She could certainly see some connection with her background; but most of it was some sort of sensational image. What made it worse was that they just wouldn't let it go. Day after day this image was raised and pushed further and further. No-one in her family had ever had an arranged marriage; and it wasn't common in her society anyway – well, not in *this* century.
>
> > 'We'd better not ask *Alicia* to help us to make a decision; she'd have to get her father's permission first'.
>
> Statements like these were always delivered with laughing; and it was expected that there would be an equally 'humorous' response, something like:
>
> > 'Well at least there'd be some *authority* present'.
>
> But Alicia really didn't want to respond, even if it would be a way of hiding how hurt she was. It seemed to her that making the expected response would mean she was giving in and adopting the norm of the banter. She had once fallen into this trap and found herself saying similarly damaging things to another newcomer. Suddenly she had understood how it worked and had thankfully stopped herself before she had been totally taken in.

Alicia tried to rise above it and to believe what other people said – that this was actually a sign of being received into the group, and even some sort of affection. Her daughter was far better integrated, and sometimes told her that she was reading too much into *some* of the incidents that she described to her.

Alicia reflected that everyone seemed either to indulge in banter or fall victim to it in the work place. Someone had said that it all began at school. She thought there must be something similar in her own society; but it didn't seem quite the same. She did, however, wonder if she didn't see it in her own society because she was an insider to it. She did have some recollection of how new children at her childhood school had suffered from something similar.

She tried to talk about it to her friend, Stefan; and he did seem to understand to a degree what she was talking about. He had travelled widely and often said that he thought immigrants were an important addition to his country's life and culture. He had seen something of the issue in what he had told her about his colleague, Roxana. But then even he would sometimes fall into what seemed to be a very tempting trap, when he laughed and said that what he liked most about her was the *drama* she brought to everything.

When she confronted him with this reference to 'drama', of course he denied that this was anything at all to do with a cultural stereotype. He then said that she really did need to get used to this mild teasing. He was laughing when he said this too; and the look in his eyes implied that coping with banter indicated some sort of moral strength which was lacking in her 'culture'.

Unlike all the other 'categories of cultural action' analyses in this book, the one in Table 8.3 presents a complete division in the **underlying universal cultural processes** domain. In both cases the division is constructed from the domains of opposition in the previous categories. It gives the impression that the entire conceptualisation of banter serves cultural opposition.

Table 8.3 Dealing with banter

Categories of cultural action	Friends and colleagues	Alicia
Statements about culture	'We are able to deal with banter because it is a characteristic of individualism and self-determination.'	'My cultural background does not fit the image projected by this banter.'
Global position and politics	The ability to make decisions independently of family sets us apart from this foreigner.	Distancing from the imagery of 'arranged marriages.'
Cultural resources	Long-standing tradition of banter.	Critical awareness of **global position and politics** (from her experience reported in Chapter 6).
Underlying universal processes	Constructing the above **global position and politics** and **cultural resources** in opposition to Alicia's presence as a foreigner.	Constructing the above **global position and politics** and **cultural resources** in opposition to the imagery implied by the banter.

The source of the conflict of perceptions which gather around banter is not surprising. While Alicia's friends and colleagues seem to think that it is special to their cultural viewpoint, banter may well exist, in essence, in other societies. An example can be seen in this description by Orhan Pamuk from 1970s Istanbul, with 'ragging' being a concept close to banter.

> 'We can stay up all night ragging one another just like we did when we were young. Mehmet is so smitten with Nurcihan he's burning up. Think of the fun we could have with him.'
>
> 'Actually the person you'd be having fun with would be me', I said. 'And anyway, Mehmet and Nurcihan are already a couple.'
>
> 'Believe me, I would never joke at your expense', Zaim said, somewhat hurt. 'Nor would I let anyone else.'
>
> (Pamuk 2011: 297)

Significant features of banter are revealed here. While it is something light-hearted between friends – making fun of Mehmet being in love with Nurcihan – it is thought to be sufficiently aggressive for Zaim to offer to protect his other friend from it. As mentioned at the beginning of the chapter, it is not so much the intention behind the act which is important as its observed effect.

The somewhat complicated Table 8.4 also takes in bullying where the concept of a group is not involved. The 'innocent banter' column has a question mark because one might question whether it is ever possible. Racist and cultural prejudice are in the same column because they are virtually the same. The reference to cohesion and morale in the bottom leftcell is significant because banter is at the core of all the processes of **small culture formation** – where the effect is to force someone into conformity. This is referred to by Alicia in the narrative where she is tempted to conform by bantering back and thus joining the discourse which it inhabits. There are indeed two main choices open to the victim of banter:

1   **Answer back** by using the same mode of banter – 'giving as good as you get' – with the effect of appearing to be undamaged by the banter, joining the group and perhaps becoming an active banterer at the expense of others.
2   **Don't answer back** and maintain the outsider, or even outcast position.

Table 8.4 For and against

	Innocent banter?	Bullying	Plus cultural or racist prejudice
Statements	Aimed at circumstances, personality, appearance, behaviour, attitudes or an individual.		... as representative of a cultural group or race.
Effect	To make fun, increase group cohesion or morale, inculcate preferred behaviour or values.	... and to demoralise, marginalise, exclude, belittle, Other.	

Banter

Analyse the examples of banter in the narrative.

- Are they really examples of cultural prejudice?
- If so, how?

What is the equivalent of banter in your own language and society? See the reference to 'playful banter' in the discussion in the Alicia narrative in Chapter 6, as well as the reference from Orhan Pamuk, above.

Recall one of your own experiences as a victim of banter.

- Is 'victim' the right term?
- How would you position your experience with regard to Table 8.4?
- What choices did you have, and what action did you take – remembering that inaction is also action?

Recall one of your own experiences of being an instigator of banter.

- What were the circumstances?
- What information did you base the banter on?
- What were your intentions?
- Was it, really, in any way innocent?

To what degree can it be argued that banter (1) can be harmless and indeed a positive contribution to moral and social cohesion, or (2) is always harmful?

Considering all of this:

- Should Alicia stop being so negative and learn to cope?
- Is she really being the victim of cultural prejudice?
- If the latter, what should she do?

Summary

- Cultural prejudice, or culturism, is closely associated with racism. It may be considered as neo-racism, or a racism which is hidden beneath references to culture.
- The paradox of cultural prejudice is that it is not recognised within innocent discourses of culture, which do not think of themselves as discourses or as products of ideology. Cultural prejudice therefore falls within the domain of easy answers and is very difficult to shake.
- Cultural prejudice is underpinned by ideology, which pervades the deep fabric of **small culture formation**.

- People who display cultural prejudice may well be the same people who distance themselves from or disapprove of it, and who may also display high principles with regard to criticality and being anti-establishment. Soft interpretations of interactions which involve cultural prejudice may divert attention from it. Both instigators and victims of cultural prejudice may benefit from soft interpretations which divert attention away from it because there are Self and Other benefits from working together.
- Cultural disbelief in the attributes and abilities of the foreign Other is a major factor in cultural prejudice. This results in a polarisation between an imagined deficient Other and an imagined proficient Self. Cultural belief is an important antidote to prejudice, but should not imply a cultural relativism in which there is not contestation.
- The struggle to make sense of cultural difference is crucial in reducing prejudice. However, this struggle can produce an ambivalence which can also result in either cultural belief or disbelief.
- Banter can be a major cause of cultural prejudice. This may not be recognised because of the contribution of banter to **small culture formation**.

Notes

1 This was a public inquiry following the murder of Stephen Lawrence in 1993, a Black British teenager from south-east London, during a racist attack.
2 This narrative is based upon an actual meeting event and the reflections of the observer and others who were consulted.
3 This is based on a number of conversations with colleagues, students and friends about being bullied under cover of banter or teasing.

Further reference

Wodak, R. (2008). 'Us and them': inclusion and exclusion. In Delanty, G., Wodak, R. and Jones, P. (eds), *Identity, belonging and migration*. Liverpool: Liverpool University Press: 54–77.
  — A discussion of the denial of racism in everyday talk which claims to be supportive.

Holliday, A.R. (2011). *Intercultural communication & ideology*. London: Sage.
  — Pages 157–62 offer an analysis of the racism issues emerging from the *Big Brother* television reality show.

If you like banter you're an idiot: http://blogs.telegraph.co.uk/news/tomchivers science/100141906/if-you-like-banter-you-are-an-idiot
  — A media discussion about the nature of banter.

John Terry case: racist abuse or sarcastic banter? http://www.guardian.co.uk/ football/2012/jul/09/john-terry-case-racist-language
  — A court case to decide whether or not a White footballer's banter was racist.

The single story phenomenon: http://www.youtube.com/watch?v=D9Ihs241zeg
  — Nigerian novelist Chimamanda Adichie talks about the problem of only having very few media or literary images to represent who you are.

Fairclough, N. (1995). *Critical discourse analysis: the critical study of language.* London: Addison Wesley Longman.
  — Page 72 provides discussion of how ideologies cut across discourse boundaries and bring together diverse forces of prejudice.

Chapter 9

Cultural travel and innovation

This chapter deals with the way in which cultural experience and competence can be carried from one location to another. It counters the common expectation that newcomers have an inherent disadvantage because cultural lines can never fully be crossed.

A significant part of the focus of this book has been the **underlying universal cultural processes** domain of the grammar within which people from varied cultural backgrounds are able to share common abilities in everyday **small culture formation**. The narratives throughout the book have involved characters from a variety of cultural backgrounds. In all cases, the final band in the 'categories of cultural action' analyses has indicated that every one of the characters have shared **underlying universal cultural processes** regardless of whether they are newcomers or original residents of the settings involved. Where there have been inequalities, these have concerned cultural Othering and prejudice rather than foreignness per se.

Figure 9.1 shows the central role of **underlying universal cultural processes** in how cultural newcomers are able to transfer experience into a new cultural environment. On the left of the figure are the sources of this experience in the places from which the newcomers originate – in the **small culture formation** which they have lived on a daily basis 'on the run', for most of us beginning with engaging with the family next door, as described in Chapter 3 and throughout the book.

The figure also refers, on the right, to the **negotiating individual versus social structure** domain of the grammar, the subject of Chapter 5. This brings the full weight of what we

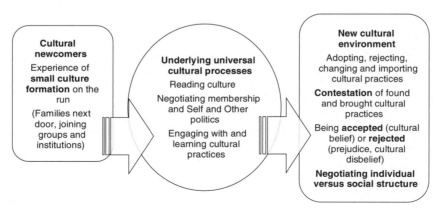

Figure 9.1 The architecture of cultural travel

bring with us as **cultural resources** when we travel to new places. This, in turn, causes us to combat or throw aside prejudices, which leads to accepting or being accepted by the people we encounter through cultural belief, or rejecting or being rejected by them through cultural disbelief, which have been discussed in Chapter 8, adopting or rejecting cultural practices themselves, and the process of cultural contestation. These elements are resonant of the politics and the personal choices which influence all aspects of intercultural behaviour.

Reading Figure 9.1

Map the different parts of the figure onto the narratives and chapters throughout the book.

Consider how the figure fits with your own life experience. What might you add to or change in the figure?

To what extent do you agree that this model of cultural travel is different from the expected? In what respect does it not represent an easy answer?

John abroad: politeness and space

An important and perhaps unexpected aspect of cultural travel is the possibility of innovation, which connects with the reference to importing cultural practices at the bottom right of Figure 9.1. The following narrative[1] exemplifies how cultural travel can result in innovation.

Act 1: Shock

The two months in which John lived with his wife's family changed his life forever. In many ways everything that he took for granted was different. Apart from food, language and climate, a lot of it was to do with space and politeness. He was lucky that his brother- and sister-in-law could speak his language, which made some meta-communication[2] possible about the things he found strange.

It began with initial greetings. In most conversations he was desperate to ask questions and get answers; but somehow this just didn't seem possible. At the beginning of every interaction there had to be some – or indeed quite a lot of – time spent asking people how they and members of their family were. This did remind him of visiting his grandparents when he was a child and always talking about the journey, how long it had taken and what the traffic was like. He also felt quite annoyed that even his wife's family referred to him as 'Mr John'.

Then there was the business of sitting down to eat. There were no place settings. Instead of having that small portion of territory marked by a squared mat and knife, fork and spoon, it was more like a sit-down buffet.[3] Everyone helped themselves from stacked plates and cutlery, and then from food in central dishes, and sat and ate where there was a space. There was, however, some conflict between this practice and a photograph he had seen the day before of a laid-out table for a formal wedding dinner. Then he thought that increasingly at home people ate on their laps in front of the television.

It was some time later, when the family were sitting around talking and his brother-in-law turned round to him and said 'excuse my back', that he began to realise that, in this place where everyone seemed to sit so close that they were almost on top of each other, this was not after all a free-for-all, and that personal space was as important as where he came from. It was something to do with this that conversations needed to begin with pleasantries. He had been told that he was being too invasive and abrupt when he wanted to begin every conversation with business.

Act 2: Reconciliation and a bigger picture

Many years later, when he was 'at home', John found he was still influenced by what he had learnt during those years of working out how to deal with a 'foreign culture'.

Even in work meetings he was conscious of considering the personal space of the people he was with – not turning his back, always at least thinking about what needed to be said before getting down to business. He had also learnt to understand that thinking that 'place settings' were all that were needed to ensure 'safe territory' was really very superficial.

He felt that he had generally become more observant of who people were and what their personal needs might be. Having got used to always placing some sort of title or honorific, like 'dear', he always used this with his wife and family, even when speaking in front of others. Although he did not use these phrases with other people, knowledge of them had somehow made him more aware of their personal status. Perhaps most important, he had made considerable progress in understanding that his wife did not after all come from a 'collectivist culture'. They just did very much the same things as he did, but in different ways.

The 'categories of cultural action' analysis in Table 9.1 tries to make sense of this narrative through 'before' and 'after' columns. Within the 'before' column there is a considerable degree of shifting between initial and eventual understanding. Significantly, in the **cultural resources** domain, there is already reference to the foreign setting in the 'before' column and this becomes very prominent in the 'after' column. Even though act 2 of the narrative takes place many years later, reference back to memories of another society remains powerful.

The key to the deeper understanding implicit in the narrative is John's ability to draw connections between the strange new cultural practices he encounters and familiar practices from his own background. This experience adds to interrogation of the 'third space' discourse. This discourse encourages the notion of an uncrossable line between two cultures. Being able to carry practices from one cultural reality to another suggests instead a very porous and negotiable line.

Table 9.1 Preparedness to engage

Categories of cultural action	'Before' – when in an unfamiliar cultural setting	'After' – on returning to a familiar cultural setting
Statements about culture	Initial: 'My culture is different to this one in that we do not begin every interaction with extended pleasantries, we have place-settings at mealtimes.' Eventual: 'We share deeper considerations regarding personal space.'	'There are deeper complexities which need to be looked for and observed.' 'Unfamiliar practices can enhance our own.'
Global position and politics	Initial expectations that the foreign culture collectivist is in opposition to his individualist culture. Eventual realisation that this is not the case.	
Cultural resources	Mode of greeting and introductions when visiting grandparents. Variations in eating styles at home. Evidence of complexity and apparent contradictions in the foreign location which resonate with his own society.	Experience in a foreign cultural location.
Underlying universal processes	Eventually seeing transferable universalities regarding personal space.	

Carrying cultural practices

Consider a foreign cultural practice you have encountered which changed your life on returning home.

- Is there anything from your own background which helped you to understand it?
- What have you taken away from the experience which has changed your own behaviour at home?

Third space?

Evaluate the proposition that John's experience goes against the notion of a third space on the basis of crossing cultural lines.

- To what extent is it possible to incorporate a new cultural practice into a cultural environment in such a way that it might integrate and enrich it?
- What chance is there that the new cultural practice might catch on and be adopted more broadly?
- Or is it instead the case that John's carrying over of a foreign cultural practice is simply an example of him creating a third space within his own culture in order to deal with the shock of return?

Eccentricity

Could it be that John is simply eccentric in his adoption of foreign practices?

Recall examples of returned travellers who have brought back 'foreign practices' – clothes, artefacts, modes of behaviour and so on. What is your opinion of them?

Cultural change

It is a major thesis of this book, which, it is claimed, is grounded in everyday reality, that 'cultural realities' have blurred boundaries with multiple opportunities for cross-over and sharing – what might be referred to as transcultural flows. While John represents an individual case of carrying practice from one place to another, the adoption, absorption, integration and mediation of foreign cultural practices is a widespread phenomenon. The following are just two examples in recent British society.

- The long-standing practice of saying 'I'm very well' when asked how one is increasingly being replaced by the American response, 'I'm good'. While 'very well' is an adverb and has always implied good health, 'good' is an adjective and would have originally implied 'good person'. Even though this new practice therefore goes against a long-standing usage, it is quickly working its way through all age groups and classes. It probably originates from popular American comedy dramas such as *Friends*.
- With the increase of café chains such as *Starbucks*, *Costa* and *Caffè Nero*, and many others, there is a growing tendency for significant numbers of people to walk around in work and public settings with tall cardboard cups of coffee. At work they bring them to even the most formal meetings; they take them on buses and trains. The word 'tall' has come to refer to a size of coffee cup. It is often thought that this trend originates in America, but it may be a far more complex worldwide phenomenon.

Cultural change and innovation

What is the difference between these two concepts?

Explain, from the cases provided so far in this chapter, which are change and which are innovation.

Think of and reconstruct examples from your own experience.

- Consider sport, fashion, clothing, food, entertainment and ceremonies.
- Try to trace their origin.
- How widespread are such changes?
- What are the features of these changes that make them sustainable?
- How did they come about?
- What impact did they have?
- In what sense are they a normal part of society?

- In what sense do they, and examples like them, take up the larger part of what is going on in society?

Evaluate the statement that society is always in a state of flux.

Wary of relativism

An important consideration in cultural change and innovation is that it should *not* be seen as cultural relativism. This is a common notion which I am going to add to the list of discourses presented in Chapter 7.

The 'cultural relativism' discourse is closely related to the 'liberal multicultural' discourse in that it projects an image of different but equal 'cultures' and encourages the view that 'anything goes'. This implication is that practices that belong to another culture are sacred to that culture and should therefore be respected. I would like to argue that this is an essentialist and an innocent discourse because it presumes that the culture and cultural practice in question are bound to each other as a solid entity and implies a negative view in which 'This is what they do; they are different to us; let them get on with it.'

Safa and her friends: cherries, paying and serving

Belief in cultural change and innovation derives from the 'critical cosmopolitan' discourse which says that we are all part of the same, bigger world. Everyone has an equal potential for cosmopolitanism. However, this cosmopolitan context brings practices from different cultural environments into a juxtaposition which might lead to contestation. This can be seen in the following narrative,[4] where three young people describe their involvement in cultural innovation.

Act 1: Integration

Safa had been a student here for three years and was enjoying her time. She had spent the first year living with a local family and now shared a flat with two local students who she felt she had a decent enough relationship with. They were all very busy and did not really get in each other's way. She also had a part-time job in a local shop and felt fairly well integrated into the society.

When she was interviewed on the topic of cultural travel and change, she talked about two specific things. When she had first arrived she had been annoyed at the way in which people here always insisted on paying for themselves in restaurants, especially when this resulted in clumsy and, in her view, embarrassing discussions about how much each person should contribute towards the bill. She had thought that this was very petty; and she missed the immense feeling of warmth and friendship when people paid for each other at home.

Then, after some time, she began to see things differently and to value the independence which the practice of sharing brought. She no longer had to worry about when she had to pay. This was especially good for students who didn't have much money, and who could, with this system, be freer in their choices.

This experience and adoption of a new cultural practice had also influenced her behaviour with her friends when she went home, and actually encouraged them to pay for themselves when they went out together. However, it wasn't just her who was instigating this cultural change. Paying for one's self was becoming the new trend among young people across her society. The practice could also be seen in television series; and waiters in restaurants were now very quick to help with the calculations. There was even a new phrase in her language which would be roughly translated as 'paying free'. One of the credit card companies had caught onto the idea and showed fashionable young people 'paying free' by placing their credit cards alongside each other on the restaurant table. When she told her friends here about this they said that there had been a similar advert on their television years before.

There was, however, a tacit limitation to this change in behaviour. It was certainly thought to be 'incorrect' practice not to share the bill equally; and this led in turn to a new social protocol – not to order items which were a lot more expensive than one's friends, so as not to have the advantage over them when paying. Hence, it had become normal, when thinking about ordering, to be openly cooperative regarding the 'level' of expense. Someone would therefore say something like, 'So what are we going to go for this evening, top, medium or low level?'. This would indicate, for example, how much wine, how many courses, and so on. It was therefore clear to Safa that even though this new practice had been brought from abroad, it had certainly taken on a distinctly indigenous flavour, which was far more elegant and less messy than the practice as she had encountered it here. She was actually quite proud of the young people in her country for their inventiveness at sorting things out.

Another thing she mentioned was a practice from home which she had only recently had the courage to introduce into her life as a foreigner here. Where she was brought up it was a tradition, when cherries came into season and were being sold in the market on the way to work, to buy some to share with one's colleagues. The reason why she had not felt she could do this here was somehow connected with the same business of paying for other people. She had noticed that people here got very embarrassed if you gave them anything without payment. They would reach into their pockets for even the smallest amount of money. She was led to believe by her friends that this attitude to money was connected to a Protestant ethos and therefore very hard to shake. Nevertheless, as with most things cultural, she had begun to learn, nothing was straightforward; and as she became more familiar with the complexities of everyday life, she did observe that there were occasions where sharing and giving took place, which was a little bit similar to what she was used to. For example, people working in the same office, if it was a small office, might offer to get coffee for each other, and may take it in turns rather than taking payment.

Safa therefore chose an office in which she knew the people very well to experiment, and took them each a small mug of cherries as an experiment. It was very well received; and she began to feel that she could at last be herself while living here.

Act 2: Conflict

After describing these developments in the interview, Safa discussed her experience with two friends who worked together in a hardware store in the main shopping area. They were also foreign students who had this job to supplement their scholarships. They said that they had been quite successful for a while in introducing a mode of serving customers which was very normal to them but surprisingly very culturally strange to people here. It was simply the practice of serving more than one customer at once. It seemed very natural to them to answer queries from the next customer who was waiting while the first customer was pausing to make a decision about something. They said that they actually found it strange to explain it like this because when they were working it was just a spontaneous thing. This was, after all, how they had always been used to being served at home. Sometimes they could even get onto a third waiting customer if the second could be dealt with quickly or also had to make a decision.

Well, it certainly was not a 'normal' thing for their employer. Even though quite a number of the actual customers seemed to like the practice, *he* certainly did not. In the end he asked that they return to the 'normal' practice of not serving a second customer until the business with the first one had been completely finished. He said that the customers wouldn't like the new practice and was worried about complaints. To keep their jobs they conformed to what he wanted. Safa shared their amazement at this. However, she had certainly noticed, while she had been spending time waiting, how people serving here would not even make eye contact with other customers who were waiting – obviously afraid of any possibility of making any sort of contact. It was so time wasting!

The 'categories of cultural action' analysis in Table 9.2 unusually does not deal with inter-actants, but with the separate experiences of Safa and her two friends. Putting this under the heading of transcendence emphasises that, more than with other narratives, the analysis shows that in each category there is a noticeable interplay between experiences from home and from the new cultural environment. There is also evidence that understanding one is helped by experience of the other.

Therefore, in the **statements about culture** domain, while Safa's statement about 'we' being sharing and warm is in opposition to what she finds in the new environment, her later observation about making things work, to be 'more civilised' is to do with how the foreign is incorporated and managed at home. While both sets of statements must be seen as easy answers, the final two are more analytical and might indicate a greater degree of maturity as a result of the experience of cultural change.

Similarly, in the **cultural resources** domain, the second, third and fourth resources listed for Safa derive either from her experience of living abroad or a comparison between this and what she had brought with her. While her knowledge of 'paying free' is from home, it could be argued that she would not have externalised this experience if it had not been brought to her attention by her experience away from home. Part of her success in introducing the foreign practice of paying is her ability to adapt it to existing norms. Also significant, the

Table 9.2 Transcendent experience

Categories of cultural action	Safa	Safa's friends
Statements about culture	Before change: 'We pay for each other in restaurants and share with each other because we value warmth and friendship.' After change: 'We have our own ways of making the "paying free" practice more civilised. 'We can sort things out and make them work.'	'This is how we normally do things.'
Global position and politics	Initial caution about being too strange and foreign. Wary of a Protestant ethic that might oppose the behaviour she brought with her.	Conforming with authority in order to keep jobs.
Cultural resources	Being part of a warm friendship group at home. Discovery of the new popular concept of 'paying free' at home. Experience of paying for oneself and a different expectation about personal space while living abroad. Mastery of new cultural practices both at home and abroad.	Experiencing the cultural practice of being served at home.
Underlying universal processes	Finding ways of being oneself in an unfamiliar cultural environment by analysing new cultural practices through experience of **small culture formation** in familiar and unfamiliar locations. Observing and waiting for sufficient knowledge and the right time and then experimenting.	Externalising tacit understandings of what is normal. Monitoring the progress of their behaviour and observing reactions. Negotiating with authority.

final resource which is listed concerns mastery of a new cultural practice. This process of successful cultural learning has not before been considered as a resource.

In the **underlying universal cultural processes** domain, both Safa and her friends are simultaneously making sense of familiar and unfamiliar cultural environments. Her friends externalise their experience of being served at home perhaps only because they have to engage with serving others in the new environment. This externalisation may indeed be the source of their own **statements about culture**.

The **global position and politics** domain in the table makes reference to the mention in the narrative of the Protestant ethic on the part of Safa. This may be a fear rather than an actuality, as may be the case in many situations. It is nevertheless significant that Safa positions herself in this way in rationalising her actions. Safa's friends, on the right, do not so much claim global and institutional politics. They give in to their employer's demand that they should behave according to the 'normal practice' allegedly preferred by the customers. In the narrative, on hearing about this, Safa does make the connection with the Protestant ethic.

Interplay of experience

Recall and describe cases in your own experience where:

- encountering unfamiliar cultural practices abroad has helped you to recall, externalise and better understand cultural practices at home;
- engagement with cultural practices abroad and understanding how they work became part of your **cultural resources**;
- knowledge of cultural practices at home has helped you to understand and engage with unfamiliar practices abroad;
- your whole perception about your home cultural environment, and your **statements about culture**, changed and deepened as a result of such experiences;
- your **cultural resources** expanded and developed as a result of cultural travel.

Recall and reconstruct a time when you took part in cultural innovation in your home society or abroad (1) with something small in your own behaviour, and (2) as part of a larger social innovation.

- What exactly happened?
- What **underlying universal cultural processes** and **cultural resources** did you employ, and what were their origins?
- How did your **statements about culture** change?
- How successful were you, and what evidence is there for this?

Values

Safa's dissatisfaction with the way in which people in her new cultural environment sorted out the bill in restaurants, even after she had decided to adopt 'paying free', seems to relate to values.

Look at the discussion of values in Chapter 2 and attempt to sort out what is going on here. Is this a negative or positive use of values? What are the reasons for your decision?

What works?

There are a number of factors connected to the three attempts at cultural innovation, both successful and unsuccessful, in the Safa narrative:

Successful:
- Sustained experience of a new practice, with insights into its deeper workings (e.g. considerable observation of behaviour and reflection regarding its consequences).
- Analysis of the new practice in the light of previous experience.
- Finding ways to adopt the new practice in a meaningful manner which is authentic to the cultural background of the adopter.

- Satisfying Self and Other identity requirements (constructing a mode of the practice which is distanced from the manner in which it is originally carried out – e.g. not messy and embarrassing).
- Integrating the new practice into existing structures and norms (e.g. applying existing behavioural norms – being organised and egalitarian).
- The development of existing behavioural norms to accommodate the new practice (e.g. new language forms – 'paying free', 'top, medium or low level').
- The innovation taking on a life of its own within the fabric of society (e.g. in the media and advertising, in the development of new language forms).

Unsuccessful:
- The first four factors above.
- Opposition from powerful stakeholders (e.g. the owner of the institution).
- Insufficient power and status to oppose this opposition (e.g. depending on employment).

It is important to note here that this is not a list of conditions for success or failure, but observations from the narrative. The movement between success and failure is implicit in the two arrows at the top and bottom of the grammar. Left to right at the top, **negotiating individual versus social structure**, is in effect what John, in the first narrative, and Safa and her two friends, in the second, are doing as they struggle to establish new practice. Right to left at the bottom, **confirming or resisting social structure**, represents supportive or oppositional response of the dominant structures into which the change is being projected. This is also in the hands of the other people involved. In the case of Safa's friends it is the shop keeper who confirms the existing social structure in the act of confirming what he considers 'normal'. In the case of Safa, it is her friends and the wider system within which the media and advertising become active which responds to this social structure and confirms the change.

Clearly significant is Safa's knowledge brought from her previous cultural experience, and her overall ability to analyse and assess based on this cultural traveller experience, as indicated in Figure 9.1. The development of the new language forms is also significant in the confirmation of the social structure. This indicates the development of a discourse, which plays a key role in **small culture formation**, as discussed with reference to the introduction of 'Smart Project Management' in Chapter 4 in the narrative about engineering conformity.

Factors in cultural change

Connect the factors in the above list with the details in the two narratives in this chapter.

Consider the role of new language, 'paying free', 'top, medium or low level' in the new practice of paying in the Safa narrative.

- Recall a case of cultural innovation in which a practice has been brought from a foreign cultural environment, which has also integrated with local practices.

- What are the details of the integration?
- What features or artefacts are taken from the local cultural environment, and how are they incorporated? What makes this incorporation successful?
- In what sense is a discourse being created? Look back at the example of baby-led weaning in Chapter 4 and compare. What are the gains and losses?

Looking back at Figure 9.1, on the right-hand side there is reference to contestation and acceptance or resistance.

Contestation, acceptance and rejection

Contestation is a normal part of cultural change and innovation. It involves the critiquing of an existing cultural practice. Indeed, it is a normal, everyday part of **small culture formation** in the sense that we are all constantly reviewing our own cultural practices and those with which we engage.

In the Safa narrative, she contests both the cultural practice of paying for oneself which she finds in her new country of residence and, subsequently, as her experience increases, the practice of paying for each other in her country of origin. Her two friends contest the practice of serving customers one-by-one in their new country of residence. Then, during the process of accepting change in her country of origin, Safa continues to contest the practice of paying in her new country; and the final version of 'paying free' contains features from both its country of origin and its new location. Safa then goes on to contest the fact that sharing with friends and colleagues is not acceptable in her new country of residence, which leads her, through further investigation, to find a way of introducing it.

Acceptance and rejection also feature from both sides. Safa's contestation of paying behaviour in her new country leads her initially to reject it, but, on further reflection, to accept it with modification. Part of this modification is Safa's continued rejection of what she considers to be the clumsy way in which people in her new country haggle over paying. There is rejection to the innovation presented by Safa's friends, the shop assistants, by their employer.

Contestation, rejection or acceptance can derive from deeper ideological factors. This is fairly mild in the Safa narrative. She is concerned about the inhibition of independence in the paying-for-each-other practice in her home country, but the stakes are relatively low. She does not anticipate the confrontation which is described in the next narrative.

Safa: 'when are you going back?'

The following narrative is an example of contestation of the cultural innovation coming not from Safa and her friends, but from people both in her new and home cultural environment. This contestation itself then takes on the form of resistance:

Safa's feeling of achievement at having found a way to be herself, in mixing the best of her experiences at home and abroad, was soon spoilt by attacks that came from both sides.

The first attack came from her old friend from home, Rita, who came to visit her while she was still studying abroad. Rita complained bitterly about how their 'culture' was changing. She referred very specifically to 'the whole business' of 'paying free', and how it was eroding their national traditions. There was something called 'return civility' which would soon be only practised by the older generation. She described how there had recently been a family gathering in a local restaurant. They had been going to this restaurant ever since the owner and her father had been childhood friends. So it was even more embarrassing, in front of people they had all known for years, when one of the younger cousins had announced in a very loud voice that she was sick and tired of this whole 'return civility' thing, and how she and her friends were so pleased to be breaking away from it. Thank God she had not started asking everyone to 'pay free'.

The young cousin had, however, mentioned Safa as someone who had inspired her and her friends – coming back to visit so confidently from living in the country where these new ideas originated. Now that she was here, Rita said that she could see that Safa fitted in too well and no longer seemed like one of them at all. She said that she knew all about globalisation and that this was a steady movement to them losing their culture and to becoming Westernised. She noted that Safa even had to think sometimes what language she was speaking in.

Safa was horrified that anyone would think that she was one of these people who forgot their native language, or, more likely, pretended to so that they could appear Westernised. Such people always looked down on where they came from. In her own view she was just the opposite to this image – a nationalist in the sense that she felt that where she came from had a huge and sophisticated culture and history – and although she loved to travel, she would always miss her home country.

This did not, however, mean that she couldn't be critical, as were so many of the younger generation. Her parents may not seem so critical at the moment, but they had carried out a revolution in their youth. She could understand where Rita was coming from because she'd met other people like her, who didn't seem to realise that the strength of their nation was far deeper than surface traditions. Anyway, as she had told the researcher during her interview, the way in which 'paying free' had been given meaning by young people and the media possessed the distinct character of her country.

From the other side, which was less painful because it happened all the time, and one just got used to it, was the response she often got from the people here, even from some of them whom she had considered to be friends. They weren't as confrontational as Rita had been, and most of it was under the veil of praise – how well she had integrated, become 'like them'. Sometimes she thought that they had been talking to Rita – when they also told her she had 'become Westernised' – except, whereas Rita took this as a sign of loss, they clearly thought it was a gain, an accomplishment. And it was certainly as though everything she did well was attributed to being 'like them', as though she had brought nothing with her. Sometimes they seemed to show disappointment that she was no longer 'authentic' – by which they seemed to mean something like 'ethnic'. Sometimes she felt that they could not accept her at all, except as being 'like them' or as being 'ethnic'.

> Certainly, there seemed to be no understanding that she could be totally herself without being 'ethnic'. In their eyes, she had to be 'wild' or 'tamed'. Loren, whom she thought she had got to know really well, showed huge surprise when she was playing the Beatles when he visited her, and not her 'own music'. Even Rita considered Frank Sinatra as her favourite musician. If Loren saw the contents on Rita's iPod he would be astonished, and think that she was no longer 'authentic' too. On one occasion she felt she made a big mistake in telling Loren about her attitudes to people paying for themselves and the development of 'paying free' in her own country. He started going on about how good it was when the 'rest of the world' learnt from 'the Western ethos of self-determination'. Safa literally felt herself collapsing inside. Who on Earth did he think he was – presuming to take such a moral high ground?
>
> This 'us–them' way of talking made it very clear to her that she would never be accepted as completely 'like them'. What really did hurt her was when this 'friend' asked her what she was 'going to do' when she 'returned home'. How dare he presume that she was ever going to 'return home'!

The points of view in this narrative have already been seen in previous narratives in the book. Rita shares a 'West versus the rest' discourse with Francisca in Chapter 2 and Jahan in Chapter 7. Safa's experience with Loren and other acquaintances in the country where she is living are similar to those of Alicia and Roxana in Chapter 6, who are facing a mixture of 'West as steward' and 'liberal multicultural' discourses. Any departure from what is considered to be 'her culture' is perceived as evidence of loss of authenticity. Safa is thought to be no longer a 'real' member of her own 'culture'.

Cultural belief and disbelief

Very prominent is the cultural disbelief which emerges on the part of Loren. It can also be argued that Rita's fear of cultural loss is a form of cultural disbelief that her cultural heritage is not more profound than its realisation in the traditions that she describes. Safa also sees cultural disbelief among her countrypeople who she feels deny their heritage, and from whom she distances herself.

To counter both Loren's cultural disbelief and Rita's anxieties, Safa nevertheless draws on a deeper engagement with her cultural background in which she does not feel that anything is lost, and to analyse Rita's perspective. She does this with a firm cultural belief in what she is doing.

Facing prejudice

Recall and reconstruct a time when you faced criticism similar to that of Loren.

- What were the circumstances?
- How effective was this in stopping what you were doing? Why or why not?
- What do you think motivated the criticism, and how justified was it?

In what sense is Loren's criticism not that unusual?

Have you ever found yourself behaving like Loren?

- What were your reasons?
- Were you aware how prejudiced you might have been?
- Are there any justifications for your actions?

The arguments

Evaluate the proposition that (1) Safa's adoption of paying for oneself, and (2) the adoption of 'paying free' in her country, are not evidence of Westernisation. What are the reasons for and against?

Evaluate Rita's argument that there is a loss of culture. What are the reasons for and against?

Which other characters in the narratives throughout the book present arguments similar to Safa's about a deeper sense of national identity which is not damaged by cultural change?

Is Safa right in thinking that Rita is hypocritical because of what she has on her iPod?

Is Safa just taking all of this too seriously? What is your justification for your judgement?

Cultural disbelief and belief

Evaluate the proposition that Rita and Loren are guilty of cultural disbelief. What are the reasons for your judgement?

On the basis of the narrative and other examples throughout the book, list the basic features of cultural disbelief and belief.

Analysis

Carry out a 'categories of cultural action' analysis of the narrative.

Achieving intercultural communication

In many ways Safa achieves the aims of this book in how she carries out and manages cultural innovation.

She demonstrates the deeper nature of what can be achieved by individual people in dialogue with the larger **particular social and political structures** across cultural boundaries. In terms of **cultural resources**, she employs multiple resources both from her home and new cultural environments. Each set are enhanced by the other, especially in cases where she understands something about the inner workings of cultural practices as they adapt themselves to innovation. In her home environment this is connected with a dynamic youth scene.

Regarding **global position and politics**, she engages with her own opinions and the opinions of others with regard to values associated with the cultural practices that concern her. Despite being positioned as non-Western or Westernised by others, she is able to negotiate this positioning and find herself within it. She nevertheless faces prejudices; and how far she is able to overcome them remains to be seen.

In her **personal trajectory**, Safa has travelled and come to terms with living in a new cultural environment. She has carried cultural preferences from her home environment and eventually learnt how to revive aspects of them in her new environment. She has also acquired a liking for new cultural practices encountered in the new environment and found ways to carry them back and integrate them into her original cultural environment.

Regarding **small culture formation**, Safa does not simply adopt or reject new cultural practices, or try to introduce cultural practices from her home environment. Finding a way to engage with new practices on her own terms leads her into analysis of how they operate and to become skilful in establishing her position. **Artefacts** play a significant role in the cultural innovation which Safa engages with – restaurant bills, credit cards, specialist language, the media, fruit, mugs and iPods.

Her **statements about culture** also change, as can be seen in Table 9.2, from a more limited 'We pay for each other in restaurants and share with each other because we value warmth and friendship' to a more sophisticated 'We have our own ways of making the "paying free" practice more civilised, and we can sort things out and make them work'. After her encounter with Rita and Loren, these will perhaps move further to something like 'Our cultural heritage is deeper than Rita believes – more than "return civility" – and is big enough to take in "paying free"'.

Negotiating individual versus social structure was discussed briefly above after the first Safa narrative. Her encounter with Rita causes Safa to further consider her position regarding the social structure of her country of origin. Whether or not she **confirms or resists this social structure** depends on which version she believes in – her own expanded one, in which case she will conform, or Rita's version, in which case she seems to be rejecting. One way of looking at this is that she and Rita live in different versions of their country of origin.

Summary

- Cultural newcomers bring everyday experience of **small culture formation** on the run from their home cultural environment, which enables them to have extended experience in engaging with the cultural practices they find in the new cultural environment.
- In achieving this extended experience, there can be a cross-referencing of **cultural resources** between the home and new cultural environments; and memories of the new environment can remain influential long after returning home.
- The potential to carry culture experience from home to new environments and back again implies a porous intercultural line which problematises the third space concept which implies an inability to succeed across cultural lines.
- In all societies cultural change is a normal part of social life. This indicates that societies are always in a state of flux.

- At the core of cultural change is the evaluation of found and brought cultural practices. This problematises the 'cultural relativism' discourse which projects the idea that 'anything goes' and implies an essentialist disbelief that what other people do can compete with one's own cultural preferences.
- The notion of cultural change instead supports a 'critical cosmopolitan' discourse. This acknowledges that, through the juxtaposition of brought and found cultural practices, contestation will be encouraged.
- **Statements about culture** and the attitudes that underpin them can change as a result of taking part in cultural innovation.
- Success in adapting to new cultural practices might be enhanced by the ability to engage with them creatively and innovatively, simultaneously making sense of the familiar and the unfamiliar.
- Successful cultural innovation needs to be authentic to the people involved, which might involve integrations into existing structures, and a knowledge of what these structures involve.
- Imported cultural practices may therefore produce new practices which have not been seen before.
- Contestation, acceptance or rejection can involve deeper ideological factors which come from **global position and politics**, as will cultural belief and cultural disbelief in the authenticity of the innovation.

Notes

1 This is based on personal experience, interviews with and observation of competent professionals and others in workplace and other settings.
2 Meta-communication is when you stand outside what you are doing and talk about it.
3 A buffet is a relatively formal eating event when diners help themselves to food laid out on a table and take it away to eat either standing or sitting away from the table.
4 This is based on interviews, observation of serving and waiting behaviour in shops, of how cultural innovation can be supported and capitalised upon by media and business, and of the way in which young people in particular cultural environments work together to organise social actions.

Further reference

Holliday, A.R. (2011). *Intercultural communication & ideology*. London: Sage.
— Pages 164–7 offer a discussion of the third space.
— Pages 170–8 offer a discussion of cultural innovation.

Holliday, A.R. (2012). Interrogating researcher participation in an interview study of intercultural contribution in the workplace. *Qualitative Inquiry* 18/6: 504–15.
— This is an analysis of the nature of an interview to explore appropriate research methodology.
— It is, however, also about the experiences of cultural travel and innovation in the workplace, looking at the experiences of a successful professional woman who arrived as an immigrant during her late teens.

Khorsandi, S. (2009). *A beginner's guide to acting English*. London: Ebury Press.
— While on the surface light-hearted, this is a deep and critical look at the experience of immigration and integration into a found society.

Shamsie, K. (2009). *Burnt shadows*. London: Bloomsbury.
— This is the story of an intensely modern Japanese woman's cultural travel from surviving the nuclear bombing of Nagasaki to integrate deeply with Pakistani society and then the US.
— The three above references are significant because they are about individuals who find themselves relatively alone in foreign locations rather than as part of immigrant communities.

Risager, K. (2011). Linguaculture and transnationality. In Jackson, J. (ed.), *Routledge handbook of language and intercultural communication*. London: Routledge: 101–5.
— This discussion of the nature of linguacultures as entities of relationship between language and cult which have the potential to travel across diverse cultural realities adds a further dimension to the content of this chapter.

Chapter 10

Epilogue

Theoretical perspective

This chapter sets out the theoretical base for the approach employed throughout the book.

The grammar and small cultures

The grammar of culture has been a developing idea over a number of years. It began with my configuration of small cultures (Holliday 1999, 2011b), and later developed into the grammar in my (2011a) book, *Intercultural Communication & Ideology*, where much of the theoretical underpinning for this book was developed. A major aim for this book is to take the grammar as developed there and provide a detailed breakdown of how it helps us to understand the working nature of intercultural communication.

There is nothing particularly new about the small cultures idea. Indeed, it has commonalities with communities of practice (Wenger 2000), though the small cultures idea distances itself from any instrumental educational purpose. Beales *et al.* (1967: 8) speak about social groupings from neighbourhoods or communities to work, friendship or leisure groups. It is at this level that we can see the detail of the building of 'normal' thinking through social construction, normalisation and reification (Berger and Luckmann 1979; Gergen 2001). Small cultures are built from the micro basics of how individuals manage image within the group (e.g. Goffman 1972). There is resonance with the New London Group's resistance to placing everything under the heading of national culture, and the emphasis on smaller entities which we all engage with as we move through life – family, school, occupations, clubs, institutions, which are partly encapsulated in the notion of 'big D discourse' (Lankshear *et al.* 1997). The importance of discourses is present in this book from Chapter 7 onwards; and the relationship or difference between discourses and small cultures continues to be unclear in my thinking. To help in this differentiation of concepts, I stick to the definition of discourse as something inherently linguistic – the place where the construction of small cultures is expressed and maintained through language, which I think is close to the views held by Fairclough (1995). Indeed, something like small cultures is referred to by Fairclough as the 'intermediate level of social structuring' in which there are identifiable discourses (1995: 37).

Small cultures were also very real to me from the perspective of social research. They are the basic entity – the social setting – in which ethnographers locate their fieldwork:

> a street where people cross, a bank window where people line up and transact business, an ocean pier where people loiter and fish, a bus door through which people enter and exit the bus, and a grocery store check-out counter where groceries are rung up, paid for, and bagged.
>
> (Spradley 1980: 40)

These settings, although they are heuristic devices selected by the researcher – slices of social life cut out for the purpose of research – contain elements of the workings of culture in which social interaction can best be observed (Holliday 2007: 40). This relationship between small cultures and everyday social settings has helped me to understand the core notion of **small culture formation** on the run, which emerged while writing the book.

Small cultures are therefore very much at the centre of the grammar; and the relationship between **small culture formation** and **underlying universal cultural processes** is at the core of every chapter. However, the heuristic element must not be forgotten. For this reason I refrain from actually defining the precise nature, content or characteristics of any particular small culture. **Small culture formation** is not the formation of a particular small culture, but rather the formation of cultural behaviour and reality at the small level of everyday interpersonal interaction, which relates to whatever is going on at the time. Therefore, wherever one looks, implicit in Spradley's statement above, **small culture formation** will be evident. Hence, in the case of Anna visiting Beatrice's family in Chapter 2, the small culture of interest is not the family, but the cultural processes which underpin how Anna deals with it.

Dealing with national culture

My preoccupation has long been with small cultures, working from the bottom up. This has caused me to break away from the dominant approach in intercultural communication studies, which has been to begin with *national* culture and work from the top down. To make sense of how to make this break, and to work out what to do with the notion of national culture, I have gone back to the sociological theory of my undergraduate days. I therefore locate the dominant approach which I wish to move away from in structural-functionalism, which has been associated with Emile Durkheim. Here, societies are unified organisms with describable working parts that mirror the characteristics of the whole and are essentially different to those which belonged to a different system, nation or culture (e.g. Durkheim 1964). This way of conceptualising social systems then influences the building of profiles for particular national cultures, and are used to predict and explain not only their behaviour traits, but also the issues which would arise when they tried to interact or communicate with each other (e.g. Hofstede 2003).

Despite its clear utility, structural-functionalism has been criticised on a number of counts. In terms of research methodology, it has been argued that its scientific neutrality is compromised by ideology. It has been accused of falling into the trap of a 'methodological nationalism' which derives from the growth of nation states in nineteenth-century Europe, and which imprints a false ideal of one nation, one language, one culture on social research (Beck and Sznaider 2006: 2; Bhabha 1994; Crane 1994; Delanty 2006; Grande 2006; Rajagopalan 1999, 2012; Schudson 1994; Tomlinson 1991). This undeclared ideological positioning leaves structural-functionalism open to the weaknesses of positivism, where national cultural profiles or theories can too easily be validated by examples because it will always be possible to find examples. When you ask people if their experience fits the profile it will always be easy for them to say yes.

Structural-functionalism has also been critiqued for the prejudicial and indeed neo-racist impact of the confining and indeed Othering nature of the cultural profiles which it has produced. This has particularly been the case with regard to individualism and collectivism, which, again, far from being neutral categories, have been accused of being ideological constructions in that they represent a veiled demonisation of a non-Western Other by an idealised Western Self, and that the collectivist attributes thus represent cultural deficiency (Kim 2005: 108, 2012; Kumaravadivelu 2007: 15; Moon 2008: 16).

These critiques of structural-functionalism, supported by my reading of Stuart Hall (1991a, 1991b), led me to emphasise in the grammar, and throughout the book, that whenever 'culture' is used, by anyone, from research theorists to anyone one might meet, it is an ideological construction which is connected in some way with a global politics. For this reason, **global position and politics** is a major feature of the grammar and is present in the 'categories of cultural action' analyses of every narrative throughout the book.

However, at the same time, it is a fact that people everywhere really do use, talk about, explain things in terms of, and present themselves with national culture profiles, despite their lack of scientific basis means. These profiles are therefore *real* in their minds and have to be taken seriously. To acknowledge the popular reality of these profiles, I place them under the heading of **statements about culture** in the first band in every 'categories of cultural action' analysis. However, these statements are also placed very firmly within inverted commas to indicate that they are 'so-believed' constructions. As constructions, they are central products of **small culture formation**; but they are artefacts of cultural realities rather than factual statements about what these realities comprise.

I also make sure that the popular use of national culture profiles is represented in the narratives in an equal voice to other views of culture. Several of the narratives present a very open discussion of these different views of culture, e.g. with Francisca, Gita and Hande in Chapters 3 and 8, and with Nada, Jahan and Osama in Chapter 7. In the latter case, the national culture profile case is presented negatively as an 'essentialist culture and language' discourse. It is important here to note the multiple reasons for appearing to agree to what amounts to a damaging stereotype which has been imposed by a dominant power. It is a phenomenon reported with regard to Chinese students in Western universities (Ryan and Louie 2007: 407), and could either be interpreted as the very normal ambivalence about one's culture background that anyone might feel (Bourn 2009: 24), as destructive self-Othering (Kumaravadivelu 2006: 22, 2012: 22–3) or as part of a long tradition of Periphery groups appearing to take on images bestowed upon them as a strategy to gain cultural capital (Grimshaw 2010a, citing Bourdieu), or as a form of resistance (Flam and Bauzamy 2008; Sawyer and Jones 2008: 245, citing Scott). The possibility of cultural resistance is represented by the voices of Francisca and Jahan in Chapter 7 within their 'West versus the rest' discourse.

In all cases I lay open my own ideologically motivated voice, as part of a 'liberal multicultural' discourse in Chapter 7; and I hope that, throughout the book, the activities allow room for readers to form their own opinions.

The need to account for social action

It cannot, however, be denied that national structures do have immense significance. The impact of their particular institutions of education, the media and politics makes the structure of nation states, and the cultural experiences they bring their citizens, very different to each other. I therefore needed to build into my grammar the space for dialogue between these **particular social and political structures** and the **underlying universal cultural processes**. Once again, looking back at basic sociological theory, I found the answer in Max Weber's social action approach (e.g. 1964: 115–17), which is very different to the

Durkheimian sociology that underpins structural-functionalism. Social action theory projects the idea that the precise nature of human behaviour can never be determined. While Weber did much to describe the social structures of Protestantism and Confucianism, it was made very clear that the social action of individuals could be expressed in dialogue with them (Bendix 1966: 261; Dobbin 1994: 118). While political and other circumstances may severely reduce the degree to which individual social action can be acted out, this does not mean that the potential is not there.

This social action approach therefore encouraged me to present the grammar as a loose arrangement in which there is room for dialogue and sometimes conflict. The **personal trajectories** domain of the grammar provides the core place where this dialogue is generated. Inspiration for **personal trajectories** is provided by the result of interviews with 32 informants from across the world (Holliday 2010, 2011a) who spoke about the ways in which their personal cultural realities developed as they moved through life, and how their ancestors and personal histories contributed to this. This interest in the trajectories and struggles of individual people is at the core of the themes that run through the book, centred around the characters in the ethnographic narratives as they try and make sense of each other against the backdrop of cultural tension. This interest in the ways in which individuals construct and struggle with culture has been considered a paradigm shift in intercultural communication studies (MacDonald and O'Regan 2011: 563).

Part of Weber's strategy against pinning things down was remembering that coherent ideas about societies should be regarded as 'ideal types' – imagined models or heuristic devices (i.e. for the purpose of investigation) – which might be used to imagine what society *might* be like but which should never be taken as descriptions of how things actually are (Stråth 2008: 33–4; Weber 1968: 23). I am therefore very careful to present my discourses of culture, from Chapter 7 onwards, as ideal types, and to invite a critique of them in the activities. Throughout I refrain from being too precise about anything, encouraging a lack of certainty. This is demonstrated throughout the narratives, where the characters constantly struggle to make sense. They hypothesise about what each other mean and sometimes present theories to each other about this for contestation.

An interesting parallel to my use of Max Weber is Nathan's (2010) use of the sociological theory of Wilhelm Dilthey, who might be said to share with Weber an interpretivist opposition to the positivism inherent in structural-functionalism. I think particularly related to the complexity of my grammar of culture, especially with regard to the **global position and politics** domain, is Nathan's emphasis on Dilthey's interest in the multiple nature of *any* society, no matter how homogeneous it may appear on the surface, which is always mediated by histories and struggles for power within smaller groups (2010: 45, citing Benhabib).

Representing a bottom-up reality

This need for a bottom-up sense-making is also inspired by the social theorists who argue that there is an unequal global order surrounding the issue of culture, in which a Centre West defines cultural norms for the rest-of-the-world, non-Western Periphery (Hannerz 1991). They argue that this marginalisation of non-Western cultural realities is part of the top-down globalisation which dominates the world with Western markets (Bhabha 1994: xiv; Canagarajah 1999: 207–9; Fairclough 2006: 40; Hall 1991a: 20, 1996). This is why there needs to be caution with the individualism–collectivism distinction as described above, as both are invested in by a Western academy (Moon 2008: 15; Shuter 2008: 38). A subtle but dangerous and seductive twist in this domination is the Western belief that everything good that happens is due to its own intervention, and an implicit ethos of a deeply patronising 'helping' of the non-Western Other (Delanty *et al.* 2008a: 9). This is then connected with a modernistic desire to tie down identities and to hide aggression beneath education, progress and civilisation (Latour 2006). An outcome of this is neo-racism, where race is rationalised, hidden and denied under the 'nice' heading of culture (Delanty *et al.* 2008a: 1; Lentin 2008: 102–3; Spears 1999).

This picture of a Western order which defines how the world ought to be while presenting itself as being good and caring is therefore a common theme in a number of the narratives in the book, particularly embodied in Christoff in Chapter 2, Ivonne in Chapter 3, Stefan and Kay in Chapter 6, Maria in Chapter 8 and Loren in Chapter 9, and is represented in the 'West as steward' discourse.

This Western defining of non-Western cultures underpins the Orientalism thesis (Said 1978) and the liberal multiculturalist agenda to represent cultural difference through superficial artefacts, festivals, ceremonies, dress, food and customs. It is asserted that this 'bland', 'indulgent' superficiality produces a commodified packaging which is far from faithful to the complexity of lived cultural experience, and instead focuses on 'the exotica of difference' which demean and alienate personal identities as though they are a 'spectacle' (e.g. Ahmad and Donnan 1994: 5; Delanty *et al.* 2008b; Hall 1991b: 55; Kubota 2004: 35; Kumaravadivelu 2007: 104–6, 109; Nathan 2010: 15, citing Benhabib; Sarangi 1995; Wallace 2003: 55). These issues are represented in a number of places in the book, through the presentation of the 'liberal multicultural' discourse, and particularly in the conversation between Nada, Jahan, Osama and Theobald in Chapter 7.

However, I appreciate the need to be cautious about pushing too strong a West–non-West theme in the book. I see the reality of this theme around me almost every day, and I meet more and more people who, sometimes reluctantly, tell me that it runs through the whole business of cultural misunderstanding. Nevertheless, there is also a body of feeling that the whole thing is an illusion, and the Orientalist thesis becomes somewhat like the global warming thesis – either underpinning everything or a groundless conspiracy. I therefore make some attempt to modify this agenda by refraining from mentioning actual countries wherever possible, and even choosing names for characters in the narratives which could indicate people from almost anywhere. I also do not want to give the impression that all the intercultural issues are to do with visiting the West or Westerners going abroad. The issue of defining and being defined therefore remains strong throughout, but not always explicitly marked as West–non-West.

There is nevertheless a need throughout to hear voices from the so-called margins, whether non-Western or elsewhere. Various theorists are relatively optimistic about a revolutionary reclaiming of cultural space from the margins – a globalisation from below (Fairclough 2006: 121), with a 'recovering' of 'hidden mysteries' (Hall 1991a: 35). This can be seen in a recent account of Pakistani cultural complexity in Qureshi (2010) and in Honarbin-Holliday's (2008) ethnography of Iranian women claiming the modern world as their own cultural heritage and tracing it back to the deep indigenous modernity implicit in the generation of their grandmothers, and even in the way in which British students learn from the working styles and attitudes brought by foreign students (Osmond and Roed 2009: 115, 120), and what the Western academy needs to learn from the experiences and traditions of non-Western research students (Robinson-Pant 2009).

Learning from the margins

The need to learn from the margins has influenced the adoption of a postmodern qualitative research methodology. I am using postmodern in its broadest sense to mean a recognition that ideology resides in everything and does not accept the stated neutrality of positivist accountable theories of difference, in the same way as Guba and Lincoln (2005: 191) to incorporate a wide range of critical and constructivist approaches, and corresponding to the 'fifth moment' in qualitative research (Denzin and Lincoln 2005: 20).

This moment involves the questioning of a postpositivist approach to qualitative research which shares key modernist features with structural-functionalism, and which is often traced back to the publication of the seminal *Writing Culture* (Clifford and Marcus 1986). In a similar manner to structural-functionalism, the dominant postpositivist paradigm in qualitative research has been criticised for naïvely clinging to the positivist principles of a detached manipulation of objective variables in the same manner as the physical sciences. Postpositivism has thus not allowed the recognition for the presence and impact of the researcher on the setting or community which is being studied, or the mediation of ideological, social and political forces, resulting in an artificially objective image with a worrying lack of researcher reflexivity (Blackman 2007; Clifford 1986: 2; Faubion 2001; Gubrium and Holstein 1997: 19–33; Hammersley and Atkinson 1995: 1; Holliday 2007: 16; MacDonald 2001; Miller *et al.* 1998; Spencer 2001). The link between this critical, postmodern turn and the critical cosmopolitan picture of culture and Weber's sociology described above is made by Rabinow (1986: 256–8).

The postmodern break from naturalism enables a far greater variety in procedure and scope in which data is presented more creatively, with more openness about who the researcher is and how she or he spins validity through argument. Janesick (2000) describes well, through an analogy with choreography, the mixing of creativity and discipline. Very much resonant of **small culture formation** on the run, it encourages a portrayal of 'people as constructing the social world', but also of researchers 'themselves constructing the social world through their interpretations of it' (Hammersley and Atkinson 1995: 11).

This co-construction between the researcher as narrator and the observed and reported realities of individuals in social life is evident in the ethnographic narratives used throughout the book. The use of such narratives was developed through two editions by Holliday *et al.* (2010) and then Holliday (2011a). The original inspiration is Kubota (2003), in which she manages skilfully to describe the complex and non-essentialist nature of culture in a far more convincing manner than any 'academic text' I have read. While I refrain from referring to these narratives as 'data', and they are clearly fictional accounts, they are carefully reconstructed from real conversations and experiences, and therefore serve as a form of real-world example. In this sense they are by no means sanitised or contrived to project particular messages. On the contrary, they generate often unexpected complexity, and lead me to consider issues which I had not thought about before. They are written with the same ethnographic disciplines of making the familiar strange, recognising and dealing with researcher prejudice, a close reading of and being faithful to the accounts and action of participants, thick description, submission, emergence and personal knowledge as more conventional forms (Holliday 2004, 2007: 107–13). Inspiration comes from Arundhati Roy, who puts aside the positivist notion that writers 'cull stories from the world':

> I am beginning to believe that vanity makes them think so – that it's actually the other way around. Stories cull writers from the world. Stories reveal themselves to us. The

public narrative, the private narrative – they colonise us, they commission us, they insist on being told.… There can never be a single story: there are only ways of seeing.

(Roy 2002: track 3)

It is of course a mistake to consider such stories to be from the margins. They might appear so because methodological nationalism has pushed them there, labelling them as exceptions to the rule. However, once methodological nationalism is put aside, these stories relate what is plain to see in ordinary and normal everyday life.

The potential for crossing intercultural lines

A key issue in intercultural studies, which the book aims to address, is the degree to which it is possible for people to cross the line between different cultural realities. The established approach to this employs the concept of a third space, in which it is possible for intercultural travellers to negotiate their position with regard to the new culture, and hybridity, where someone at the same time maintains the attributes of their own culture while taking on in a limited way those of another. These concepts are used to struggle with the problems of essentialism, especially in the search for postcolonial spaces (e.g. Bhabha 1994: 5; Canagarajah 1999: 208; Delanty 2006: 33; Fay 1996: 55ff.; Guilherme 2002: 167; Kramsch 1993; Young 2006: 159; Zhu 2008). However, following Kumaravadivelu (2007: 5, 12, 112) and my analysis in Holliday (2011a: 164ff), in various parts of the book I oppose these notions of third space and hybridity by saying that they, in effect, confine the individual within essentialist concepts of culture. This critique also leads me to analyse the issue of values in Chapter 2, which seem so often to be the heralding cry for the cultural incompatibility which underpins the third space idea (e.g. Spencer-Oatey and Stadler 2009).

I therefore make it a leading theme in the book, culminating in Chapter 9, that individuals are not only very capable of crossing intercultural lines, but that they can do this creatively and innovatively given the potential. Indeed, this is presented as an extension to the normal cultural creativity within **small culture formation**. The possibility for transcending cultural lines can be seen in Angouri and Harwood's (2008) discussion of how people co-construct multiple writing genres in response to different communities of practice; in Baumann's (1996) ethnographic study of how people in the multicultural London borough of Southall construct different discourses of culture in different ways at different times, depending on who and what they are relating to; and also in schoolchildren playing creatively with culture in urban classrooms and adults playing similarly in everyday multicultural lives (Rampton 2011; Rampton *et al.* 2008). There is also evidence of the expended cultural sophistication of diverse transnational communities of university students (Montgomery and McDowell 2009; Thom 2009).

People do not, however, cross intercultural lines without carrying important cultural identities and structures with them. These **cultural resources** are the major connection with big national cultural realities; but the relationship with them is never fixed or even easily predictable. The power of their reality can be seen in the conversation between Francisca, Hande and Gita in Chapter 8. There is little reference to language in the book, though a lot to discourse. This is because, trying to escape from the 'essentialist culture and language' discourse implicit in structural-functionalism, placing language becomes a very complex matter. Helpful here is the notion of elements of linguaculture being carried from place to place, by means, I think, of the **personal trajectories** domain of the grammar and engaging with diverse settings in complex and transformative ways (Risager 2011).

There is, however, a dark side to this carrying of **cultural resources**, which arises from the prejudices coming out of the closely connected **global position and politics** domain of the grammar. This is the opposition to transcultural innovation which comes from the people that cultural travellers encounter in their new cultural environments, evidence for which can be found in studies of what happens between foreign and home university students. On the part of home students and lecturers, there is fear of the unknown, a fear of offending contravening political correctness and 'having to walk on "eggshells"' (Osmond and Roed 2009: 118; Ryan and Viete 2009: 307). Moreover, despite a surface tolerance and stated rejection of stereotypes, there is an Othering of foreign students through 'unequal dialogue', referring to people as indiscriminate members of groups rather than as individuals, and reference to 'language problems' as a euphemism for difference (Caruana and Spurling 2006: 8; Harrison and Peacock 2009: 133, 136). On the part of foreign students, there are feelings of isolation, rejection of friendship and exclusion from activities outside the classroom (Clifford 2009: 173; Leask 2009). Some attention is given in the book to people who believe they are being friendly and accommodating when in fact they are not, the final example being Loren in Chapter 9, who fails to appreciate how Safa can be successful on her own cultural terms. This derives partly from the 'West as steward' discourse referred to earlier, which is unaware of its patronising effect and possible hidden racism (Wodak 2008: 65).

Of course, this type of discussion is full of interpretation. An interesting point of focus here is Eva Hoffman's (1998) seminal description of being a Polish immigrant in North America. Whereas this is often cited as an example of the problems with crossing cultural lines, my own reading of Hoffman did not begin from my own preoccupation with an indelible intercultural line and therefore inspired me with accounts of someone struggling to write herself into and taking ownership of a new and strange cultural universe. Once again, I invite the particular experience of readers in this respect in the activities throughout the book; and these issues are debated strongly by the characters in the narratives.

Cultural realism

The conviction, which runs throughout the book, that everything to do with culture is motivated by ideologies, embedded within the **global position and politics** domain of the grammar, which are realised through everyday Self and Other politics and social construction within the **small culture formation** domain, indicates an underlying postmodern approach. I find this label meaningful as an antidote to the modernist thrust of structural-functionalism described above. It is part of a major paradigm change taking place within the area of applied linguistics and intercultural studies (e.g. Kumaravadivelu 2012).

At the same time, I shy away from the cultural relativism which some theorists associate with postmodernism. Indeed, I critique a 'cultural relativism' discourse in Chapter 9 in my justification for the contestation of brought and found cultural practices on universal humanistic grounds, following Delanty (2008). I therefore also subscribe to a cultural realism such as that described by Kumaravadivelu (2007: 143). This means that I can come out and assert that the realities of the emergent, the margins, the Periphery have more value than the falsely conscious imaginations of the Centre West. This is not due to a patronising liberationism, but, in the words of Berger and Luckmann (1979: 18), to recover 'the real social being of the [Centre-Western] thinker' as someone who recovers dignity through engaging with and putting aside demeaning prejudices. In this respect I have been very careful not to be seen to be speaking for people who feel culturally misunderstood. Instead, I speak with the authority of one who knows what it is like to have deep-seated cultural prejudice because of his Centre-Western upbringing (Holliday 2005a).

Kumaravadivelu (2007: 143) claims social constructivism in his cultural realism, which it is important to contrast with the more extreme constructionist analysis of society in which everything is constructed and no reality is left. Fairclough (2006: 18) underlines this distinction and also maintains the constructivist position in his engagement with the realism of actual social structures and their fine balance with social agency:

> Human beings engage in social activity in a preconstructed social world which is largely beyond their control. They have to come to terms with it, accept that they can only act within certain parameters and constraints. Yet human beings are agentive, strategic and reflective beings, and the preconstructed social world is a socially, humanly, constructed world, the outcome of past and continuing human agency, strategy and reflexivity. Wherever people engage in social activity, they reflexively produce representations of it and of their own place within it; these representations may (given certain social conditions) be consolidated and stabilized in diverse shared discourses, and they may include imaginaries for possible alternative forms of social activity, and may (always subject to particular social conditions) come to be parts of strategies for social change.
>
> (Fairclough 2006: 163)

Glossary

Banter 'Joking, kidding (informal), ribbing (informal), teasing, jeering, quipping, mockery, derision, jesting ... pleasantry, repartee, wordplay, ... raillery' (*Collins English Dictionary*), 'the playful and friendly exchange of teasing remarks' (Google definitions), 'supple term used to describe activities or chat that is playful, intelligent and original ... something you either possess or lack, there is no middle ground' (Urban dictionary), 'an exchange of light, playful, teasing remarks; good-natured raillery' (Dictionary.com – http://dictionary.reference.com/browse/banter).

Centre Being in such a position of global power that the rest of the world feels defined politically, economically and culturally by it.

Collectivist A label used to characterise an imagined cultural type in which the collective is thought to dominate behaviour at the expense of the individual.

Critical reading Reading texts to find the hidden nature of historical narratives, discourses and ideologies and the **global position and politics** which they carry with them.

Cultural belief When we perceive the cultural background of any person to be rich and resourceful to the extent that it can be engaged with, learnt from and indeed expanded into.

Cultural contestation When we critique an existing cultural practice – a normal part of **small culture formation** as well as cultural innovation – the questioning of cultural practices which may appear opposed to the human rights which underpin cultural belief.

Cultural disbelief When we imagine that while 'other cultures' have the right to be themselves, they present a 'problem' because they are incompatible with an imagined Western world view.

Cultural environment A geographical or psychological entity from which an individual derives a sense of cultural identity at a particular point in time.

Cultural practice A way of doing things which is particular to a cultural environment.

Culturism Any thought or act which reduces people to something less than what they are according to an essentialist view of culture.

Discourse A way of using language which represents ideas about how things are.

Discourses of culture, innocent discourses Those which do not recognise ideology: 'Essentialist culture and language'; 'Third space'; 'Liberal multiculturalism'; 'West as steward'; 'Cultural relativism'.

Discourses of culture, Discourses recognising culturist ideology 'West vs. the rest'; 'Critical cosmopolitan'.

Dominant discourse A powerful way of looking at things which marginalises competing ways of looking at things.

Easy answers   The most common, default ways of making sense of cultural difference, most often associated with unacknowledged, essentialist, innocent discourses and therefore easily fall into the trap of cultural prejudice.

Essentialist   Explaining people's behaviour as the essence of their culture, and that all people from that culture will behave in that way.

Exoticising   Seeing something as having a strange or bizarre allure, beauty or quality (*Collins English Dictionary*).

Facebook   A social networking site developed in America.

Globalisation, bottom-up   Where people, especially but not only, from the Periphery claim and make use of global trends to make them their own in their own terms.

Globalisation, top-down   Where the world is dominated by Centre global trends.

Historical narratives   Powerful narratives which are long-standing and implicit in the **particular social and political structures** of nation, religion and ideology, and the **global position and politics** that collect around them.

Ideology   A system of ideas which supports a particular set of interests.

Individualist   A label used to characterise an imagined cultural type in which the individual is thought to dominate behaviour at the expense of the individual.

Innocent discourses   Discourses which deny an ideological presence in their structure.

Manners   Good 'social conduct' or 'a socially acceptable way of behaving' (*Collins English Dictionary*).

Marked   Emphasising strong and exclusive boundaries, characteristics, identities and so on – more effective in pushing arguments and making political impact. (Related to, e.g. statements, interpretations, historical narratives, or discourses).

Neo-racism   Any form of rationalising the subordination of a defined group of people on the basis of culture even though race is not an explicit agenda in the minds of the people concerned.

Non-essentialist   Not trying to explain behaviour in terms of culture, or of any other stereotypical idea.

Other   A demonised or glorified image of others which strengthens the personal identity of the Self.

Othering   Reducing a group of people to a negative stereotype.

Positive Othering   Othering can be positive, when the Self positions itself against a superior Other.

Self-Othering   People taking on negative labels of who they are which are imposed by a dominant discourse.

Periphery   Lacking power in such a way that there is a feeling of being defined politically, economically and culturally by others.

Prejudice   Images built on prior formulae for Self and Other representation.

Political correctness   A strategy to undo a discourse of prejudice by changing key aspects of its language.

Reification   Making real something which is not initially seen to be so – similar to institutionalisation.

Routinising   Establishing a piece of behaviour to the degree that it becomes normal and routine, part of the thinking-as-usual, or part of the everyday institutional processes of an organisation – similar to 'normalising' and 'embedding'.

Self   An idealised image of who you are which strengthens your personal identity.

Sociological blindness   The inability to see what is happening in front of you because you are preoccupied with a theoretical perspective which contradicts it.

Soft interpretation   Naïve, not seeing the full implications. (Not to be confused with 'unmarked' below).

Small culture   A cultural environment which is located in proximity to the people concerned.

Small culture formation   Reading and making culture, constructing rules and meanings, imagining Self and Other.

Small culture formation on the run   The process which takes place every day, everywhere, with whoever we meet or think about, through which we construct and deal with cultural realities.

Stereotype   Theory about the nature of a particular culture – a cultural profile.

Thick description   Interconnecting different facets of a social phenomenon to arrive at a deeper complexity of meanings.

Unmarked   Acknowledging negotiable boundaries, characteristics, identities and so on. (Not to be confused with 'soft', above, related to, e.g. statements, interpretations, historical narratives or discourses).

Values   'The moral principles and beliefs or accepted standards of a person or social group' (*Collins English Dictionary*).

References

Abrams, J.J., Lieber, J. and Lindelof, D. (2005). *Lost*. US: ABC.

Adichie, C.N. (2007). *Half of a yellow sun*. Kindle edition. London: Harper Collins e-books.

Ahmad, A.S. and Donnan, H. (1994). Islam in the age of postmodernity. In Ahmad, A.S. and Donnan, H. (eds), *Islam, globalization and postmodernity*. London: Routledge: 1–20.

Al Sheykh, H. (1998). *I sweep the sun off the rooftops*. London: Bloomsbury.

Andrić, I. (1995). *Bridge over the Drina*. Edwards, L.F., Trans. London: Harvill Press.

Angouri, J. and Harwood, N. (2008). This is too formal for us...: a case study of variation in the written products of a multinational consortium. *Journal of Business and Technical Communication* 22/1: 38–64.

Armenta, I. (in progress). *An ethnographic study of how a small group of English teachers and students, in a language department in a Mexican university, construct 'culture'*. Unpublished PhD thesis, Department of English & Language Studies, Canterbury Christ Church University, Canterbury.

Baumann, G. (1996). *Contesting culture*. Cambridge: Cambridge University Press.

Beales, A.R., Spindler, G. and Spindler, L. (1967). *Culture in process*. New York: Holt, Rinehart.

Beck, U. and Sznaider, N. (2006). Unpacking cosmopolitanism for the social sciences: a research agenda. *British Journal of Sociology* 57/1: 1–23.

Bendix, R. (1966). *Max Weber: an intellectual portrait*. London: Methuen.

Berger, P. and Luckmann, T. (1979). *The social construction of reality*. Harmondsworth: Penguin.

Bhabha, H. (1994). *The location of culture*. London: Routledge.

Blackman, S.J. (2007). 'Hidden ethnography': crossing emotional borders in qualitative accounts of young people's lives. *Sociology* 41/4: 699–716.

Bourn, D. (2009). Students as global citizens. In Jones, E. (ed.), *Internationalisation and the student voice: higher education perspectives*. London: Routledge: 18–29.

Byram, M. (2008). *From foreign language education to education for intercultural citizenship: essays and reflections*. Clevedon: Multilingual Matters.

Canagarajah, A.S. (1999). On EFL teachers, awareness and agency. *ELT Journal* 53/3: 207–14.

Caruana, V. and Spurling, N. (2006). The internationalisation of UK higher education: a review of selected material. *The Higher Education Academy*. Retrieved from http://www.heacademy.ac.uk/resources/detail/the_internationalisation_of_uk_he (6 July 2010).

Chatziefstathiou, D. and Henry, I. (2007). Hellenism and Olympism: Pierre de Coubertin and the Greek challenge to the early Olympic movement. *Sport in History* 27/1: 24–43.

Clifford, J. (1986). Introduction: partial truths. In Clifford, J. and Marcus, G.E. (eds), *Writing culture: the poetica of politics of ethnography*. Berkeley, CA: University of California Press: 1–26.

Clifford, J. and Marcus, G.E. (eds) (1986). *Writing culture: the poetica of politics of ethnography*. Berkeley, CA: University of California Press.

Clifford, V. (2009). The internationalized curriculum. In Jones, E. (ed.), *Internationalisation and the student voice: higher education perspectives*. London: Routledge: 169–80.

Clifford, V. and Montgomery, C. (eds) (2011). *Moving towards internationalisation of the curriculum for global citizenship in higher education*. Oxford: OCSLD and CICIN (Centre for International Curriculum Inquiry and Networking), Oxford Brookes University.

Costner, K. (1990). *Dances with wolves*. US: Majestic Films International.

Crane, D. (1994). Introduction: the challenge of the sociology of culture to sociology as discipline. In Crane, D. (ed.), *The sociology of culture*. Oxford: Blackwell: 1–19.

Delanty, G. (2006). The cosmopolitan imagination: critical cosmopolitanism and social theory. *British Journal of Sociology* 57/1: 25–47.

——(2008). Dilemmas of secularism: Europe, religion and the problem of pluralism. In Delanty, G., Wodak, R. and Jones, P. (eds), *Identity, belonging and migration*. Liverpool: Liverpool University Press: 78–97.

Delanty, G., Wodak, R. and Jones, P. (2008a). Introduction: migration, discrimination and belonging in Europe. In Delanty, G., Wodak, R. and Jones, P. (eds), *Identity, belonging and migration*. Liverpool: Liverpool University Press: 1–20.

——(eds) (2008b). *Identity, belonging and migration*. Liverpool: Liverpool University Press.

Denzin, N.K. and Lincoln, Y.S. (2005). The discipline and practice of qualitative research. In Denzin, N.K. and Lincoln, Y.S. (eds), *Handbook of qualitative research*. 3rd edn. Thousand Oaks: Sage: 1–30.

Dobbin, F.R. (1994). Cultural models of organization: the social construction of rational organizing principles. In Crane, D. (ed.), *The sociology of culture*. Oxford: Blackwell: 117–41.

Doshi, T. (2010). *The pleasure seekers*. Kindle edition. London: Bloomsbury.

Durkheim, E. (1964). *The division of labour in society*. Simpson, G., Trans. New York: Free Press.

Fairclough, N. (1995). *Critical discourse analysis: the critical study of language*. London: Addison Wesley Longman.

——(2006). *Language and globalization*. London: Routledge.

Faubion, J.D. (2001). Currents of cultural fieldwork. In Atkinson, P., Coffey, A., Delamont, S., Lofland, J. and Lofland, L. (eds), *Handbook of ethnography*. London: Sage: 39–59.

Fay, B. (1996). *Contemporary philosophy of social science: a multicultural approach*. Oxford: Blackwell.

Flam, H. and Bauzamy, B. (2008). Symbolic violence. In Delanty, G., Wodak, R. and Jones, P. (eds), *Identity, belonging and migration*. Liverpool: Liverpool University Press: 221–40.

Ge, J. (2004). *An investigation of perceptions and attitudes held by Chinese language teachers toward western influence on English language teaching in China*. Unpublished PhD thesis, Department of English and Language Studies, Canterbury Christ Church University, Canterbury.

Geertz, C. (1993). *The interpretation of cultures*. London: Fontana.

Gergen, K.J. (2001). *Social construction in context*. London: Sage.

Goffman, E. (1972). *Relations in public*. Harmondsworth: Penguin.

Golding, W. (1954). *Lord of the flies*. London: Faber & Faber.

Grande, E. (2006). Cosmopolitan political science. *British Journal of Sociology* 57/1: 87–111.

Grimshaw, T. (2002). *Discursive struggle: linguistic imperialism and resistance on Chinese university campuses*. Unpublished PhD thesis, Department of English and Language Studies, Canterbury Christ Church University, Canterbury.

——(2010a). *Stereotypes as cultural capital: international students negotiating identities in British HE*. Paper presented at the British Association of Applied Linguistics Annual Conference: Applied Linguistics: Global and Local, University of Aberdeen.

——(2010b). Styling the occidental other: interculturality in Chinese university performances. *Language & Intercultural Communication* 10/3: 243–58.

Guba, E.G. and Lincoln, Y.S. (2005). Paradigmatic controversies, contradictions, and emerging confluences. In Denzin, N.K. and Lincoln, Y.S. (eds), *Handbook of qualitative research*. 3rd edn. Thousand Oaks: Sage: 191–215.

Gubrium, J.F. and Holstein, J.A. (1997). *The new language of qualitative research*. New York: Oxford University Press.

Guilherme, M. (2002). *Critical citizens for an intercultural world: foreign language education as cultural politics*. Clevedon: Multilingual Matters.

——(2007). English as a global language and education for cosmopolitan citizenship. *Language & Intercultural Communication* 7/1: 72–90.

Hall, S. (1991a). The local and the global: globalization and ethnicity. In King, A.D. (ed.), *Culture, globalization and the world-system*. New York: Palgrave: 19–39.

——(1991b). Old and new identities, old and new ethnicities. In King, A.D. (ed.), *Culture, globalization and the world-system*. New York: Palgrave: 40–68.

——(1996). The West and the rest: discourse and power. In Hall, S. and Held, D. (eds), *Modernity: an introduction to modern societies*. Oxford: Blackwell: 184–228.

Hammersley, M. and Atkinson, P. (1995). *Ethnography, principles and practice*. 2nd edn. London: Routledge.

Hannerz, U. (1991). Scenarios of peripheral cultures. In King, A.D. (ed.), *Culture, globalization and the world-system*. New York: Palgrave: 107–28.

Harrison, N. and Peacock, N. (2009). Interactions in the international classroom: the UK perspective. In Jones, E. (ed.), *Internationalisation and the student voice: higher education perspectives*. London: Routledge: 125–42.

Hoffman, E. (1998). *Lost in translation*. London: Vintage.

Hofstede, G. (2003). *Culture's consequences: comparing values, behaviours, institutions and organizations across cultures*. 2nd edn. London: Sage.

Holliday, A.R. (1999). Small cultures. *Applied Linguistics* 20/2: 237–64.

——(2004). The value of reconstruction in revealing hidden or counter cultures. *Journal of Applied Linguistics* 1/3: 275–94.

——(2005a). How is it possible to write? *Journal of Language, Identity & Education* 4/4: 304–9.

——(2005b). *The struggle to teach English as an international language*. Oxford: Oxford University Press.

——(2007). *Doing and writing qualitative research*. 2nd edn. London: Sage.

——(2010). Complexity in cultural identity. *Language & Intercultural Communication* 10/2: 165–77.

——(2011a). *Intercultural communication & ideology.* London: Sage.

——(2011b). Small cultures. In Zhu, H. (ed.), *The language and intercultural communication reader.* London: Routledge: 196–218. (Also in (1999) *Applied Linguistics* 20/2, 237–64).

Holliday, A.R., Hyde, M. and Kullman, J. (2010). *Intercultural communication: an advanced resource book for students.* 2nd edn. London: Routledge.

Honarbin-Holliday, M. (2008). *Becoming visible in Iran: women in contemporary Iranian society.* London: I.B. Tauris.

Janesick, V.J. (2000). The choreography of qualitative research design: minuets, improvisations, and crystallization. In Denzin, N.K. and Lincoln, Y.S. (eds), *Handbook of qualitative research.* 2nd edn. Thousand Oaks: Sage: 379–400.

Jones, E. (2009). 'Don't worry about the worries': transforming lives through international volunteering. In Jones, E. (ed.), *Internationalisation and the student voice: higher education perspectives.* London: Routledge: 83–97.

Jones, J. (2007). *Northanger Abbey.* UK: Granada Television.

Khorsandi, S. (2009). *A beginner's guide to acting English.* London: Ebury Press.

Kim, M.-S. (2005). Culture-based conversational constraints theory. In Gudykunst, W.B. (ed.), *Theorizing about intercultural communication.* Thousand Oaks: Sage: 93–117.

——(2012). *Trends in intercultural communication research: from a research culture of war to a research culture of peace.* Paper presented at the BAAL Special Interest Group in Intercultural Communication: intercultural communication in international contexts – training and development, practice and research, Open University, Milton Keynes.

King, A.D. (ed.) (1991). *Culture, globalization and the world-system.* New York: Palgrave.

Kramsch, C. (1993). *Context and culture in language teaching.* Oxford: Oxford University Press.

Kubota, R. (2003). Unfinished knowledge: the story of Barbara. *College ESL* 10/1–2: 84–92.

——(2004). Critical multiculturalism and second language education. In Norton, B. and Toohey, K. (eds), *Critical pedagogies and language learning.* Cambridge: Cambridge University Press: 30–52.

Kuhn, T. (1970). *The structure of scientific revolutions.* Chicago, IL: University of Chicago Press.

Kumaravadivelu, B. (2006). Dangerous liaison: globalization, empire and TESOL. In Edge, J. (ed.), *(Re)locating TESOL in an age of empire: language and globalization.* London: Palgrave: 1–26.

——(2007). *Cultural globalization and language education.* New Haven, CT: Yale University Press.

——(2012). Individual identity, cultural globalization, and teaching English as an international language: the case for an epistemic break. In Alsagoff, L., Renandya, W., Hu, G. and McKay, S. (eds), *Principles and practices for teaching English as an international language.* New York: Routledge: 9–27.

Laing, R.D. (1961). *Self and Others.* London: Tavistock Publications.

Lankshear, C., Gee, J.P., Knobel, M. and Searle, C. (1997). *Changing literacies.* Buckingham: Open University Press.

Latour, B. (2006). War of the worlds: what about peace? *Matrix, Bridge the Gap*. Retrieved from http://www.btgjapan.org/catalysts/bruno.html, (19 August 2006).

Leask, B. (2009). 'Beside me is an empty chair': the student experience of international-isation. In Jones, E. (ed.), *Internationalisation and the student voice: higher education perspectives*. London: Routledge: 3–17.

Lentin, A. (2008). Racism, anti-racism and the Western state. In Delanty, G., Wodak, R. and Jones, P. (eds), *Identity, belonging and migration*. Liverpool: Liverpool University Press: 101–19.

Longinotto, K. and Mir-Hosseini, Z. (1999). Divorce Iranian style. UK: Channel 4 Television.

MacDonald, M.N. and O'Regan, J.P. (2011). A global agenda for intercultural communi-cation research and practice. In Jackson, J. (ed.), *Routledge handbook of language and intercultural communication*. London: Routledge: 553–67.

MacDonald, S. (2001). British social anthropology. In Atkinson, P., Coffey, A., Delamont, S., Lofland, J. and Lofland, L. (eds), *Handbook of ethnography*. London: Sage: 60–79.

Mernissi, F. (2001). *Scheherazade goes West: different cultures, different harems*. New York: Washington Square Press.

Miller, S.M., Nelson, M.W. and Moore, M.T. (1998). Caught in the paradigm gap: qualita-tive researchers' lived experience and the politics of epistemology. *American Educational Research Journal* 35/3: 377–416.

Montgomery, C. (2010). *Understanding the international student*. Abingdon: Palgrave Macmillan.

Montgomery, C. and McDowell, L. (2009). Social networks and the international student experience: an international community of practice? *Journal of Studies in International Education* 13/4: 455–66.

Moon, D.G. (2008). Concepts of 'culture': implications for intercultural communication research. In Asante, M.K., Miike, Y. and Yin, J. (eds), *The global intercultural communi-cation reader*. New York: Routledge: 11–26.

Naghibi, N. (2007). *Rethinking global sisterhood: Western feminism and Iran*. Minneapolis, MN: University of Minnesota Press.

Nathan, G. (2010). *Social freedom in a multicultural state: towards a theory of intercultural justice*. Basingstoke: Palgrave Macmillan.

Oral, Y. (in progress). Unpublished Paper, Department of English Language Teaching, University of Istanbul, Istanbul.

Osanloo, A. (2009). *The politics of women's rights in Iran*. Princeton, NJ: Princeton University Press.

Osmond, J. and Roed, J. (2009). Sometimes it means more work.... In Jones, E. (ed.), *Internationalisation and the student voice: higher education perspectives*. London: Routledge: 113–24.

Pamuk, O. (2011). *The museum of innocence*. Freeley, M., Trans. Kindle edition. London: Faber & Faber.

Qureshi, R. (2010). Ethical standards and ethical environment: tension and a way forward. In Shamim, F. and Qureshi, R. (eds), *Perils, pitfalls and reflexivity in qualitative research in education*. Karachi: Oxford University Press Pakistan: 78–100.

Rabinow, P. (1986). Representations are social facts: modernity and postmodernity in anthropology. In Clifford, J. and Marcus, G.E. (eds), *Writing culture*. London: University of California Press: 234–61.

Rajagopalan, K. (1999). Of EFL teachers, conscience and cowardice. *ELT Journal* 53/3: 200–6.

——(2012). *Hybridity as the hallmark of transcultural interaction: implications for language policy.* Paper presented at the CALPIU 2nd International Conference, Higher education across borders: Transcultural interaction and linguistic diversity, Roskilde University, Denmark.

Rampton, B. (2011). From 'multi-ethnic adolescent heteroglossia' to 'contemporary urban vernaculars'. *Language & Communication* 31/4: 276–94.

Rampton, B., Harris, R., Georgakopoulou, A., Leung, C., Small, L. and Dover, C. (2008). *Urban classroom culture and interaction: end-of-project report.* Unpublished Working Papers in Urban Language and Literacies, Kings College, London University, London.

Rapley, G. and Murkett, T. (2008). *Baby-led weaning: helping your baby to love good food.* London: Random House.

Risager, K. (2011). Linguaculture and transnationality. In Jackson, J. (ed.), *Routledge handbook of language and intercultural communication.* London: Routledge: 101–5.

Roberts, C. (2009). Cultures of organisations meet ethno-linguistic cultures: narratives in job interviews. In Feng, A., Byram, M. and Fleming, M. (eds), *Education and training: becoming interculturally competent.* Clevedon: Multilingual Matters: 15–31.

Robinson-Pant, A. (2009). Changing academies: exploring international PhD students' perspectives on 'host' and 'home' universities. *Higher Education Research & Development* 28/4: 417–29.

Rostami-Povey, E. (2007). *Afghan women: identity and invasion.* London: Zed Books.

Roy, A. (2002). *Come September: in conversation with Howard Zinn.* Santa Fe: Lensing Performing Arts Centre, Lannan Foundation.

Ryan, J. and Louie, K. (2007). False dichotomy? 'Western' and 'Confucian' concepts of scholarship and learning. *Educational Philosophy & Theory* 39/4: 404–17.

Ryan, J. and Viete, R. (2009). Respectful interactions: learning with international students in the English-speaking academy. *Teaching in Higher Education* 14/3: 303–14.

Said, E. (1978). *Orientalism.* London: Routledge & Kegan Paul.

Samy Alim, H. and Pennycook, A. (2007). Glocal linguistic flows: hip-hop culture(s), identities, and the politics of language education. *Journal of Language, Identity & Education* 6/2: 89–100.

Sangari, K. (1994). Relating histories: definitions of literacy, literature, gender in early nineteenth century Calcutta and England. In Joshi, S. (ed.), *Rethinking English.* Delhi: Oxford University Press.

Sarangi, S. (1995). Culture. In Vershueren, J., Östman, J. and Blomaert, J. (eds), *Handbook of pragmatics.* Amsterdam: John Benjamins: 1–30.

Sawyer, L. and Jones, P. (2008). Voices of migrants: solidarity and resistance. In Delanty, G., Wodak, R. and Jones, P. (eds), *Identity, belonging and migration.* Liverpool: Liverpool University Press: 241–60.

Schudson, M. (1994). Culture and the integration of national societies. In Crane, D. (ed.), *The sociology of culture.* Oxford: Blackwell: 21–43.

Schutz, A. (1964). The stranger. *Collected papers, Volume 2.* The Hague: Martinus Nijhoff: 91–5.

Shamsie, K. (2009). *Burnt shadows.* London: Bloomsbury.

Shuter, R. (2008). The centrality of culture. In Asante, M.K., Miike, Y. and Yin, J. (eds), *The global intercultural communication reader.* New York: Routledge: 37–43.

Spears, A.K. (1999). Race and ideology: an introduction. In Spears, A.K. (ed.), *Race and ideology; language, symbolism, and popular culture*. Detroit: Wayne State University Press: 11–58.

Spencer, J. (2001). Ethnography after postmodernism. In Atkinson, P., Coffey, A., Delamont, S., Lofland, J. and Lofland, L. (eds), *Handbook of ethnography*. London: Sage: 443–52.

Spencer-Oatey, H. and Stadler, S. (2009). Sino-British interaction in professional contexts. *Warwick Occasional Papers in Applied Linguistics, 6*. Retrieved from http://www.globalpeople.org.uk/, http://www.warwick.ac.uk/al (June 2009).

Spradley, J.P. (1980). *Participant observation*. New York: Holt, Rinehart & Winston.

Stråth, B. (2008). Belonging and European identity. In Delanty, G., Wodak, R. and Jones, P. (eds), *Identity, belonging and migration*. Liverpool: Liverpool University Press: 21–37.

Tarantino, Q. (1994). *Pulp fiction*. US: Miramax.

Thom, V. (2009). Mutual cultures. In Jones, E. (ed.), *Internationalisation and the student voice: higher education perspectives*. London: Routledge: 155–65.

Thorpe, V. (2012). *Homeland*'s troubled CIA agent. *Guardian*, 3 March. Retrieved from: http://www.guardian.co.uk/tv-and-radio/2012/mar/03/homeland-claire-danes-carrie-mathison?fb=native (accessed 10 November 2012).

Tomlinson, J. (1991). *Cultural imperialism*. London: Pinter Publications.

Triandis, H.C. (1995). *Individualism and collectivism*. Boulder, CO: Westview Press.

Wallace, C. (2003). *Critical reading in language education*. Basingstoke: Palgrave Macmillan.

Weber, M. (1964). *The theory of social and economic organization*. New York: The Free Press. (Originally published as *Wirtschaft und gesellschaft*, 1922).

——(1968). Ideal types and theory construction. In Brodbeck, M. (ed.), *Readings in the philosophy of the social sciences*. London: Macmillan: 496–507. (Originally published as *The methodology of the social sciences*, 1949).

——(1977). *The Protestant ethic and the spirit of capitalism*. London: Allen and Unwin.

Wenger, E. (2000). Communities of practice and social learning systems. *Organization* 7/2: 225–46.

Wodak, R. (2008). 'Us and them': inclusion and exclusion. In Delanty, G., Wodak, R. and Jones, P. (eds), *Identity, belonging and migration*. Liverpool: Liverpool University Press: 54–77.

Wu Ming (2009). *Mantuana*. Whiteside, S., Trans. London: Verso.

Young, R. (2006). The cultural politics of hybridity. In Ashcroft, B., Griffiths, G. and Tifflin, H. (eds), *The post-colonial studies reader*. London: Routledge: 158–62. (Originally published as *Colonial Desire*, 1995).

Zhu, H. (2008). Duelling languages, duelling values: codeswitching in bilingual intergenerational conflict talk in diasporic families. *Journal of Pragmatics* 40/10: 1799–816.

Zimmerman, A.L. (2006). *Innocents abroad*. Cambridge, MA: Harvard University Press.

Index